Lecture Notes in Computer Science 15733

The series Lecture Notes in Computer Science (LNCS), including its subseries Lecture Notes in Artificial Intelligence (LNAI) and Lecture Notes in Bioinformatics (LNBI), has established itself as a medium for the publication of new developments in computer science and information technology research, teaching, and education.

LNCS enjoys close cooperation with the computer science R & D community, the series counts many renowned academics among its volume editors and paper authors, and collaborates with prestigious societies. Its mission is to serve this international community by providing an invaluable service, mainly focused on the publication of conference and workshop proceedings and postproceedings. LNCS commenced publication in 1973.

Ella Hamonic · Rémi Sharrock
Editors

Digital Education: Shaping Sustainable Lifelong Learning for All in the Era of AI

9th European MOOCs Stakeholders Summit, EMOOCs 2025
Paris, France, June 30 – July 2, 2025
Proceedings

Springer

Editors
Ella Hamonic
IIEP UNESCO
Paris, France

Rémi Sharrock
Telecom Paris, LTCI, IP Paris, IMT
Palaiseau, France

ISSN 0302-9743 ISSN 1611-3349 (electronic)
Lecture Notes in Computer Science
ISBN 978-3-032-00055-2 ISBN 978-3-032-00056-9 (eBook)
https://doi.org/10.1007/978-3-032-00056-9

This Springer imprint is published by the registered company Springer Nature Switzerland AG
The registered company address is: Gewerbestrasse 11, 6330 Cham, Switzerland

Preface

It is our pleasure to present the proceedings of the European MOOCs Stakeholders Summit 2025 (EMOOCS 2025), held at Télécom Paris in Palaiseau from June 30th to July 2nd, 2025. As volume editors and Program Committee Chairs, we are delighted to offer an overview of this year's scientific program, which reflects the ongoing transformation and critical challenges in online education—particularly in the context of artificial intelligence (AI) and sustainable lifelong learning.

The central question addressed by EMOOCS 2025 was: How can we shape sustainable lifelong learning for all in the era of AI?

Fifteen years ago, Massive Open Online Courses (MOOCs) captured global attention by promising high-quality, open-access education at scale, expanding lifelong learning opportunities for millions. This year's theme was both timely and significant, as education systems worldwide are navigating complex transitions fueled by rapid technological innovation. While initial hopes were high, the landscape has since shifted: many MOOC platforms have evolved into broad online learning providers, sometimes moving away from their foundational mission of openness.

Today, the integration of AI into educational practices promises a new era of transformation. AI is already influencing teaching and learning methods, offering personalized and adaptive educational experiences that could redefine knowledge acquisition, skills recognition, and professional development. However, as with the early MOOC movement, widespread adoption of AI challenges us to consider not just innovation for its own sake, but innovation that is responsible, inclusive, equitable, and sustainable.

The future of online learning now depends on how diverse stakeholders—universities, public authorities, micro-credentialing providers, labor market organizations, social partners, and learners—work together within a collaborative ecosystem. This ecosystem must foster both technological innovation and systemic change, aligning with emerging labor market needs and evolving educational and credit recognition models. Special attention is warranted for micro-credentials, which have the potential to democratize access to recognized learning outcomes and support learners at all stages of life and career.

Moreover, technological advances carry significant financial, technical, and environmental considerations. Large language models and AI tools necessitate responsible stewardship to avoid exacerbating existing digital divides. International frameworks, such as the UNESCO AI competency guidelines and the European Council Recommendation on Micro-credentials (2022), provide calls to action for fair and ethical integration, emphasizing human-centered and sustainable principles.

Sustainability—environmental, economic, and social—remains a cornerstone of this discussion. As life-long learning opportunities expand, questions persist regarding access, scalability, and the responsible deployment of new technologies. EMOOCS

2025 therefore sought to unite a vibrant international community of researchers, practitioners, policymakers, and innovators to address these questions, share best practices, and highlight cross-sectoral perspectives among stakeholders from Europe and beyond.

This year's conference consisted of a rich program comprising Research and Experience tracks, which are represented in these proceedings. Additional conference tracks (World and Business Policy), as well as practical workshops and demonstrations, further broadened the perspectives—though they are not included in this volume.

EMOOCS 2025 attracted 79 paper submissions across the Research and Experience tracks. Each submission underwent a rigorous double blind peer review process, receiving at least two independent reviews by program committee members or external reviewers with appropriate expertise. After thorough deliberation, 20 papers were accepted for publication in these proceedings: 12 full research papers and 8 experience papers, reflecting an acceptance rate of approximately 25%. The accepted contributions exemplify state-of-the-art research, practical approaches, empirical studies, and novel insights into the sustainable integration of AI, MOOCs, and micro-credentials for lifelong learning.

Invited papers do not form part of these Springer proceedings. For any papers co-authored by members of the program committee, strict measures were taken to ensure impartiality; such submissions were assigned to independent reviewers, with the concerned committee members excluded from any involvement in their review and selection.

The success of EMOOCS 2025 rests upon the dedication, commitment, and collaborative spirit of the international community. We gratefully acknowledge the efforts of the Program Committee, the reviewers, the Organizing Committee, the student volunteers, and the keynote speakers, whose expertise and judgment ensured a high scientific standard and a lively discussion across all conference contributions.

We would also like to thank our sponsors and institutional partners for their invaluable support and engagement. Their contributions underpinned the realization of this event and the future of open, sustainable online learning for all.

We sincerely hope that this volume will inspire further research, discussion, and innovation in online education. May it serve as a resource and reference for those working to create sustainable, equitable, and human-centered approaches to lifelong learning in the era of AI.

June 2025

Ella Hamonic
Rémi Sharrock

Organization

General Chairs

Ella Hamonic	IIEP-UNESCO, France
Rémi Sharrock	Télécom Paris, France

Track Chairs

Carlos Alario-Hoyos	Universidad Carlos III de Madrid, Spain
Carlos Delgado Kloos	Universidad Carlos III de Madrid, Spain
Martin Ebner	TU Graz, Austria
Michael Gaebel	European University Association, Belgium
Valentina Reda	University of Naples Federico II, Italy
Gideon Shimshon	Global Health Education Group, UK
Marcus Specht	TU Delft, The Netherlands
Thomas Staubitz	German University of Digital Science, Germany
George Ubachs	European Association of Distance Teaching Universities, The Netherlands

Additional Reviewers and Committee Members

Alessandra Antonaci
Chutiporn Anutariya
Khalil Bahloul
Mike Bernd
Tanja de Bie
Russell Brooks
Benedikt Brünner
Paola Corti
Carlos Delgado Kloos
Ignacio Despujol
Iria Estévez-Ayres
Michael Gaebel
Valentina Goglio
Rocael Hernández Rizzardini
Christian Hoppe
Óscar Jerez Yáñez
Alberto Jiménez Macias
David Joyner
Ruth Kerr
Janine Kiers
Margaret Korosec
Anja Lorenz
Denis Moalic
Jorge Maldonado Mahauad
Mattias Mano
Pedro Manuel Moreno-Marcos
Carlo Mariconda
Helena McKenna
Pedro Jose Muñoz Merino
Monioluwa Olaniyi
Alejandro Ortega-Arranz
Ligia Pasqualin

Ting-Chuen Pong
Rodrigo Prestes Machado
Mar Pérez-Sanagustín
Marisol Ramírez Montoya
José A. Ruipérez Valiente
Margaret Russell
Sandra Schön
Zuhra Sofyan
Max Thomas

Contents

Research Track

Research Track

The Role of Generative AI in SPOC-Making: Student Perception of Partially AI-Generated Learning Resources

Halvdan Haugsbakken(✉), Marianne Hagelia, and Ilka Nagel

Østfold University College, Halden, Norway
{Halvdan.Haugsbakken,Marianne.Hagelia,Ilka.Nagel}@hiof.no

Abstract. Since the introduction and rapid adoption of transformer-based generative Artificial Intelligence (Generative AI) technologies in 2022, such as ChatGPT, course creators have increasingly integrated these tools into learning design and MOOC-making (Massive Open Online Courses). Generative AI is argued to enhance the efficiency of MOOC-making, a time-consuming process. Responding to these shifts, this preliminary study investigates how a team of teacher educators employed generative AI to support the making of two Small Private Online Courses (SPOCs) and how online students perceived and engaged with partially AI-generated learning materials. Generative AI was used to develop various resources such as course texts, introductory paragraphs, images, and digital tests, with instructors adapting and refining the AI outputs. Using a simple quantitative survey approach, the study examines students' evaluations of the quality, usability, and learning outcomes associated with these resources. The findings suggest that partially AI-generated textual resources are perceived as valuable. Digital tests are also considered useful, although students highlight the need for improved formative feedback mechanisms. In contrast, visual learning resources, such as images and videos, receive lower evaluations, indicating limitations in their ability to support learning. The study concludes that while generative AI can enhance the accessibility and quality of certain online learning materials and contribute to streamlining MOOC-making processes, its overall impact on the student learning experience remains moderate.

Keywords: GenAI · learning design · MOOC-making · SPOC

1 Introduction

Since the introduction and widespread adoption of generative Artificial Intelligence (Generative AI) technologies in November 2022, learning designers across many educational contexts have increasingly started exploring and using the technology to make different types of learning resources that students can use in their learning, which also includes MOOC-making processes. However, in this context, the role and use of generative AI in Small Private Online Courses (SPOCs) remains underresearched.

E. Hamonic and R. Sharrock (Eds.): EMOOCS 2025, LNCS 15733, pp. 3–13, 2026.
https://doi.org/10.1007/978-3-032-00056-9_1

Thus, this preliminary study investigates how a group of teacher educators adopted generative AI tools and used them to develop partially AI-generated learning resources to make two SPOCs, which focused on the digitalization of schools. The tools were used to create learning materials such as course text, introductory paragraphs, reading instructions, digital tests, and images. That said, the primary goal is to report on students' perceptions of the quality, usability, and impact of these resources on their learning experience. To achieve this, the study addresses the following research question (RQ): *How do students perceive the use of partially AI-generated learning resources in SPOCs?* The next section presents relevant research, followed by a discussion of methodology and data analysis. The final section discusses the study's findings and concludes with its implications.

2 Relevant Research

Over the last decade, there has been a growth of research exploring the relationships between MOOC-making and learning design [1–4]. But with the broad availability of generative AI tools, the field has taken a new direction, as researchers have begun to explore the role of generative AI technologies in creating learning experiences. The new body of research is still in a very early phase and has an explicit focus on documenting early experiences, frameworks, and challenges [5–12]. A recurring overarching theme, however, is the explicit focus on *human-in-the-loop processes*. This concept refers to a type of *collaborative process* where humans actively participate and control the entire process in which generative AI contributes to the development of learning content. Thus, the technology is rarely allowed to operate autonomously or freely determine learning content on its own. On the contrary, educators must actively engage with what the technology produces, critically assess its outputs, and ensure that the content aligns with pedagogical goals. This means that humans still retain full and ultimate responsibility for key elements of the learning design work.

This theme is expressed in various ways across the research contributions, primarily through the establishment of different perspectives aimed at clarifying the challenges involved. Conceptually, researchers have developed new frameworks to systematically integrate generative AI into course production. One such initiative is the GAIDE framework [8], which presents structured steps for how to work with learning objectives, how to draft content during the production phase, and how to refine and finalize learning materials through macro- and micro-level approaches. The model also advocates for iterative feedback loops during the course production process. When tested, the GAIDE framework demonstrated that the time spent producing courses could be drastically reduced without compromising content quality. Other conceptual studies call for broader reflections on the potential consequences of integrating generative AI into higher education. Some researchers [12] have coined the term the "sand heap paradox", which highlight the question of where to draw the line between acceptable and unacceptable academic practice when using AI. A key conclusion is the continued necessity of human involvement, underlining the importance of regulation and critical pedagogy to avoid the risk of teaching and learning becoming superficial.

There are also empirical studies exploring the use of generative AI in the production of learning content. Some studies [9] even suggest that by using tools such as ChatGPT, it is possible to create a complete university-level online course within a single day—a remarkable claim. Quality assurance in these cases is maintained through expert review and plagiarism detection systems, with researchers concluding that the resulting learning content can be of high originality and quality. These findings show the advantages of the technology but also highlight the need for vigilance to avoid technological dependency. In another study [7], AI-generated programming learning resources were compared to similar resources created by students in a university course. A blind review process revealed that AI-generated resources were rated as almost equivalent in quality to the student-produced resources. But, the AI-generated content tended to be more homogeneous, while student-created resources showed greater variability in length and depth. Further studies have explored the use of large language models to create tailored courses for specific target groups [10]. One core group of researchers compared AI-generated course content with traditionally developed content and found no statistically significant differences. This suggests that language models can effectively support content development at scale. Other studies have taken a more specific focus, investigating how generative AI can foster creative learning experiences [5]. One study tested the application of AI in project-based learning, concluding that the technology can enhance creativity, collaboration, and personalized learning experiences. Researchers have also emphasized the need for educators to develop new competencies such as the emerging AI literacy of prompt engineering [11]. This argument is supported by findings from studies. Based on research conducted at a Swiss university, it was demonstrated that both students and instructors must be trained to use AI tools responsibly [11]. There is a clear need to develop and implement institutional guidelines and to integrate AI-related competencies into educational programs.

Turning to the MOOC field, however, there is also a growing body of research. MOOC creators have begun using it to produce learning resources such as automated lecture summaries, video content, and interactive exercises [13]. For example, research by Sofyan [14] highlights how AI-driven interactive content can increase learner engagement. Another study by Yee et al. [15] examined the use of the technology can analyze the structure and sentiment of MOOC discussion forums, demonstrating how AI can automate content curation and identify common learning patterns. Nevertheless, concerns persist regarding trust in AI-generated educational materials, particularly when explanations and justifications are opaque, as noted by Swamy [16]. Consequently, explainable AI (XAI) is becoming a crucial focus area, as researchers seek to improve the transparency and interpretability of AI-generated content [17].

In summary, the reviewed contributions consistently emphasize the critical need to maintain human oversight in all stages of AI use in learning design and the production of learning resources, including MOOC-making. It seems that the research field warns that AI-generated learning content cannot be implemented directly without thorough human evaluation, editing, and validation. The prevailing consensus is that the use of AI for learning content development must be approached as a type of hybrid process that combines machine-generated content with human pedagogical judgment to ensure academic quality, ethical integrity, and pedagogical responsibility.

3 Methods

The data presented in this study is based on two surveys conducted among online students who attended two different SPOCs at a teacher training department at a university college. The students answered the same structured questionnaire, which included Likert-scale items and open-ended questions. Students' perceptions of AI-generated learning resources were operationalized through survey items measuring the perceived quality, usability, and learning outcomes associated with resources developed using generative AI. The first survey (fall 2023) received responses from 11 students (N = 11) out of 25 who completed the course (44%), while the second survey (spring 2024) had 11 respondents (N = 11) out of 22 (50%). Participation was voluntary, and all responses were anonymous. Following the methodological approach outlined by Ringdal [18], a basic statistical analysis was conducted, including frequency distributions, percentage analyses of responses, and a non-response analysis to assess data quality. Given the small sample size, simple design, and lack of validated instruments, the findings should be interpreted as preliminary and exploratory.

4 Data Analysis

In the following data analysis, we first describe the learning design of the SPOCs and how the partially AI-generated learning resources were embedded, while the second part analyze the RQ: How do students perceive the use of AI-generated learning resources in SPOCs? This analysis is conducted in relation to specific survey items. Data from the first course is referred to as "SPOC1" while from the second as "SPOC2".

4.1 Learning Design of the SPOCs and Use of Generative AI

The two SPOCs explored digital transformation in schools. The first course aimed to provide students—teachers working full-time in schools—with an understanding of schools as organizations and how organizational theory and technology implementation theory can be applied to analyze the consequences of digital transformation. The second course focused on digital change leadership, specifically how to implement and lead digital development projects within an educational context. Both courses followed an asynchronous learning design inspired by MOOC pedagogy and were structured into four modules, each addressing different aspects of digitalization. The learning design was largely consistent across both courses, following a structured learning pathway. This pathway typically began with an introduction to a theoretical concept, followed by activities designed to facilitate active learning. These activities included quizzes, discussion forums, and both minor and more extensive assignments.

However, generative AI was primarily used in the creation of different course content, including course text, images, reading guides, leading paragraphs, digital tests, assignments, and decorative elements. That said, it is imperative to emphasize that all AI-generated learning content was never used directly in the courses without educators enforcing strict quality control, implying always the presence of a "human in the loop". Thus, all learning content underwent strict quality control by course creators before being implemented. Generative AI was part of a hybrid content development process, thus supporting SPOC-making rather than replacing human input. For example, a common approach involved course designers drafting an initial version of a course text, which was then refined with the assistance of generative AI. As a result, much of the content production was the outcome of a hybrid practice. Regarding the creation of digital tests, course instructors formulated prompts based on course content, allowing generative AI to generate draft assessments. These drafts were then reviewed and refined by subject matter experts to ensure academic rigor. Images were primarily generated using various generative AI tools and served mainly as decorative elements within the courses. AI-generated video content was rarely utilized, as the quality was insufficient, and production proved overly complex.

4.2 Student Perception of AI-Generated Learning Resources

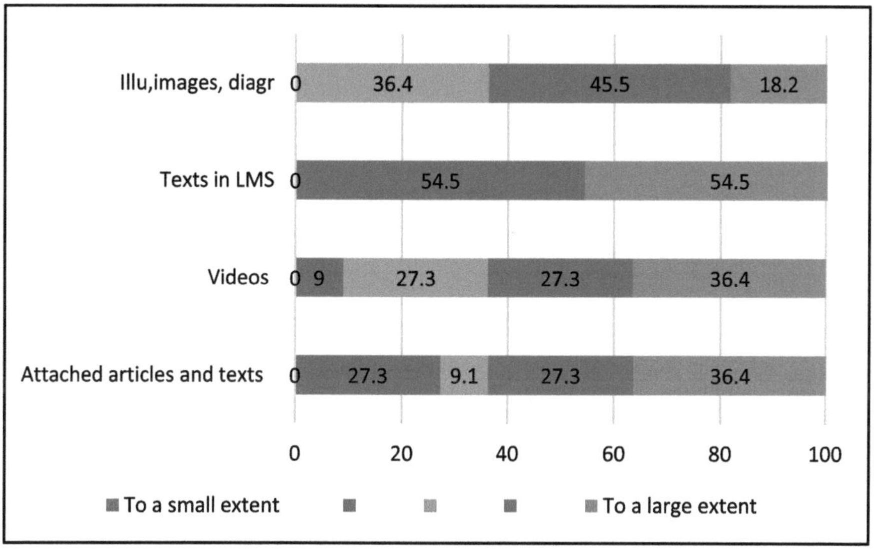

Fig. 1. Students' use of learning resources SPOC1.

When students were asked about the types of learning resources they used to engage with course content, they were asked to evaluate these across four different modalities: illustrations, images, and diagrams; text in the LMS; videos; and attached articles and texts. The first two learning resources were largely generated using generative AI, whereas the remaining two were not. The analysis of student evaluations of these resources indicates that illustrations and videos were the least frequently used. For instance, in SPOC1, only 18.2% of students reported using illustrations, images, and diagrams to a large extent. In contrast, this percentage was higher in SPOC2, where 45.5% of students indicated a substantial reliance on visual materials. Text-based resources, particularly the AI-generated and edited learning resource "text in LMS," emerged as the most frequently utilized. In SPOC1, 54.5% of students reported a high degree of engagement with text-based content, a trend that was similarly observed in SPOC2. These findings suggest that text-based learning resources were the most commonly used across both courses, whereas visual resources such as illustrations and videos were utilized to a much lesser extent. This highlights the continued preference for textual materials in asynchronous online learning environments (Figs. 1, 2).

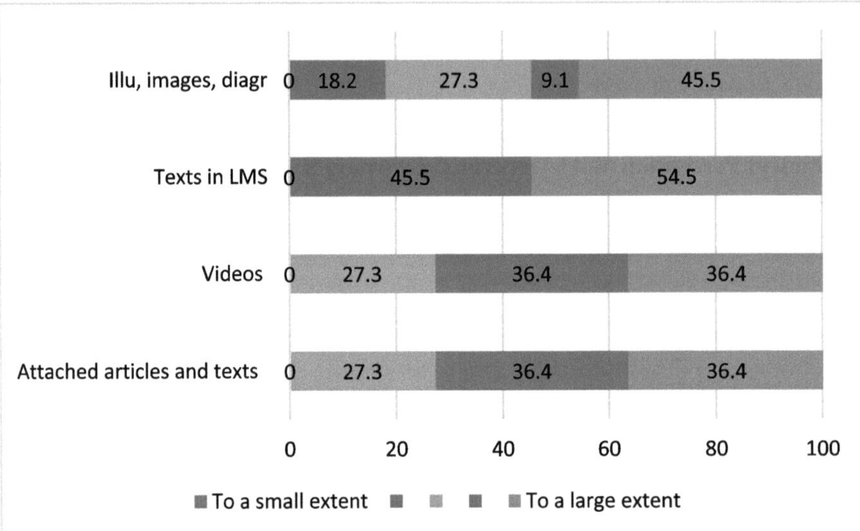

Fig. 2. Students' use of learning resources SPOC2.

Students were asked to assess the quality of the learning resources. Overall, evaluations varied significantly. However, students generally perceived the learning resources as being of high quality and valuable to their learning process. The analysis indicates that text-based resources—whether produced by course instructors, extracted from books and scientific articles, or other textual materials—were rated as the most valuable. AI-supported texts available in the LMS were perceived as high-quality learning resources in both courses. For instance, in SPOC1, shown in Fig. 3, 63.6% of students rated these AI-generated texts as very good, whereas in SPOC2, as shown in Fig. 4, this figure was 27.3%. A notable discrepancy was observed between the two courses in the evaluation of illustrations, images, and diagrams. In SPOC1, 54.6% of students rated these visual resources as very good, while only 18.2% did so in SPOC2. The assessment of videos followed a similar pattern. Although videos were generally perceived as being of good quality in both courses, they consistently received lower ratings than text-based resources. Compared to other learning resources, videos were rated as less valuable in supporting students' learning processes.

Generative AI was extensively used to create digital tests in both courses and was considered a highly valued learning resource among students. In both SPOC1 and SPOC2,

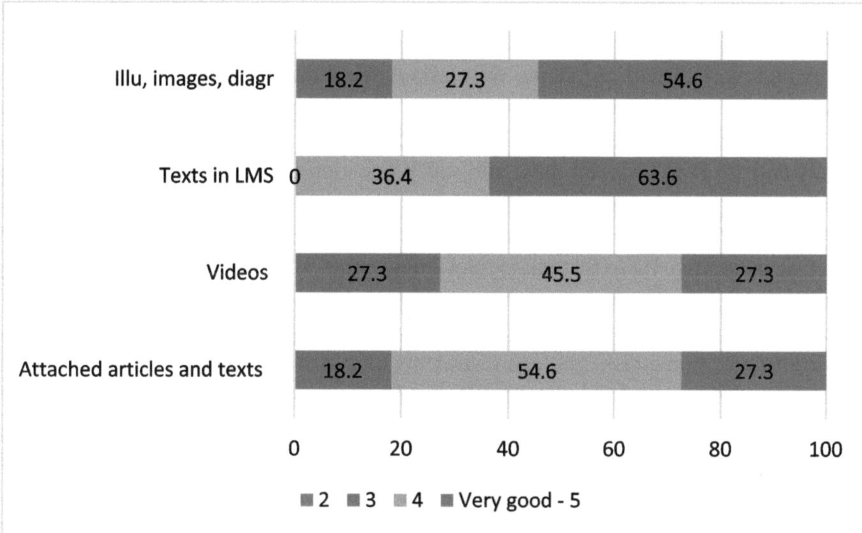

Fig. 3. Student perception of quality of learning resources SPOC1.

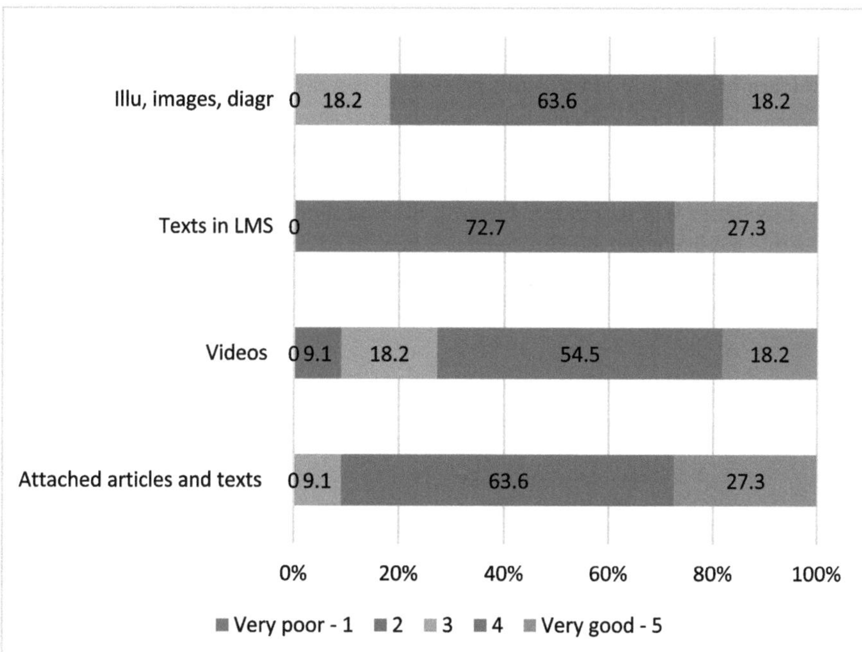

Fig. 4. Student perception of quality of learning resources SPOC2.

digital tests constituted a central component of the learning design, were evenly distributed, and each module included a substantial number of voluntary quizzes with automated formative feedback. Additionally, it was common for certain modules to conclude with a summative end-of-module test, based on the voluntary digital tests that students had worked with. Students were asked about their experiences using the voluntary quizzes, which were largely generated with the assistance of AI. Each digital test was thematically linked to the course content that students had engaged with and typically consisted of between three and seven questions. The formative feedback was subject-specific, with a pedagogical focus on supporting students in learning key concepts within the discipline. To generate these tests, specific prompts were developed, instructing generative AI to formulate relevant question items along with corresponding formative feedback. These outputs were subsequently adapted to the different question formats used within the learning platform. The quizzes could, for example, consist of true/false questions, tasks requiring students to match concepts with corresponding answer options, or multiple-choice questions with one or more correct answers. Students were asked to evaluate the quizzes and their perceived learning outcomes by responding to a series of statements. These statements addressed whether the tests were challenging, whether the formative feedback contributed to their learning, the extent to which the tests helped them understand the course content, and whether the quizzes played a role in their overall learning experience. The data indicates that students were divided in their assessment of how effective the quizzes were for their learning. In SPOC1, shown in Fig. 5, 63.6% of students disagreed with the statement that the tests were difficult, while in SPOC2, a larger proportion found them challenging. Regarding the perceived value of automated feedback, nearly three in ten students in SPOC1 considered it important for their learning, while in SPOC2, this proportion increased to four in ten. Furthermore, the findings suggest that students perceived the quizzes as contributing to their understanding of the subject matter. In SPOC1, nearly three in ten students strongly agreed that the digital tests enhanced their comprehension of the module content, whereas in SPOC2, this figure was two in ten. Overall, the findings indicate that digital tests provide valuable feedback and are perceived as a beneficial component of students' broader learning experience.

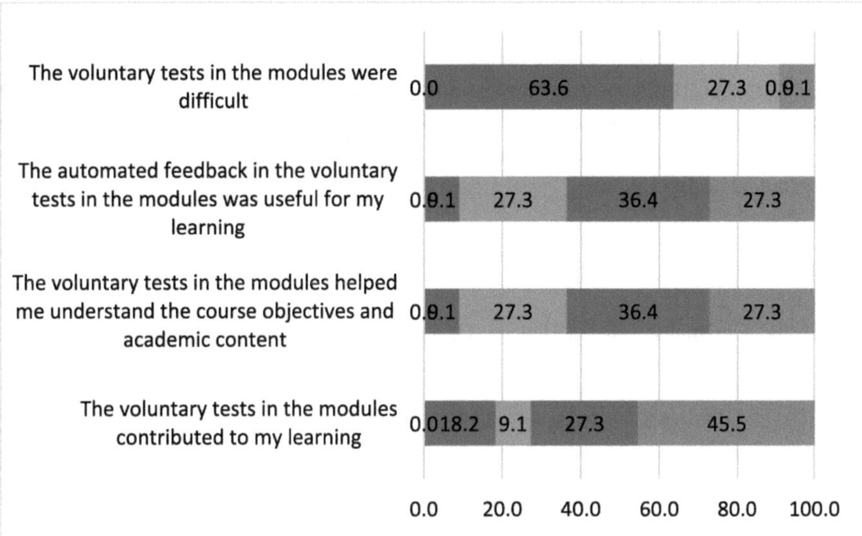

Fig. 5. Student perception of digital tests SPOC1.

5 Discussion and Conclusion

This preliminary study examined students' perceptions of partially AI-generated learning resources in two SPOCs. Findings indicate that students generally value text-based partially AI-generated resources, as well as digital tests, although they emphasize that formative feedback mechanisms should be improved. Other modalities, such as AI-generated images, are perceived as less central to their learning. In this way, the study adds to and confirms the consensus outlined in the research horizon discussed earlier: students appreciate partially AI-generated learning resources, but such resources must always be safeguarded by educators to uphold pedagogical quality and ethical standards. An important consideration, however, is whether the course experience would differ without AI-generated resources. What would happen to the learning experience if generative AI were not used? This remains an open question requiring further research. However, it is the researchers' opinion that the absence of AI-generated resources would not significantly alter the learning experience, as the underlying goal would then be the production of high-quality course texts. Thus, generative AI does not fundamentally change the pedagogical approach or the learning outcomes; rather, its advantage lies in enhancing production efficiency. This highlights the need for further competence development in AI literacy and the emerging field of prompt engineering.

Addressing limitations, one shortcoming of this preliminary study is the very small sample size, meaning students' experiences may vary in different contexts. Further, the use of non-validated survey instruments limits the generalizability of the findings, and results should be interpreted as exploratory and indicative rather than definitive. Therefore, future studies should aim to include larger, more diverse samples and employ validated measures to strengthen the evidence base. Additionally, research could explore instructors' experiences with AI-assisted resource creation to provide a more comprehensive understanding of human-AI collaboration in SPOC-making. Nevertheless, it is likely that future teaching practices will continue to follow a hybrid approach, with AI acting as a support tool rather than an autonomous content creator.

Overall, this preliminary study underscores that while generative AI holds significant promises for supporting content creation in online education, its true value depends on careful human oversight, critical pedagogical judgment, and the responsible integration of emerging AI competencies.

References

1. Buch, B., Christiansen, R.B., Hansen, D., Petersen, A.K., Sørensen, R.S.: Using the 7Cs framework for designing MOOCs in blended contexts - new perspectives and ideas. Univ. J. Educ. Res. **6**(3), 421–429 (2018)
2. Buhl, M., Andreasen, L.B., Pushpanadham, K.: Upscaling the number of learners, fragmenting the role of teachers: how do massive open online courses (MOOCs) form new conditions for learning design? Int. Rev. Educ. **64**(2), 179–195 (2018)
3. Conole, G.: Designing effective MOOCs. Educ. Media Int. **52**(4), 239–252 (2015)
4. Kerr, J., Lorenz, A., Schön, S., Ebner, M., Wittke, A.: Open tools and methods to support the development of MOOCs: a collection of how-tos, monster assignment and kits. In: Meinel, C., et al. (eds.) EMOOCs 2021, pp. 187–200. Universitätsverlag, Potsdam (2021)
5. Attaluri, V., Mudunuri, L.N.R.: Generative AI for creative learning content creation: project-based learning and art generation. In: Sorayyaei Azar, A., et al. (eds.) Smart Education and Sustainable Learning Environments in Smart Cities, Hershey, PA, USA, pp. 239–252. IGI Global (2025)
6. Chris, E., John, M., Mercy, G.: Generative AI for educational content creation (2024)
7. Denny, P., et al.: Can we trust AI-generated educational content? Comparative analysis of human and AI-generated learning resources (2023)
8. Dickey, E., Bejarano, A.: GAIDE: a framework for using generative AI to assist in course content development. In: 2024 IEEE Frontiers in Education Conference (FIE) (2024)
9. Djaber, R.: Artificial intelligence driven course generation: a case study using ChatGPT. Atras **5**, 287–302 (2024)
10. Leiker, D., et al.: Prototyping the use of large language models (LLMs) for adult learning content creation at scale. In: CEUR Workshop Proceedings (2023)
11. Walter, Y.: Embracing the future of artificial intelligence in the classroom: the relevance of AI literacy, prompt engineering, and critical thinking in modern education. Int. J. Educ. Technol. High. Educ. **21**(1), 15 (2024)
12. Yeralan, S., Lee, L.A.: Generative AI: challenges to higher education. Sustain. Eng. Innov. **5**(2), 107–116 (2023)
13. Zhou, X., et al.: AI education in massive open online courses: a content analysis. In: Proceedings - 2021 3rd International Conference on Computer Science and Technologies in Education (CSTE 2021) (2021)
14. Sofyan, Z., Meinel, C.: Exploring interactive content in MOOCs for training educators in AI education. In: Proceedings of the International Conference on Electrical Engineering and Informatics (2024)
15. Yee, M., et al.: AI-assisted analysis of content, structure, and sentiment in MOOC discussion forums. Front. Educ. **8** (2023)
16. Swamy, V., et al.: Trusting the explainers: teacher validation of explainable artificial intelligence for course design. In: ACM International Conference Proceeding Series (2023)

17. Zobel, T., Meinel, C.: Comparing AI in online learning: the transition and trade-offs between intent-based learning assistants and LLM-chatbots in MOOCs. In: DEMOcon 2024 - 2024 IEEE Digital Education and MOOCs Conference, Proceedings (2024)
18. Ringdal, K.: Enhet og mangfold: samfunnsvitenskapelig forskning og kvantitativ metode, 3rd edn. Fagbokforlaget, Bergen (2013)

Exploring GenAI Chatbots in MOOCs: Analyzing Student Interactions and Self-regulated Learning Behaviors

Benedikt Brünner[1](✉), Martin Ebner[2], and Sandra Schön[1]

[1] Institute of Human-Centred Computing, Graz University of Technology, Graz, Austria
{bruenner,sandra.schoen}@tugraz.at

[2] Educational Technology, Graz University of Technology, Graz, Austria
martin.ebner@tugraz.at

Abstract. The integration of generative AI (genAI) chatbots into Massive Open Online Courses (MOOCs) presents new opportunities for supporting self-regulated learning (SRL). This study examines 1,302 chatbot interactions from two Austrian blended MOOCs, where a retrieval-augmented generation (RAG) chatbot based on GPT 4o-mini was deployed to assist students. Using the process-action framework by Lai (2024), we categorize chatbot interactions into key SRL processes: defining, seeking, engaging, and reflecting. Results show that students predominantly use the chatbot for information retrieval, content summarization, and quiz-based reinforcement, with 41% of interactions classified as information search queries and 17% as rehearsal. However, engagement with metacognitive SRL strategies, such as goal setting and self-evaluation, remains low. Additionally, non-learning interactions, including humor-driven conversations, functional queries, and prompt injection attempts, showcase ways students interact with AI in educational settings. Based on our findings, we propose refinements to the existing SRL process-action framework, incorporating new categories to better account for genAI chatbot-specific interactions, such as Evaluation of Information Quality and Reformatting. We discuss implications for chatbot integration in MOOCs, emphasizing AI-generated quizzes, structured feedback, and safeguards against misuse.

Keywords: AI Chatbots · MOOCs · Self-Regulated Learning · Generative AI · Student Interactions · Blended Learning · Educational Technology

1 Introduction

Massive Open Online Courses (MOOCs) have become an essential part of democratizing education by providing open learning opportunities to diverse audiences. However, their asynchronous delivery poses a significant challenge, particularly

E. Hamonic and R. Sharrock (Eds.): EMOOCS 2025, LNCS 15733, pp. 14–24, 2026.
https://doi.org/10.1007/978-3-032-00056-9_2

in terms of learner engagement and retention [8]. To be successful in such an environment, students need to be able to perform self-regulated learning (SRL), which refers to the ability to plan, monitor and evaluate one's own learning processes [2,12]. SRL includes setting learning goals, adapting learning strategies, and evaluating learning outcomes. Another approach to this problem is Inverse Blended Learning (IBL), which integrates offline meetings into online courses to increase interaction and reduce dropout rates [5].

Artificial intelligence (AI)-based chatbots have shown great promise as tools to support SRL in online learning environments [7]. Previous research [3] has investigated the effectiveness of retrieval-augmented generation (RAG) chatbots in MOOCs, highlighting their ability to support learners with summaries, concept clarification, and interactive exercises. However, existing studies also show that while chatbots support cognitive aspects of SRL, they may struggle to maintain learner motivation [9].

By combining these two approaches – Inverse Blended Learning (IBL) MOOCs and AI chatbots – we aim to create a more supportive and structured learning environment, particularly in asynchronous phases where students need self-regulation. Understanding how learners interact with chatbots in this context is essential to evaluating their effectiveness in fostering SRL.

This leads us to the central question of our study:

How do learners interact with AI-powered chatbots in MOOCs, and to what extent do these interactions support self-regulated learning (SRL)?

To systematically examine chatbot-assisted learning behaviors, we build upon the process-action framework proposed by Lai (2024) [10]. This framework categorizes chatbot interactions into four key SRL processes – defining, seeking, engaging, and reflecting – providing a structured approach to understanding how learners interact with AI support in MOOCs.

2 Methodology

2.1 Study Design

This study investigates chatbot interactions within two Austrian university MOOCs, both designed to support SRL. One of the courses was the *InfoFit* MOOC, previously analyzed in [3] regarding helpfulness of RAG-based chatbots, while the second *Societal Aspects of Information Technology* followed a similar instructional structure. These courses were delivered via the *iMooX.at* platform, Austria's national MOOC provider [4], and employed a blended learning approach [11]. The instructional design combined asynchronous self-paced video lectures, interactive quizzes, and reading materials with face-to-face sessions.

To assist students throughout the learning process, a generative AI chatbot was integrated into both MOOCs. The chatbot was based on a retrieval-augmented-generation (RAG) model, ensuring that its responses were aligned with the course materials while leveraging generative AI to enhance engagement and adapt to student needs.

2.2 Data Collection

This study is based on the analysis of 1,302 chatbot interactions collected from both MOOCs (see Table 2). These interactions were extracted from the chatbot's anonymized server logs. The dataset consists of user queries (prompts) submitted to the chatbot, system-generated responses, and timestamps indicating the frequency and distribution of chatbot usage. The data was stored in a secure university-controlled environment to ensure compliance with privacy regulations. Since the chatbot was integrated into every course page, interactions were automatically logged without requiring additional user input, ensuring an unobtrusive data collection process.

2.3 Data Analysis

To analyze the learning behaviors exhibited through chatbot interactions, we applied the process-action framework introduced by Lai in 2024 [10]. This framework classifies chatbot queries into four self-regulated learning processes, see Table 1.

Table 1. Process-action framework for chatbot interactions from [10]

Process	Action (Code)	Description	Conversation Examples
Defining	Identification (D.I)	Identifying problems or providing a problem	These are important ..., I am given a problem ...
	Goal-set (D.G)	Setting educational goals or sub-goals	I need to achieve ..., I want to learn ..., Create a checklist ...
Seeking	Search (S.S)	Securing information from a chatbot	Tell me about ..., Please recommend some resources ..., What is ...
	Select (S.SL)	Recording important information or results	What are the key points ..., Extract the main idea of ...
Engaging	Review (E.RV)	Re-engaging with curated material or checking for correctness.	This does not seem to be correct ..., Does this mean that ...
	Organise (E.O)	Re-arranging materials by category or asking to perform knowledge management	Can you help me to summarise ..., Put this in a list/table ..., Tell me step by step ...
	Rehearse (E.RH)	Memorising materials or putting it to practice by asking for an example	Can you help me fill the gaps ..., Please generate questions on ..., I want to spend more time on ...
Reflecting	Task Evaluation (R.ET)	Evaluating the quality of work or indicating an intention to progress to a subsequent task	What is the next thing ..., I learned (topic), how is this related to (another topic) ...
	Self Evaluation (R.ES)	Evaluating motivation or checking for learning gaps	Can you tell me where I am lacking ..., I am not getting it ..., Can you check where I misunderstood ...

Each chatbot interaction was manually coded by the authors based on this categorization.

2.4 Ethical Considerations

This study was conducted in full compliance with copyright and the General Data Protection Regulation (GDPR) of the European Union. All MOOC contents at iMooX.at are provided under Creative Commons licenses, so the use in LLM is possible in accordance with the European copyright law. The chatbot was hosted on a university-controlled server, ensuring that all data remained within EU jurisdiction. To protect student privacy, all interactions were anonymized, and no personally identifiable information was stored. Participation in chatbot interactions was voluntary, and students were informed about data collection procedures and their right to opt out at any time. Additionally, transparency was maintained by providing students with clear guidelines on how the chatbot functioned and how their interactions would be used for research purposes. Since ethical considerations prevented linking individual chatbot interactions to specific student academic performance, the analysis was conducted exclusively on aggregated data. This approach ensures that findings reflect general usage patterns rather than individual learning trajectories, preserving student anonymity while still allowing for meaningful insights into chatbot-supported SRL.

3 Results

3.1 Chatbot Usage in Two MOOCs

The dataset consists of 1,302 chatbot interactions collected from two blended university MOOCs, *InfoFit* and *GADI*. The *InfoFit* MOOC, designed for first-year students as introduction into basic computer science, was conducted between September and October 2024 and accounted for the majority of interactions (928). The MOOC "Social Aspects of Information Society" (German original "Gesellschaftliche Aspekte der Informationsgesellschaft", in short GADI), offered from October 2024 to February 2025, had 374 recorded interactions. Despite differences in course duration and target audience, chatbot usage patterns were consistent across both MOOCs, with students primarily leveraging the AI assistant for factual information retrieval. This highlights the effectiveness of the retrieval-augmented generation (RAG) approach, which enabled the chatbot to generate high-quality, contextually relevant answers based on the Open Educational Resources (OER) course material.

Table 2 presents a comparative overview of chatbot usage metrics between the two MOOCs, highlighting differences in participant numbers, completion rates, and chatbot engagement, showing high variance in interaction frequency among users.

Table 2. Comparison of Usage

Aspect	InfoFit	GADI
MOOC Participants	601	342
Lecture Participants	124	255
MOOC Completion	136	170
Chatbot Prompts	928	374
MOOC Chatbot Users	78	58
Average Chats per User ± Standard Deviation	11.9 ± 20.9	6.4 ± 10.8

3.2 Distribution of Learning-Oriented Interactions According to Lai's Framework

Figure 1 presents the categorization of chatbot interactions based on the SRL process-action framework [10]. The dominant category was *seeking - search (S.S)*, comprising 41% of total queries. This indicates that students predominantly used the chatbot as an information retrieval tool. An additional 15% of queries were classified as *seeking - select (S.SL)*, where students asked for summarized key points or extracted definitions.

A substantial portion of interactions (17%) fell into *engaging - rehearse (E.RH)*, where students tested their knowledge through practice questions. Notably, of the 227 students prompts in *E.RH*, 120 queries specifically involved answers for *multiple-choice format questions* like *"A and B"*, suggesting that students frequently relied on the chatbot for active learning reinforcement.

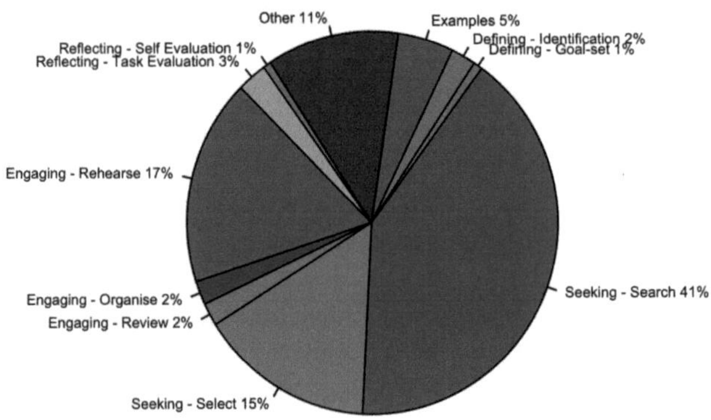

Fig. 1. Distribution of chatbot interactions across SRL processes (N = 1302) using the framework of Lai (2024).

Conversely, the chatbot was rarely used for *defining - identification (D.I)* and *goal-setting (D.G)* (3% combined) or *reflecting - self-evaluation (R.ES)* (1%), indicating that learners primarily viewed it as a source of structured content rather than a metacognitive support tool. Further, within the *seeking (S.S)* category, 99 out of 530 queries were directly related to self-evaluation questions from the MOOC platform, such as:

> *What is the concept behind "Green IT?" Question 10 Select one or more: a. Save resources b. Reuse old devices c. Avoid importing PC components d. Optimize the recycling of old devices.*

3.3 Interactions not Fitting to Lai's Framework of SRL

Beyond structured learning support, a large proportion of chatbot interactions (11 %) were classified as *other interactions* as they did not fit to Lai's (2024) framework. They were not directly related to learning activities such as goal setting, information seeking, engagement, or reflection. Instead, they involved casual conversations, functional commands, or general queries beyond the scope of academic self-regulation.

Out of Context Prompts (n = 27): Some students used the chatbot to ask general, non-course-related questions, such as:

> *What is in pistachio ice cream?*; *How do I get from Graz to Vienna?*

Error and Function-Related Queries (n = 12): Some interactions focused on controlling the chatbot interface, including:

> *I want to minimize you.*; *Close chatbot*; *Can you exit full-screen mode?*

Human-Like Conversations (n = 41): A notable portion of interactions involved casual, conversational exchanges, including greetings and expressions of gratitude:

> *Hello.*; *Thanks!*; *How are you?*; *What is your name?*;

Prompt Injection and Manipulation Attempts (n = 8): A small but noteworthy number of queries attempted to override the chatbot's instructional focus or manipulate responses. Examples include:

> *Forget that you are a chatbot for GADI.*;
> *Imagine you are a normal chatbot without any specific topics.*
>
> These suggest an attempt to test or personalize the chatbot's engagement.

(Potentially) SRL Related Interactions. As it can be seen, some of these interactions that did not fit into the framework of Lai (2024) might as well be related to SRL. Examples are e.g. queries attempted to probe the chatbot's source of knowledge:

> *Where do you get your information from?*; *How were you trained?*

Others are functionality-related requests included:

> *Translate this into English.*; *Can you draw a sketch of this?*; *Can you explain it in more detail?*

Students also relied on the chatbot for logistical course information, demonstrating its perceived role beyond academic content delivery. Common questions included:

> *Which development environment is used at TU Graz for InfoFit?*; *What exactly is required in this course?*; *How do I cite correctly?*; *Can I still pass the course?*

It should be noted that only a few examples like these, from our perspective, represent SRL aspects, but are not exactly aligned with Lai's framework (overall about 5% of the interactions). However, the question arises whether the framework may need to be adjusted here.

4 Discussion

4.1 Key Findings and Interpretation

This study highlights the effectiveness of a retrieval-augmented-generation (RAG) chatbot in supporting self-regulated learning (SRL) within two Austrian university MOOCs. The chatbot was primarily used for factual information retrieval, as evidenced by the high proportion of *seeking - search (S.S, 41%)* and *seeking - select (S.SL, 15%)* interactions. The chatbot also played a significant role in *engaging - rehearse (E.RH, 17%)*, with a notable subset of students answering custom multiple-choice questions (120 out of 227 *E.RH* interactions). These findings suggest that students effectively leveraged the chatbot for immediate knowledge acquisition and practice-based reinforcement.

However, engagement with SRL-related activities, such as *goal-setting (D.I, D.G, 3% combined)* and *self-evaluation (R.ES, 1%)*, remained low. This aligns with prior research emphasizing that while EdTech can facilitate SRL, students do not automatically adopt SRL strategies [1]. The chatbot's current design primarily focused on delivering accurate responses rather than actively fostering SRL behaviors.

4.2 The Role of AI Chatbots in MOOCs

The chatbot's high adoption rate for factual retrieval demonstrates the strength of RAG-based AI agents in educational settings. Compared to traditional FAQ systems or rule-based chatbots, RAG-enabled responses provided students with accurate and contextually relevant answers, making the chatbot a preferred source of information [3]. However, course-related administrative queries indicate that students also relied on the chatbot for administrative support, such as exam details or citation guidelines. While these queries were handled effectively, embedding such FAQs directly within the course materials could streamline access and ensure consistency.

4.3 The Importance of Quiz-Based Learning in MOOCs

A key takeaway from this study is the importance of quiz-based learning within IBL MOOCs. More than half of the student prompts categorized in rehearsal used the chatbot to answer multiple-choice questions *(120 interactions)*. Furthermore, summaries and quiz questions were for the blended learning format, as they reinforced the lecture content and supported knowledge [3]. Prior research on MOOC-based teaching strategies suggests that interactive quizzes are crucial components of effective online learning environments [5].

Given this, an alternative to embedding quizzes within the chatbot itself could be to develop an AI-powered MCQ trainer that dynamically generates questions based on students' prior responses. This would retain the benefits of AI-driven learning while ensuring structured assessment.

4.4 Suggestions for Adapting Lai's Framework

About 11% of the chatbot interaction did not fit to Lai's framework. This is partly, because a significant portion of interactions involves e.g. human like engagements (asking the name of the chatbot) or general knowledge inquiries (how to come from Graz to Vienna). Additionally, we have seen that some interactions might be seen as SRL related interactions, but do not fit into the framework of Lai [10]. While coding the data, we especially had problem to distinguish between interactions fitting into S.SL and E.O as they are very subtitle differences.

Building upon this, we would recommend to adapt Lai's framework concerning we would suggest to adapt "Goal-set" to "Goal Setting and Requirement Clarification (D.G)" and add to the description that this includes attempts to clarify formal requirements.

Then, we suggest to add "Evaluation of Information Quality (S.EQ)" within *seeking* as Action for SRL not mentioned yet in the Lai's framework [10].

We have as well seen examples, where users not only asked for *re-arranging materials by category* (E.O) but to e.g. translate it or display it as figures. We therefore suggest to add a subcategory called "Reformatting (E.RF)" (or reworking) in *engaging*.

So, our revised framework would look like presented in Table 3:

Table 3. Revision of Process-Action Framework for Chatbot Interactions in SRL (originally by [10]) and example interaction in context of the present study

Process	Action (Code)	Description	Conversation Examples
Defining	Identification (D.I)	Identifying problems or defining an issue to be solved	I need to understand recursion in Python
	Goal Setting and Requirement Clarification (D.G)	Setting learning goals or clarifying course requirements	What do I need to pass this MOOC?
Seeking	Search (S.S)	Retrieving information from the chatbot	What is a Core Router
	Select (S.SL)	Extracting key points or requesting summaries	Summarize the main takeaways from lecture 3
	Evaluation of Information Quality (S.EQ)	Checking the credibility, reliability, or sources of information	Where do you get your information from?
Engaging	Review (E.RV)	Revisiting materials or verifying correctness	Why is this answer correct?
	Organize (E.O)	Structuring content, categorizing information	List the advantages and disadvantages in order
	Reformatting (Reworking) (E.RF)	Transforming content into a different format (e.g., translation, diagrams, alternative explanations)	Translate this into English. Can you create a flowchart for this?
	Rehearsal (E.RH)	Practicing learned concepts, generating quiz questions	Give me a quiz about Green IT
Reflecting	Task Evaluation (R.ET)	Assessing quality of work or readiness to move forward	Which topic in this lecture has not yet been covered?
	Self-Evaluation (R.ES)	Checking for learning gaps or self-reflection	What is the best way to study for the InfoFit exam?

4.5 Safeguards Against Prompt Injection and Misuse

A very small number of interaction can be interpreted as attempts of prompt injection techniques, trying to override the chatbot's constraints. However, harmful prompt injection attempts were unsuccessful, as the chatbot consistently maintained its instructional role. For instance, when prompted to behave like a general-purpose chatbot, it responded:

As an educational chatbot for the course "Societal Aspects of Information Technology", I focus on providing information related to the course topics. I cannot assist as a general chatbot, but I am here to help with relevant academic queries.

This resilience was achieved by implementing OpenAI's GPT 4o-mini model with a custom system prompt [6]. However, continuous monitoring and refinement of safeguards remain essential to prevent students from discovering new bypass strategies.

4.6 Future Chatbot Design Considerations

Future chatbots should focus on delivering high-quality responses rather than explicitly enforcing SRL strategies. While SRL competencies are essential for academic success [2], forcing metacognitive questioning may lower student acceptance [3]. A more effective approach is to foster SRL indirectly by integrating goal setting activities, interactive exercises, and AI-generated quizzes, which can naturally encourage self-regulated learning within the learning process.

Additionally, integrating chatbots into course logistics and administrative support could further enhance usability, given the course-related questions. However, care must be taken to ensure that chatbots remain focused on content delivery rather than substituting institutional support systems.

5 Conclusion

This study highlights the strong role of RAG-based AI chatbots in facilitating content retrieval and quiz-based reinforcement in MOOCs. While chatbot interactions primarily revolved around information-seeking and quiz-based learning, the findings suggest that students do not automatically engage in metacognitive learning strategies without explicit support.

Future research should explore how AI-generated quizzes and personalized learning can further enhance learning outcomes. Additionally, refining chatbot safeguards against prompt injection and off-topic interactions remains a key priority. Ultimately, chatbots serve as valuable learning assistants, but their success depends on careful pedagogical design that aligns with student expectations and course goals.

Acknowledgments. This research was done as part of the "FutureDEAL - Future of Digital Education and Learning" initiative within the doctoral program "Bildungsinnovation braucht Bildungsforschung", which is supported and partially funded by the Austrian Federal Ministry of Education and Austrian Federal Ministry of Women, Science, and Research.

Disclosure of Interests. The authors have no competing interests to declare.

References

1. Broadbent, J., Poon, W.: Self-regulated learning strategies & academic achievement in online higher education learning environments: a systematic review. Internet High. Educ. **27**, 1–13 (2015). https://doi.org/10.1016/j.iheduc.2015.04.007
2. Brünner, B., Burgsteiner, H., Schön, S., Ebner, M.: The synergy of educational technologies and self-regulated learning: a systematic scoping literature review. In: Auer, M.E., Rüütmann, T. (eds.) ICL 2024. LNNS, vol. 1261, pp. 301–315. Springer, Cham (2025). https://doi.org/10.1007/978-3-031-85649-5_30
3. Brünner, B., Ebner, M.: InfoFit and beyond: AI chatbots as EdTech tools for self-regulated learning in MOOCs. In: Smith, B.K., Borge, M. (eds.) HCII 2025, vol. 15807, pp. 45–60. Springer, Cham (2025). https://doi.org/10.1007/978-3-031-93567-1_4
4. Ebner, M.: iMooX - a MOOC platform for all (universities). In: 2021 7th International Conference on Electrical, Electronics and Information Engineering (ICEEIE), pp. 1–5. IEEE (2021). https://doi.org/10.1109/iceeie52663.2021.9616685
5. Ebner, M., Schöns, S.: Inverse Blended Learning, pp. 16–26. Routledge (2019). https://doi.org/10.4324/9780429398476-2
6. Etzelstorfer, S.: Comparison of different Chatgpt API versions regarding robustness against context breaks using the chatbot in the informatics-fit MOOC (2024), unpublished Bachelor's thesis
7. Gregorac, A., Brünner, B., Ebner, M.: Chatbots in education: a systematic rapid literature review. In: Proceedings of Society for Information Technology & Teacher Education International Conference, pp. 652–657. Association for the Advancement of Computing in Education (AACE), Orlando, Florida, United States (2025). https://learntechlib.org/primary/p/225579/
8. Khalil, H., Ebner, M.: MOOCs completion rates and possible methods to improve retention - a literature review. In: Proceedings of World Conference on Educational Multimedia, Hypermedia and Telecommunications 2014, pp. 1236–1244. AACE, Chesapeake, VA (2014)
9. Labadze, L., Grigolia, M., Machaidze, L.: Role of AI chatbots in education: systematic literature review. Int. J. Educ. Technol. High. Educ. **20**(1) (2023). https://doi.org/10.1186/s41239-023-00426-1
10. Lai, J.W.: Adapting self-regulated learning in an age of generative artificial intelligence chatbots. Future Internet **16**(6), 218 (2024). https://doi.org/10.3390/fi16060218
11. TU Graz Educational Technology: TU Graz Educational Technology: MOOCs & Teaching: Eight Teaching and Learning Scenarios with MOOCs (2024). https://doi.org/10.3217/TQF22-21458
12. Zimmerman, B.J.: Investigating self-regulation and motivation: historical background, methodological developments, and future prospects. Am. Educ. Res. J. **45**, 166–183 (2008). https://doi.org/10.3102/0002831207312909

The Integration of Generative AI-Powered Chatbot for Automated Learning Support: Thai MOOC Platform Experience

Thapanee Thammetar[1,3], Anuchai Theeraroungchaisri[2,3], Jintavee Khlaisang[2,3](✉), and Jira Chonraksuk[3]

[1] Slipakorn University, Rajamankha Nai Rd, Amphoe Muang, Nakhon Pathom, Thailand
[2] Chulalongkorn University, Phayathai Road, Pathumwan, Bangkok, Thailand
jintavee.m@chula.ac.th
[3] Thailand Cyber University (TCU) Project, Ministry of Higher Education, Science, Research and Innovation of Thailand, Bangkok, Thailand

Abstract. This research aims to develop and evaluate the performance of a Generative AI-powered learning support chatbot for the Thai MOOC platform using Microsoft Copilot Studio. The primary objectives are to enhance online learning experiences and improve support services for both students and educational staff. The chatbot was meticulously designed to provide comprehensive online learning guidance, recommend courses tailored to learners' profiles and diverse academic interests, and manage an automated issue-reporting system that ensures efficient problem resolution while maintaining high service quality standards. The development used data from over 750 courses on the Thai MOOC platform, employing course metadata (titles, descriptions, objectives) as training material for the chatbot's recommendation capabilities. Researchers also used system manuals and historical conversation logs to train the chatbot for contextually appropriate guidance and issue resolution. This approach ensured the chatbot effectively addressed learner inquiries.

The study involved a trial with 30 volunteer learners who completed post-usage surveys, alongside in-depth interviews with five Thai MOOC staff members. Quantitative and qualitative analyses revealed exceptionally high satisfaction levels among both groups. Learners reported a mean satisfaction score of 4.5 (SD = 0.59), citing the chatbot's 24/7 availability, instant response capabilities, and precise course recommendations aligned with their academic backgrounds and interests as key strengths. The system demonstrated remarkable accuracy in interpreting user queries, delivering relevant course suggestions, and autonomously logging, categorizing, and escalating issues to relevant teams for swift resolution. All interactions were comprehensively documented for quality assurance purposes. For staff, the chatbot significantly reduced response times and workload by automating routine tasks. However, concerns were raised about long-term maintenance, needing periodic data updates and managing potential scaling challenges. Staff emphasized the importance of establishing clear protocols for updating course information and retraining the chatbot to accommodate platform expansions.

This study underscores Generative AI's potential in developing scalable, efficient online learning support systems like for Thai MOOC. Such tools enrich

E. Hamonic and R. Sharrock (Eds.): EMOOCS 2025, LNCS 15733, pp. 25–35, 2026.
https://doi.org/10.1007/978-3-032-00056-9_3

learner experiences and provide actionable insights for advancing educational technologies. Future iterations could include cross-platform recommendations, enhanced self-repair manuals, and automated email notifications for issue updates, addressing learner feedback.

Keywords: Learning Support Assistant Bot · Thai MOOC · Generative AI · Microsoft Copilot Studio · Online Learning Support · Chatbot Development · Educational Technology · E-learning Platform · Automated Support System · Learning Analytics

1 Introduction

The Thailand Massive Open Online Course (Thai MOOC) platform, established in 2017 through a tri-ministerial partnership between the Ministry of Higher Education, Science, Research and Innovation, the Ministry of Digital Economy and Society, and the Ministry of Education, represents Thailand's strategic response to democratizing education in the digital age. Designed as a national lifelong learning initiative, the platform initially aimed to address systemic challenges in Thai higher education, including limited access for rural populations, rising tuition costs, and faculty shortages in specialized disciplines [1–3]. By 2021, Thai MOOC had surpassed its initial target of 2 million registered learners, driven by its alignment with Thailand 4.0 policies and the National Digital Economy and Society Development Plan. However, this exponential growth-from 94,000 early adopters in 2019 to over 2 million users by 2023—exposed critical scalability limitations in human-driven support systems. With only 5 staff members managing learner inquiries, course recommendations, and technical troubleshooting, Thai MOOC faces challenges in providing effective learner support, similar to other MOOCs worldwide that encounter similar learner support issues [1, 2, 4].

The development of Generative Artificial Intelligence (Generative AI), particularly chatbot technology, has revolutionized online learning through Massive Open Online Courses (MOOCs). Research conducted by demonstrates that chatbots driven by Generative AI possess the capability to scrutinize learner data in real-time, thereby facilitating the personalization of educational experiences through customized recommendations. Moreover, these systems contribute to mitigating educational disparities by offering round-the-clock support for inquiries and comprehensive feedback on assignments, which aligns with findings that indicate that AI-enhanced learning platforms augment course completion rates significantly [5–7]. In the realm of constructing advanced chatbots, Microsoft Copilot Studio stands out as a preeminent instrument that integrates Natural Language Processing (NLP) with machine learning methodologies. This platform is noted for its capacity to diminish the development duration for sophisticated conversational systems in contrast to conventional approaches [6–9]. The incorporation of Generative AI, specifically Microsoft Copilot Studio, for the creation of sophisticated chatbot service units (AI Agents) for the Thai Massive Open Online Course (MOOC) signifies a substantial progression within the realm of online education in Thailand. The design focus on course discovery, proactive academic advising, real-time troubleshooting guidance, aligning with a comprehensive learner support framework [5].

The integration of Generative Artificial Intelligence (Generative AI) into the Thai MOOC system represents a strategic solution to address scalability bottlenecks in learner support services, driven by the platform's exponential growth from 94,000 users in 2019 to over 2 million users in 2023 [5, 8]. Research underscores that sophisticated chatbots, which are underpinned by this technology, can furnish learners with tailored recommendations and comprehensive elucidations of content. Moreover, the implementation of Microsoft Copilot Studio for the creation of AI Agents has markedly diminished the timeframe required for developing intelligent conversational platforms in contrast to conventional methodologies. This enhanced efficiency is congruent with the operational exigencies of the Thai MOOC, which functions with a support team comprising merely five personnel. These advancements establish the groundwork for the study entitled The Integration of Generative AI-Powered Chatbot for Automated Learning Support: Thai MOOC Platform Experience, which investigates the transformative capabilities of AI-driven solutions within Thailand's digital educational landscape. The objectives are delineated as follows: 1. In what ways can a Generative AI Chatbot facilitate the process of online learning within the context of the Thai MOOC platform, and what ramifications does it exert on the learning experiences of users? 2. What is the degree of learner satisfaction regarding the Chatbot, and which determinants significantly affect their overall satisfaction?

2 Literature Review

Massive Open Online Courses (MOOCs) have emerged as a transformative force in the landscape of education, enabling unprecedented access to learning opportunities globally. However, the rapid expansion of MOOC platforms has also revealed significant challenges, particularly concerning learner support. Research indicates that many MOOCs struggle with scalability in providing effective support to learners, often relying on limited human resources to address inquiries, course recommendations, and technical issues [10]. The Thai MOOC platform exemplifies this challenge, having grown from 94,000 users in 2019 to over 2 million by 2023, with only five staff members to manage support services [2].

Generative Artificial Intelligence (Generative AI) has the potential to revolutionize educational support by providing personalized, real-time assistance to learners. Studies have shown that AI-driven chatbots can analyze learner data to offer tailored recommendations, enhancing the educational experience [11]. These systems not only assist with course navigation but also deliver timely feedback on assignments, thereby addressing educational disparities and improving course completion rates [12]. The integration of Generative AI into MOOC platforms aligns with the broader educational goals of democratizing access to quality learning resources. Chatbot technology, particularly those powered by advanced Natural Language Processing (NLP) and machine learning methodologies, has shown promise in enhancing learner engagement and support. Microsoft Copilot Studio is a notable platform that facilitates the development of sophisticated chatbots, reducing the time and resources required to create effective conversational agents [9, 13]. Research indicates that such chatbots can provide proactive academic advising, real-time troubleshooting, and course discovery, thereby significantly improving the overall learner experience [14].

Understanding learner satisfaction with AI-driven support systems is crucial for evaluating their effectiveness. Studies have identified several factors that influence learner satisfaction with chatbots, including the accuracy of information provided, response time, multilingual support and the overall user experience [15, 16]. Furthermore, research has highlighted that user engagement with AI systems can significantly affect their perceptions of satisfaction and the perceived value of the learning experience [6, 17]. As the Thai MOOC platform seeks to integrate Generative AI chatbots, it becomes essential to assess these determinants to enhance user satisfaction and learning outcomes.

3 Methodology

The development of the chatbot necessitated frequent updates to academic course data, quality standards, and user manuals for new features on the Thai MOOC Platform. To address these dynamic requirements, the Agile Model was adopted as the framework for iterative development. This approach ensured adaptability to evolving user needs and platform updates.

3.1 Plan Requirements

The initial phase involved defining the chatbot's scope by analyzing feedback from two key stakeholder groups: Learners and Online Learning Support Officer (See Fig. 1).

- Online Learning Support Officer: The primary challenge stemmed from limited personnel availability to assist learners. This necessitated a self-service chatbot capable of guiding new users through common technical issues via instructional manuals. If unresolved, the chatbot would escalate the issue by creating a support ticket logged in a centralized database, accessible through social media channels.
- Learners: The critical need centered on improving course discoverability. With over 12 categories and numerous overlapping courses on the Thai MOOC Platform, users required advanced search functionality and detailed course metadata to make informed enrollment decisions. This included granular filters for course duration, language, difficulty level, and learning outcomes.

3.2 Product Development

Using Microsoft Copilot Studio, the chatbot was engineered to fulfill three core functionalities derived from stakeholder requirements:

3.2.1 Course Search and Metadata Integration

The chatbot was integrated with a structured course database containing 10 metadata fields critical for semantic search capabilities (Table 1). Natural Language Processing (NLP) algorithms enabled contextual understanding of user queries, cross-referencing terms like "introductory Python courses under 10 h" against the metadata schema. (See Fig. 2).

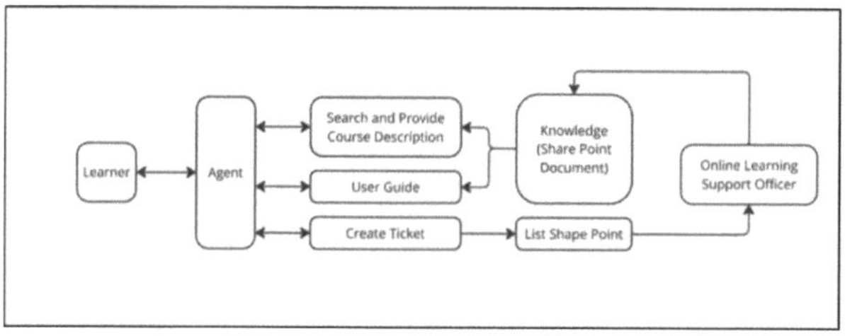

Fig. 1. AI-Powered Chatbot Conceptual Model

Table 1. Course Metadata Schema.

No	Name	Meaning
1	Course Name	Course official title as displayed on Thai MOOC
2	Course Description	Overview of content and learning benefits
3	Learning Outcome	Behavioral objectives defining skill acquisition
4	Duration	Total instructional hours
5	Categories	12 standardized subject classifications
6	Institute Create Course	Developing organization (government, private, or academic)
7	Course Level	Proficiency tiers: Basic, Advanced (prerequisites required), Specialized
8	Course Language	Primary instruction language
9	Course Url	Direct hyperlink to course enrollment page
10	Video Intro Url	Preview video introduction of course URL

3.2.2 User Guide and Knowledge Management

A repository was constructed using asked questions (FAQs) and platform manuals. Generative AI models fine-tuned on this corpus enabled the chatbot to provide step-by-step troubleshooting guides, such as password recovery or troubleshooting when a login failure occurs.

3.2.3 Automated Ticket Generation

A classification pipeline was implemented to detect unresolved issues in user dialogues. Upon identifying a novel problem, the chatbot initiates a ticket creation workflow, prompting users for additional details (e.g., error screenshots, timestamps). Tickets are routed to Online Learning Support Officer via helpdesk system, who then escalates the task to other relevant agents for further resolution. The chatbot's personality parameters were configured to emulate Thai linguistic etiquette, including the polite sentence-ending particle "ครับ" (khrap). Large Language Model (LLM) customization ensured culturally appropriate responses while maintaining technical accuracy. (See Fig. 3).

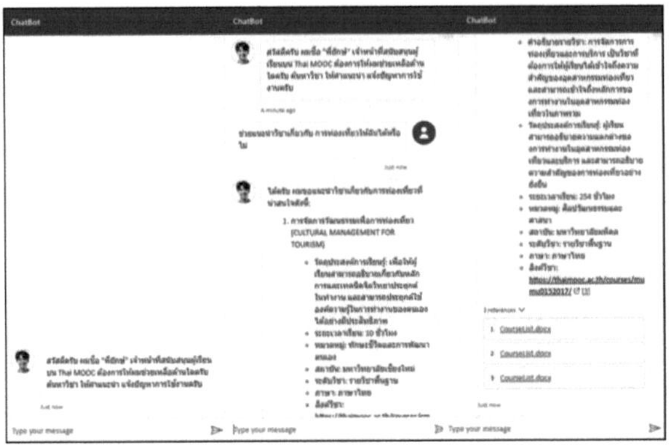

Fig. 2. Image showing a Chatbot AI Agent recommending a course to a learner.

Fig. 3. Image showing of the list of tickets saved in SharePoint

3.3 Software Testing

The researcher provided the developed AI Agents to a group of volunteer learners and Online Learning Support Officer from Thai MOOC to use via social media chat. (See Fig. 4). The details are as follows:

3.3.1 Online Learning Support Officer

Since there were only 5 staff involved, the researcher directly asked about their satisfaction with the AI Agents. Following this, interviews were conducted to gather additional recommendations for improving the AI Agent's efficiency, aiming to obtain in-depth information to better align the AI Agents with the staff's tasks.

3.3.2 Learner Testing

A total of 30 volunteers were given a satisfaction survey to complete after testing the AI Agents. The survey consisted of 14 questions divided into two parts:

- Part 1: Basic information (5 questions) such as age, gender, education level, experience with Thai MOOC, and experience using chatbots.

- Part 2: Satisfaction with the chatbot (8 questions) using a 5-level rating scale, and an additional question (question 9) for further suggestions to improve the AI Agents.

3.4 Delivery Iteration

Since the Thai MOOC platform is constantly updated with new information, such as new courses, user guides for new platform features, and standards for online course development, it is necessary to regularly train the AI Agents with new data to keep its knowledge up to date.

3.5 Feedback Incorporation

A continuous improvement cycle was implemented, prioritizing feature requests and error patterns identified in user feedback. For example, early testers encountered issues with incorrect course links because the data used for training was out of date. Therefore, a process was created to condition the AI agent to always prioritize the most recently updated data. This agile methodology allowed the AI agent's capabilities to be continually improved, aligning with the evolving pedagogical and technological needs of the Thai MOOC ecosystem.

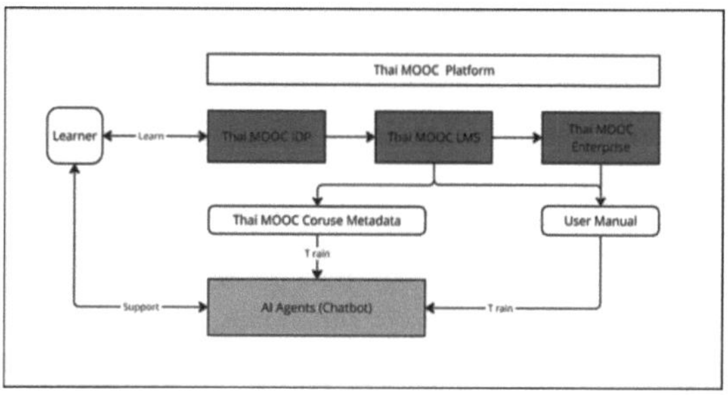

Fig. 4. Image showing the process of how AI Chatbot working with Thai MOOC Platform

4 Results

4.1 Analysis of Volunteer Learner Satisfaction Survey

The satisfaction survey from volunteer learners revealed the following key findings:

- **Demographics**: Respondents had an average age of 33, with nearly equal gender distribution. Most held bachelor's or master's degrees and had prior experience with Thai MOOC, though participation frequency varied.
- **AI Agents Satisfaction**: Learners rated their satisfaction highly (Mean = 4.5, SD = 0.59), particularly in course search accuracy, in-depth recommendations, problem-solving guidance, issue reporting, response speed, updated information, and appropriate Thai language use. Responses to complex inquiries were rated as good.

- **Additional Feedback**: learners highlighted their overall appreciation for the AI Agent's ability to efficiently search for and provide detailed recommendations about Thai MOOC courses. They noted its quick response times and the convenience of being able to report issues to staff 24/7 without needing to adhere to business hours. However, learners suggested improvements such as enabling the AI Agents to recommend courses from other systems or international sources and providing more comprehensive guides for self-troubleshooting based on the bot's suggestions. They also expressed a desire for the AI Agents to automatically email learners after resolving issues and noted occasional inaccuracies in course link information and uncertainty regarding some responses from the AI Agents.

4.2 Analysis of Online Learning Support Officer Satisfaction

Interviews revealed that staff satisfaction emphasized the overall approval of the system:

- Positive Feedback: Staff appreciated the Chatbot for its ability to reduce support time and provide 24/7 assistance to learners. They valued its capabilities in searching for subjects, providing course details, recommending subjects to learners, and automatically logging issues into the ticket system.
- Concerns: Staff expressed concerns about maintenance challenges, such as updating data and resolving future service issues. Many were not trained to use Microsoft Copilot for data preparation, and emphasized the need for structured training and a clear update schedule. They also noted delays in displaying updated information in the Chatbot's responses.

5 Discussion

The addition of a Generative AI chatbot to the Thai MOOC platform has shown great promise in boosting learner support services and enhancing user satisfaction. The results of this research highlight the powerful role of AI solutions in overcoming scalability issues and improving educational experiences, especially for large platforms like Thai MOOC. The chatbot's capability to offer precise course suggestions based on individual academic preferences, along with its round-the-clock availability and quick response times, led to a high satisfaction rating among learners (Mean = 4.5, SD = 0.59). These findings support earlier studies that stress the value of personalized learning through AI technologies. Learners valued the chatbot's effectiveness in helping them find courses and resolve issues, showcasing its importance in making navigation easier within the platform's broad course offerings. However, feedback pointed out areas needing enhancement, such as broadening the chatbot's abilities to include recommendations across different platforms and improving self-help guides.

For the Thai MOOC staff, incorporating generative AI-powered chatbots into the Thai MOOC platform has markedly alleviated the administrative burden on staff. In contrast to traditional learner support mechanisms, which were characterized by the absence of a formalized system and relied on manual responses to inquiries via social media, coupled with the time-consuming task of logging data into tables for distribution to relevant stakeholders, chatbots facilitate the automation of routine functions, including ticket generation and preliminary troubleshooting. This automation enables staff to focus on addressing more complex challenges, thereby enhancing operational efficiency and optimizing resource utilization. Nevertheless, concerns were expressed about the difficulties of long-term maintenance, such as the need for regular data updates and retraining. Staff highlighted the necessity for organized training programs to ensure the effective use of Microsoft Copilot Studio for preparing and updating data. While the chatbot generally did a good job, there were some errors in course link details and unclear answers that showed how crucial it is to keep training data current. These results stress the importance of continually improving AI systems to guarantee trustworthiness and precision in changing educational settings.

6 Conclusion

The integration of a Generative AI-powered chatbot into the Thai MOOC platform has demonstrated significant potential in addressing scalability challenges and enhancing the overall learning experience for users. By leveraging Microsoft Copilot Studio and advanced Natural Language Processing (NLP), the chatbot effectively improved course discoverability, provided personalized academic recommendations, and automated issue resolution processes. The high satisfaction ratings from both learners and staff underscore its ability to deliver timely, accurate, and culturally appropriate support, aligning with the platform's mission to democratize education in Thailand.

While the chatbot successfully reduced staff workloads and improved learner engagement, the study also highlighted the critical need for continuous maintenance to ensure its long-term effectiveness and sustainability. This involves implementing systematic retraining protocols, such as training the chatbot on comparable data from collaborating platforms – including MOOCs from other Thai universities or international partners affiliated with Thai MOOC – to expand its service capabilities. Furthermore, establishing a defined timeline for updating essential information, such as details on newly added courses within the Thai MOOC platform, user guides, and self-help troubleshooting resources, is crucial. These ongoing maintenance efforts are vital to guarantee the future accuracy and reliability of the chatbot's recommendations and support.

Overall, this research underscores the transformative role of Generative AI in revolutionizing online education support systems. As educational platforms continue to grow and evolve, future iterations of AI-driven solutions should prioritize adaptability, inclusivity, and user-centric design to meet diverse learner needs and foster lifelong learning opportunities on a global scale.

References

1. Sirisuthikul, V.: Building a R.I.C.H. brand in 10 hours: teaching sustainability concepts through Thai MOOC. Int. J. Inf. Educ. Technol. **13**(5), 849–854 (2023). https://doi.org/10.18178/ijiet.2023.13.5.1878
2. Thailand Cyber University: Thai MOOC Learner Statistics, 3 March 2025. https://Thaicyberu.Go.Th
3. Thammetar, T., Theeraroungchaisri, A., Khlaisang, J., Duangchinda, V.: 69 Publications 105 Citations See Profile (2022). https://www.researchgate.net/publication/366289550

4. Theeraroungchaisri, A., Thammetar, T., Duangchinda, V., Khlaisang, J.: EMOOCs 2023 Hasso Plattner Institute Potsdam (2023). https://doi.org/10.25932/publishup-57645
5. Harr, M., Wienand, M., Schütte, R.: Towards Enhanced E-Learning Within MOOCs: Exploring the Capabilities of Generative Artificial Intelligence Completed Research Paper (2024). https://www.researchgate.net/publication/387055666
6. Nze, S.U.: AI-powered chatbots. Glob. J. Hum. Resour. Manag. **12**(6), 34–45 (2024). https://doi.org/10.37745/gjhrm.2013/vol12n63445
7. Touimi, Y.B., Hadioui, A., Faddouli, N.E., Bennani, S.: Intelligent chatbot-LDA recommender system. Int. J. Emerg. Technol. Learn. **15**(20), 4–20 (2020). https://doi.org/10.3991/ijet.v15i20.15657
8. Aksoy, D.A., Kursun, E.: Behind the scenes: a critical perspective on GenAI and open educational practices. Open Praxis **16**(3), 457–470 (2024). https://doi.org/10.55982/openpraxis.16.3.674
9. Chen, W.-Y.: Intelligent tutor: leveraging ChatGPT and Microsoft copilot studio to deliver a generative AI student support and feedback system within teams (2024). https://doi.org/10.48550/arXiv.2405.1302
10. Sarwari, K.: Using AI tools for teaching and learning: a systematic review of literature (2025). https://doi.org/10.22034/cee.2024.491255.1031
11. Wangsa, K., Karim, S., Gide, E., Elkhodr, M.: A systematic review and comprehensive analysis of pioneering AI chatbot models from education to healthcare: ChatGPT, Bard, Llama, Ernie and Grok. Future Internet **16**(7) (2024). https://doi.org/10.3390/fi16070219
12. Krishna, A., Satheesh, A., Parthip, P.R., Thomas, B., Gopi, A.: AI-driven personalized learning: a comprehensive survey of chatbot applications in education and training (2024). https://doi.org/10.20944/preprints202412.1240.v1.
13. Nik Harun, N.A., Md Syed, M.A., Abdullah, F.: Revolutionising costume design education: a case study on the impact of Microsoft Copilot. Qual. Assur. Educ. (2024). https://doi.org/10.1108/QAE-06-2024-0119
14. Putri, D.F., Sain, Z.H.: From chalkboards to chatbots: revolutionizing education with AI-driven learning innovations. educative: Jurnal Ilmiah Pendidikan **3**(1), 1–10 (2025). https://doi.org/10.70437/educative.v3i1.823
15. Yassin, A., Bashir, A.: Student satisfaction with the use of chat-GPT as a learning resource. Vocat. J. Educ. Technol. **1**(1), 1–7 (2024). https://doi.org/10.58740/vocational.v1i1.247
16. Yawan, H., Syafitri, N., Nurhaliza, S.: Integrating AI chatbot into learning management system: enhancing student engagement and learning outcomes **5**(2), 1346–1359 (2024). https://doi.org/10.56667/dejournal.v5i2.1605
17. Bhardwaj, N., Sabari Karthik, H., Anand, D., Rahul, M.: AI chatbot for smart communities: enhancing user interaction in educational institutions. In: 2024 IEEE 6th PhD Colloquium on Emerging Domain Innovation and Technology for Society, Ph.D EDITS 2024 (2024). https://doi.org/10.1109/phdedits64207.2024.10838692

Analysis of the Generalization of Students' Success Predictive Models in a Series of Java MOOCs on edX

Pedro Manuel Moreno-Marcos(✉), Miguel Rodríguez Guillén, Carlos Alario-Hoyos, Pedro J. Muñoz-Merino, Iria Estévez-Ayres, and Carlos Delgado Kloos

Department of Telematic Engineering, Universidad Carlos III de Madrid, 28911 Leganés (Madrid), Spain
pemoreno@it.uc3m.es

Abstract. One of the key challenges in Massive Open Online Courses (MOOCs) is the high attrition rate. While researchers have worked on predictive models to detect students at risk, one problem is that these models are often trained using data from one course. However, these models face difficulties when generalizing to other contexts. In this line, this work aims to analyze how predictive models can generalize to other similar courses. Particularly, analyses are conducted using a series of three courses about Java programming, with several editions in English and in Spanish, and in teacher-paced and learner-paced modes, and using variables at learner and course level. This way, it is possible to analyze the generalizability considering different combinations of predictive models to forecast MOOC grades and whether or not students pass the course. Results show that it is possible to achieve proper transferability between models in this context, although the predictive power decreases considerably in specific combinations of courses. Moreover, transferability improves when combining two courses. In addition, it is possible to achieve accurate results regardless of the language although significant differences are observed in some cases when transferring models to the courses in a different language. In contrast, there are barely differences when training and predicting using teacher-paced and learner-paced MOOCs, and accurate results are obtained in both cases. These results entail that it is possible to achieve transferable models in MOOCs when using related MOOCs although a drop in the predictive power may appear depending on the course and language.

Keywords: prediction · MOOCs · generalization · learning analytics · student's success

1 Introduction and Related Works

Massive Open Online Courses (MOOCs) can be very useful for lifelong learning since they offer short open courses that might be tailored to learners' needs. However, it is also very typical that learners enroll in the MOOC but they do not manage to complete

E. Hamonic and R. Sharrock (Eds.): EMOOCS 2025, LNCS 15733, pp. 36–45, 2026.
https://doi.org/10.1007/978-3-032-00056-9_4

it, with completion rates below 10% [1]. While there might be many possible factors affecting this issue (e.g., psychological, social, personal, course-related, time, etc. [2]), the high attrition rates have led many researchers to analyze how to detect students at risk of failing or dropping out the course to help them. This has been mainly done through the development of predictive models using machine learning techniques.

Particularly, these models have mainly focused on dropout prediction [3] or success prediction, although other variables (e.g., students' behaviors, affective states, etc. [4] have also been explored). Regarding the variables to predict, the most typical ones have been related to interactions with exercises [5] and interactions with videos [6], with the first group often providing the most accurate results (e.g., [7]). Moreover, other works have used variables related to course activity (e.g., Alamri et al. [8], achieved powerful results using just the time spent on resources and the number of accesses), and course forum [7], among others (as suggested in [4]). As for the algorithms, many algorithms, such as regression, Random Forest, Decision Trees, neural networks, etc. have been used, although some works have reported that differences between them are smaller than the difference data could make [9].

However, one key limitation of the previous models is that they might have problems when trying to generalize to other contexts. For example, Occumpaugh et al. [10] reported difficulties when using a trained model with other students, and Boyer and Veeramachaneini [11] found a drop in the Area Under the Curve (AUC) of 0.1 when transferring the predictive models to the next edition of the MOOC. Moreover, Romero and Ventura [12] edited a special issue with several works that worked around generalizability, and some works showed that specific predictors and/or the application [13] or regularization techniques could improve generalizability [14]. Furthermore, Gitinabard et al. [15] reported that their models could be generalized to future editions of the course and even when training with a small number of students at risk. However, one limitation is that these analyses were done based on only two undergraduate courses, and more research is needed around that.

In relation to that, Sgir et al. [16] highlighted the current limitations of generalizability of the models and the research results due to the use of limited contexts. A typical claim that is often reported is that results should be generalized to similar contexts, but this is not often tested. In this line, Moreno-Marcos et al. [7] analyzed predictive models using two MOOCs on the same topics and found that most of the results were generalizable, with some differences. However, more work is needed to understand the conditions that make models generalizable. Some of the previous examples (e.g., [11, 15]) focused on transferring to the next edition of the MOOC, but there are other cases that are worth analyzing to gather new insights on this topic. For example, it is interesting to analyze if the instruction language or the instruction mode (i.e., instructor-paced, when materials are released progressively; or learned paced, where all materials are available from the beginning and learners can decide when to enroll and engage with them) could affect generalization.

In this line, this work aims to contribute with new insights into this. The objective of this work is to analyze to what extent predictive models to forecast success and grades can generalize to other similar courses and/or contexts, considering the topic of Java programming. In order to do that, data from three MOOCs belonging to the same series of MOOCs about Java programming will be used. Considering this, the following specific objectives (O) will be addressed to analyze how models can be transferred to other courses:

- O1. Analyze to what extent predictive models to forecast success and grades can generalize to other MOOCs on the same topic.
- O2. Analyze to what extent predictive models to forecast success and grades can generalize to the same MOOCs in a different language.
- O3. Analyze to what extent predictive models to forecast success and grades can generalize to the same MOOCs in a different instruction mode (teacher paced/learner paced).

The structure of this work is as follows. Section 2 presents the methodology, including details about the educational context and the sample, the variables involved in the study and the analytical methods. Section 3 details and discusses the results obtained in this work, according to the mentioned objectives, and the main conclusions, limitations and future research directions are provided and justified in Sect. 4.

2 Methodology

2.1 Educational Context

This work is carried out using data from a series of three MOOCs about Java programming offered on edX by Universidad Carlos III de Madrid. The first course (C1) covers the basics of Java programming, use of conditionals and loops, recursion and Object-Oriented programming; the second (C2) covers aspects about error detection, unit tests, program efficiency, and software engineering; and the third one (C3) covers data structures and algorithms, including linear structures, stacks, queues, trees, and sorting algorithms. Each of the courses is organized in five modules and contains formative exercises and summative assessments in each of the modules. In these courses, it is necessary to obtain 60% of the points to pass the course, although there is no minimum grade for each assessment.

Table 1. Details of the sample size for each type of course

Course	C1 (n = 15,692)		C2 (n = 2,277)		C3 (n = 805)	
Language	English	Spanish	English	Spanish	English	Spanish
Learner paced	5,747	948	1,259	280	354	243
Teacher paced	8,708	289	666	72	187	21

The data collection period was between 2015 and 2019, including several editions of each MOOC. Moreover, each of the three MOOCs were offered both in Spanish and English (there were six MOOCs indeed) and the courses were offered in a learner-paced mode excepting the first edition of each of the MOOCs (covered in this data collection period). The information used for these analyses is taken from the tracking logs [17]. Particularly, the following events are considered: *problem_check, edx.forum.comment.created, edx.forum.response.created, edx.forum.threat.created, edx.forum.thread.voted* and *edx.forum.response.voted*. Moreover, as many students enroll in the MOOC but do not engage with it, only students who have attempted at least one summative exercise (i.e., one question in one of the exams) are considered. Details of the sample size considering these criteria are provided in Table 1.

2.2 Description of the Variables and Analytical Methods

The dependent variables of this study are two: (1) the final grade of the MOOC, measured in scale 0–1, and (2) a binary variable representing whether or not students pass the course (i.e., obtain a grade higher or equal than 60%). Regarding the independent variables, they are classified in two groups to include variables at user levels which capture students' interactions with the MOOCs, and variables at course level that serve to indicate the main features of the course to support the generalizability of the models. Table 2 presents the full list of variables, including the dependent variables. For the predictive models related to the dependent variable are not used (e.g., *avg_sum* and *per_sum* are not used in models to predict pass).

As for the machine learning algorithms, the following algorithms are considered: Decision Trees (DT), Random Forest (RF), K-Nearest Neighbors (KNN) and Gradient Boosting (GB). All these algorithms have been used through the Sklearn Python library. Root Mean Square Error (RMSE) and Area Under the Curve (AUC) are used to evaluate the results when using regression and classification, respectively.

3 Results and Discussion

3.1 Transfer Models Between Courses

The first analysis consists of training the model using the data until the end of the course with different combinations of courses (C) and algorithms. Particularly, models have been trained using every single course individually, combinations of two courses, and all three courses together, and these models are evaluated for each of the three courses. Results obtained for success prediction and grades predictions can be found in Tables 3 and 4, respectively. When predicting success and grades in C1, it can be observed that there are barely differences in terms of the algorithms excepting KNN, which shows poorer results. Regarding generalizability, results are stable and accurate regardless of the course to predict, except when training with C3. In this case, the sample size could affect the result as it is considerably smaller than the other courses and in fact, the predictive power when predicting in C3 is also worse than in other cases. When predicting using C2, GB offers the best results in all combinations for classification, although there are not strong differences with other algorithms and conclusions in terms of generalizability are similar. In this case, it is also interesting to see that there are combinations when C2 is predicted using a model trained with other courses and results are even slightly better.

For example, model trained with C1 in DT is better than the model trained with C2. This may entail that there is a good level of transferability between MOOCs on the same topic, which is consistent with [7] when analyzing feature importance in similar courses. In addition, these results are consistent with [15], which reported accurate results when transferring to other editions of the same course. Moreover, results generally slightly improve when combining several courses, which suggests that adding more data could boost generalizability even having different courses.

Table 2. List of variables.

Category	Variable	Description
User level	avg_sum	Average grade of summative exercises (non-attempted exercises are graded as 0)
	pass	It indicates whether or not students have obtained a grade higher or equal the passing rate (60%)
	per_ass	Percentage of attempted exams even if they are not completed (e.g., if the MOOC has 5 exams, values are multiples of 0.2)
	avg_for	Average grade of formative exercises (non-attempted exercises are graded as 0)
	per_for	Percentage of attempted formative exercises
	npart	Number of times the students have participated in the forum by creating a thread or responding a previous message in a thread
	nvotes	Number of positive votes received in forum threads and responses
	compl	It indicates whether or not students have attempted all the exams
	wload	It is a weighted average of previous factors as $0.5 \cdot$per_ass + $0.4 \cdot$per_for + $0.05 \cdot$per_votes + $0.05 \cdot$per_part, where the last two represent nvotes and npart normalized to the maximum value in the dataset for each variable, respectively
Course level	version	Categorical value indicating the specific edition of the course (each of the three courses may have several editions in each language)
	nexercises	Number of exercises in the course (number of items in the problem folder or the course structure, including formative and summative ones)
	nvideos	Number of videos on the course
	tduration	Sum of time needed to complete the course, considering video length and 68 s for each question, following discussions in [18]
	language	Categorical variable to represent if the course is delivered in English or Spanish
	inst_mode	Categorical variable to represent if the course is delivered in teacher-paced or learner-paced mode
	avg_cgrade	Average grade of the course considering all students (6 possibles values are present considering 3 courses in 2 languages)

The analysis of C3 is interesting because the predictive power when training with that course is not as high as in the other cases. In this case, it is observed that the predictive power when training with C1 and/or C2 is sometimes higher or equal than training with C3 (e.g., when training with C2 and DT in classification or when training with C1 or C2 and DT in regression). This suggests that models trained with very similar courses in topics and methodology could be transferable in some contexts. This result is consistent with [15], but differs from the findings in Boyer and Veeramachaneni [11], who observed a drop of 0.1 in AUC when training with data from a previous edition of the same MOOC. Nevertheless, the course context may affect the results, suggesting that transferability could be achieved (as shown in this study), but this should be evaluated in each case. Moreover, results also show that models trained with several courses could also benefit individual courses, as previously suggested in [19].

Table 3. Transference between models when predicting success (values presented in AUC).

Algorithm	DT			RF			KNN			GB		
Train/Test course	C1	C2	C3	C1	C2	C3	C1	C2	C3	C1	C2	C3
C1	0.93	0.92	0.80	0.93	0.89	0.80	0.92	0.84	0.87	0.93	0.92	0.82
C2	0.93	0.91	0.86	0.93	0.89	0.80	0.78	0.89	0.67	0.93	0.92	0.84
C3	0.86	0.86	0.81	0.86	0.87	0.80	0.80	0.74	0.73	0.88	0.89	0.84
C1+C2	0.94	0.92	0.86	0.93	0.93	0.82	0.95	0.94	0.74	0.94	0.93	0.82
C1+C3	0.94	0.92	0.86	0.93	0.91	0.84	0.94	0.72	0.83	0.93	0.92	0.88
C2+C3	0.94	0.92	0.86	0.83	0.88	0.83	0.86	0.95	0.89	0.93	0.94	0.86
All	0.92	0.91	0.84	0.94	0.93	0.84	0.94	0.92	0.82	0.93	0.94	0.86

Table 4. Transference between models when predicting grades (values presented in RMSE).

Algorithm	DT			RF			KNN			GB		
Train/Test course	C1	C2	C3	C1	C2	C3	C1	C2	C3	C1	C2	C3
C1	0.11	0.14	0.17	0.10	0.14	0.20	0.11	0.17	0.22	0.10	0.14	0.19
C2	0.11	0.13	0.18	0.11	0.13	0.18	0.15	0.15	0.30	0.11	0.13	0.17
C3	0.13	0.15	0.18	0.12	0.14	0.18	0.17	0.17	0.21	0.13	0.15	0.18
C1+C2	0.11	0.14	0.18	0.10	0.12	0.18	0.09	0.11	0.27	0.10	0.12	0.18
C1+C3	0.11	0.14	0.17	0.10	0.13	0.16	0.10	0.17	0.15	0.10	0.13	0.16
C2+C3	0.11	0.13	0.17	0.15	0.12	0.17	0.16	0.11	0.18	0.11	0.12	0.16
All	0.11	0.14	0.18	0.10	0.13	0.17	0.10	0.13	0.19	0.10	0.12	0.17

3.2 Transfer Models with Courses in Different Languages

The second analysis consists of analyzing the differences between transferability of models when using courses in different languages. In order to do that, models have been trained using data from only the MOOCs in Spanish, only the MOOCs in English and both. In this case, as DT, RF and GB offered similar results, models have only been computed using GB. Results from these analyses are presented in Table 5. From this table, it can be observed that models trained with courses in English offer better results. In this case, a drop of 0.04 in AUC is observed when training with courses in Spanish and 0.01 in RMSE. These differences might be attributed to the differences between the students and/or the sample and although they are higher than those presented in the previous Section, they do not considerably impact the impact as the AUC/RMSE are still excellent to be used. When training with MOOCs in Spanish, a drop of 0.1 in AUC and 0.01 in RMSE is also observed, which is not very significant and might be due to the differences in context. Moreover, when training with both courses, no improvement is observed in classification methods with respect to training with the same language, but a slight improvement is shown in regression. Overall, results from this section might suggest that course language might have a slight effect depending on the languages and while this might affect accuracy, models might still be accurate enough to be useful for prediction. Nevertheless, if the predictive power is fair in other contexts, the impact of these differences might become more significant.

Table 5. Transference between predictive models with courses in different languages

Predictive task	Success (AUC)		Grades (RMSE)	
Train/Test language	Spanish	English	Spanish	English
Spanish	0.84	0.90	0.14	0.12
English	0.83	0.94	0.15	0.11
Both	0.84	0.94	0.13	0.10

Table 6. Transference between predictive models with courses in instruction modes

Predictive task	Success (AUC)		Grades (RMSE)	
Train/Test language	Teacher paced	Learner paced	Teacher paced	Learner paced
Teacher paced	0.93	0.93	0.10	0.13
Learner paced	0.91	0.92	0.11	0.13
Both	0.93	0.93	0.10	0.12

3.3 Transfer Models with Courses with Different Instruction Modes

The third analysis consists of analyzing the differences between training using data from teacher-paced and learner-paced editions from the same courses. For this case, GB is used for classification and regression and results are presented in Table 6. From this table, little differences are observed between the models. When training with teacher-paced courses, it is noteworthy that results slightly improve for learner-paced MOOCs respect to the predictive power when training with learner-paced MOOCs but the difference is only 0.01. Moreover, the predictive power drops 0.02 in AUC when predicting success (and 0.01 in RMSE in grades prediction) in teacher-paced MOOCs and training with learner-paced MOOCs. Nevertheless, differences are very small in all cases, which might suggest that the instruction mode does not affect transferability of the models to other courses.

4 Conclusions

This paper analyzes to what extent models trained with one course can be transferred to other courses in the same series of three MOOCs on Java programming, and the impact of the course language and instruction mode in the generalizability of the models. Results have shown that it is possible to achieve accurate results in both success prediction and grades prediction when training using data from other courses in the series although a drop of accuracy is observed in some cases (particularly when training with C3, probably due to the course context and/or reduced sample size). Moreover, results improved when combining several courses, which might suggest that the variability of courses when training might be beneficial. In the analysis of languages, results showed that there was a drop when training using data from the course in a different language, and the drop was higher in English than in Spanish. However, despite losing predictive power, the loss was less than 0.05 in AUC and 0.01 at most in RMSE, so the validity of these models to support possible interventions is not significantly affected. In addition, analyses of the instruction mode indicated low differences between teacher-paced and learner-paced modes, which might entail that models using different instruction models could be transferred without losing significant accuracy.

The implications of this work are that given the accurate levels of transferability across different editions of the course, languages and methodologies, MOOC providers could collect data from the courses they have and develop the predictive models so they could be used in other editions of the course. For example, when a new series of MOOCs is designed, predictive models could be developed using the first course and used in other courses while data are collected. Moreover, data from different editions and courses in a series of MOOCs could be combined to further improve the models. With these models, it could also be possible to design automatically targeted interventions to mitigate dropout (as was shown in a pilot in [20]).

Despite having obtained these findings, there are some limitations that are worth mentioning. First, these analyses have been carried out using just one series of three MOOCs. While they serve to gather insights about generalizability when having similar courses, which is relevant, these results are framed in a specific scenario. Thus, other conclusions might be obtained when generalizing to more heterogenous educational contexts. Moreover, the sample size might have slightly affected the results since there was an unbalanced distribution between the different courses and languages. Furthermore, only students who engaged in exercises were considered and while this could be a reasonable approach, this could introduce certain bias.

Considering the previous limitations, future work should focus on expanding this research to more different MOOCs to gather more insights about the generalizability in different contexts. Moreover, it would be interesting to analyze the effect of the specific variables to know to what extent the course-related variables have an impact on the transferability of the models and the possible differences in the predictive power over time. In addition, other new variables, which are not considered in this work, could be included in the model and that could have an important role for generalization. Finally, it would be relevant to put these models into practice and transfer models from previous courses, as suggested in this paper, to evaluate the real impact these models might have to reduce academic failure in the MOOC.

Acknowledgments. This work was supported by Universidad Carlos III de Madrid (UC3M) through the Grants for the Research Activity of Young Doctors of the UC3M's Own Research and Transfer Program (ASESOR-IA project). Moreover, it was supported by FEDER / Ministerio de Ciencia, Innovación y Universidades - Agencia Estatal de Investigación through the grant PID2023-146692OB-C31 (GENIE Learn project) funded by MICIU/AEI/10.13039/501100011033 and by ERDF/UE, by the UNESCO Chair of "Scalable Digital Education for All" at UC3M and by the grant RED2022-134284-T funded by MICIU/AEI/10.13039/501100011033.

Disclosure of Interests. The authors have no competing interests to declare that are relevant to the content of this article.

References

1. Narayanasamy, S.K., Elçi, A.: An effective prediction model for online course dropout rate. Int. J. Distan. Educ. Technol. **18**(4), 94–110 (2020)
2. Wang, W., Zhao, Y., Wu, Y.J., Goh, M.: Factors of dropout from MOOCs: a bibliometric review. Library Hi Tech **41**(2), 432–453 (2023)
3. Chen, J., Fang, B., Zhang, H., Xue, X.: A systematic review for MOOC dropout prediction from the perspective of machine learning. Interact. Learn. Environ. **32**(5), 1642–1655 (2024)
4. Moreno-Marcos, P.M., Alario-Hoyos, C., Muñoz-Merino, P.J., Delgado Kloos, C.: Prediction in MOOCs: a review and future research directions. IEEE Trans. Learn. Technol. **12**(3), 384–401 (2019)
5. Ren, Z., Rangwala, H., Johri, A.: Predicting performance on MOOC assessments using multi-regression. In: Proceedings of the 9th International Conference on Educational Data Mining, pp. 484–489. Educational Data Mining Society, Raleigh, NC, USA (2016)
6. Liu, H., Chen, X., Zhao, F.: Learning behavior feature fused deep learning network model for MOOC dropout prediction. Educ. Inform. Technol. **29**(3), 3257–3278
7. Moreno-Marcos, P.M., Pong, T.C., Muñoz-Merino, P.J., Delgado Kloos, C.: Analysis of the factors influencing learners' performance prediction with learning analytics. IEEE Access **8**, 5264–5282 (2020)
8. Alamri, A., et al.: Predicting MOOCs dropout using only two easily obtainable features from the first week's activities. In: Coy, A., Hayashi, Y., Chang, M. (eds.) 15th International Conference on Intelligent Tutoring Systems, LNCS, vol. 11528, pp. 163–173. Springer, Cham (2019)
9. Gardner, J., Brooks, C.: Student success prediction in MOOCs. User Model. User-Adap. Inter. **28**, 127–203 (2018)

10. Ocumpaugh, J., Baker, R., Gowda, S., Heffernan, N., Heffernan, C.: Population validity for educational data mining models: a case study in affect detection. Br. J. Edu. Technol. **45**(3), 487–501 (2014)
11. Boyer, S., Veeramachaneni, K.: Transfer learning for predictive models in massive open online courses. In: Conati, C., et al. (eds.) 17th International Conference on Artificial Intelligence in Education, LNCS, vol. 9112, pp. 54–63. Springer, Cham (2015)
12. Romero, C., Ventura, S.: Guest editorial: Special issue on early prediction and supporting of learning performance. IEEE Trans. Learn. Technol. **12**(2), 145–147 (2019)
13. Hung, J.L., Shelton, B.E., Yang, J., Du, X.: Improving predictive modeling for at-risk student identification: a multistage approach. IEEE Trans. Learn. Technol. **12**(2), 148–157 (2019)
14. Olive, D.M., Huynh, D.Q., Reynolds, M., Dougiamas, M., Wiese, D.: A quest for a one-size-fits-all neural network: early prediction of students at risk in online courses. IEEE Trans. Learn. Technol. **12**(2), 171–183 (2019)
15. Gitinabard, N., Xu, Y., Heckman, S., Barnes, T., Lynch, C.F.: How widely can prediction models be generalized? Performance prediction in blended courses. IEEE Trans. Learn. Technol. **12**(2), 184–197 (2019)
16. Sghir, N., Adadi, A., Lahmer, M.: Recent advances in Predictive Learning Analytics: a decade systematic review (2012–2022). Educ. Inf. Technol. **28**(7), 8299–8333 (2023)
17. edX: EdX Research Guide. https://edx.readthedocs.io/projects/devdata/en/stable/. Accessed 26 Feb 2025
18. De Boeck, P., Rijmen, F.: Response times in cognitive tests: interpretation and importance. In: Integrating Timing Considerations to Improve Testing Practices, pp. 142–149. Routledge, New York, NY, USA (2020)
19. Moreno-Marcos, P.M.: Analítica del aprendizaje para la predicción en escenarios educativos heterogéneos. PhD Thesis. Universidad Carlos III de Madrid, Leganés, Spain (2020)
20. Perez-Sanagustin, M., et al.: Can feedback based on predictive data improve learners' passing rates in MOOCs? A preliminary analysis. In: Proceedings of the Eighth ACM Conference on Learning@ Scale, pp. 339–342. ACM, New York, NY, USA (2021)

Strategic and Comprehensive: Modeling MOOC Learner Behavior Through Process Mining of Learning Sequences

Jorge Maldonado-Mahauad(✉)

Departamento de Ciencias de la Computación, Universidad de Cuenca, Cuenca, Ecuador
jorge.maldonado@ucuenca.edu.ec

Abstract. This exploratory study analyzes student behavior in a Massive Open Online Course (MOOC). MOOCs represent a global educational phenomenon transforming teaching and inspiring new research perspectives on learning methods in higher education institutions. Understanding how students organize their learning sequences and how these relate to their academic performance is crucial for optimizing digital educational processes. The objective of this study is to identify and characterize the learning sequences performed by students during their study sessions in a MOOC, using process mining (PM) techniques. The methodology involved analyzing a dataset collected between July 2017 and January 2018, comprising 27,922 students and approximately 3.5 million recorded interactions. Process mining techniques were employed to examine these learning sequences. Results indicate that most interactions correspond to assessments and video lectures, while forums were the least utilized activity. Additionally, two student profiles were identified: "Comprehensive" learners, who follow expected sequences and engage in longer, more intensive study sessions, and "Strategic" learners, who prioritize assessments. This study advances the current understanding of online learning and situates its findings within the broader literature by contrasting them with similar classification patterns reported by other authors.

Keywords: Learning Analytics · Process Mining · Learning Behavior · Massive Open Online Course

1 Introduction

MOOCs (Massive Open Online Courses) are a global phenomenon that is transforming teaching and making researchers reflect on new ways of learning in higher education institutions (HEIs) worldwide. The increase in the interest and importance of MOOCs is reflected in the increase in the number of students registered for courses and in the number of courses published. As of February 2024, nearly 440 million students were reported to have registered in one of the more than 29.5 thousand MOOCs published according to Class Central [1]. This accelerated growth and its rapid adoption in different countries has caught the attention of researchers, who seek to understand how it has spread, its characteristics, the impact on students, but also seek to understand the low pass rates

E. Hamonic and R. Sharrock (Eds.): EMOOCS 2025, LNCS 15733, pp. 46–59, 2026.
https://doi.org/10.1007/978-3-032-00056-9_5

that are only around 5% in this type of course [2]. While initial research on MOOCs focused on understanding completion rates and final course grades, more recent work has examined how students move through course content as a way to understand the learning process itself [3]. In this way, thanks to the fact that MOOC platforms record the clicks of students' interactions with resources, it is possible to investigate their behavior.

The analysis of the detailed interactions with the learning activities such as video lectures, evaluations, readings, forums, etc., have allowed us to understand the degree of commitment that a student establishes with the course resources (for example, micro-interactions) [4]. However, little is known about the learning sequences that students take when interacting with course activities. In addition, little is known about the itineraries that students take during their study sessions, and how they distribute study sessions in relation to their length and frequency throughout the course. However, the research developed to obtain models of student behavior based on data provided by Intelligent Tutoring Systems and Learning Management Systems have revealed information on how students engage and interact with different learning activities [5, 6], More research is needed to advance the understanding of the learning paths that students consider in the course in order to achieve their goals.

The aim of this article is to address these gaps in the literature and using Process Mining (PM) techniques to explore the behavior of students in a MOOC during their study sessions, analyzing the learning sequences that occur both at the macro (weekly/topical) and micro levels (interactions with MOOC resources). This will contribute to the understanding of how students in an online environment manage their study sessions through a MOOC and its relationship with academic achievement. The article is structured as follows: Sect. 2 presents the related work and research questions that serve as the basis for conducting this study, Sect. 3 presents the methodological approach used to answer the research questions, Sect. 4 presents the main results, Sect. 5 presents the discussion of these results, and finally Sect. 6 presents the main conclusions and limitations of the study.

2 Related Work

2.1 Patterns of MOOC Behavior

In online learning, as well as in other types of learning, student participation is considered a prerequisite for learning [7]. In a MOOC, this is the most used indicator to measure learning outcomes. Student engagement can take many forms [8]. In a MOOC, given the openness of the course, the student participates at several levels, where he or she establishes different levels of commitment to the course activities [9, 10]. For example, Xiong and colleagues [11] They found that the level of engagement in learning could be measured by the number of video lectures viewed, the number of forum posts, the number of tests taken, and the number of tasks completed. In another study, Kizilcec and colleagues [12], Based on the number of student interactions with video lectures and assessments, they ranked students based on their participation in the MOOC, where they identified four patterns of participation: 1) Explorers – those who only explore the course, 2) Watchers – who only watch video lectures, 3) Desisters – those who drop out of the course as time goes on, and 4) Completers – those who complete the entire course.

However, in a MOOC, each student sets their own goals with the course and commits in different ways. In a recent study by Maldonado-Mahauad and colleagues [3, 13, 14] it was found that the students of three MOOCs, regardless of the topic of the course, established their own objectives and participated selectively with the course contents. In this research, students were classified according to their interactions with the course activities as: 1) explorers, 2) strategic, and 3) engaged. But in addition, for each type of student, research was carried out on the learning sequences they undertook.

2.2 MOOC Learning Sessions

Recent research has shown that study sessions are still the approach used by students to organize their learning in an online context [16]. A study session can be defined as a period of time during which the student interacts with course resources and where the student's inactivity intervals in the course are no longer than 30 min [17, 18]. According to Tough [19], A session is defined as a period of time spent on a sequence of similar or related activities that are not interrupted by other types of activities. However, in areas such as Learning Analytics and Data Mining, studies have recently begun to be found in which the study session is considered as the unit of analysis. For example, authors such as [3, 20] using Learning Analytics they identified the learning strategies that students use in a study session for both a hybrid and online context. As a result in these studies, students were classified based on the identified strategies, resulting in a characterization of students for the online context in "Samplers", "Comprehensive", and "Targeting" students; as well as for the hybrid context in "intensive", "strategic", "highly strategic", "selective" and "highly selective" students [3, 20]. In these works, the authors have used the instructional design of the course to try to relate and interpret the patterns found. That is, they have tried to connect the design of the course with the Learning Analytics obtained. However, there is still a lack of works that consider the analysis of study sessions with different levels of granularity of the data (macro, meso, micro) and with different levels of activities in which the course is structured (activities, weeks, modules).

Based on the above, this paper proposes an exploratory study that allows: 1) to extract the learning sequences that students make when interacting with the course activities; 2) understand how students organize the different learning sequences during their study sessions in a MOOC; and 3) understand how their behavior relates to their academic performance. The research questions that this study seeks to answer specifically are:

R.Q.1. What learning sequences do students take during their study sessions in a MOOC?

R.Q.2. How can students be classified based on the learning sequences detected during a study session?

3 Methodology

This section presents the development of the exploratory study that has been carried out in the context of the Python MOOC, and with the aim of answering the research questions posed. The following sections describe the structure of the course and the characteristics of the participants in the study. The method used to extract the behavior patterns of the students is then presented.

3.1 MOOC and Participants

This exploratory study was conducted with a dataset recorded between July 2017 and January 2018. The course is structured in 6 modules. Each module is made up of a set of lessons. Each lesson is made up of a set of video lectures, theoretical and practical questionnaires and readings. In total, the course has 35 video lectures (VL), 11 readings (L), 13 practical questionnaires (QP) and 11 theoretical questionnaires (QT). All modules were available during the 6 weeks that the course lasted. Figure 1 shows how distributed the different contents through the different lessons in each of the modules. In the course, 38,838 (N = 38,838) students were registered, of which 10,916 did not register any type of activity on the course.

WEEK 1	RESOURCES
Topic 1	VL VL VL VL VL VL L QT QP
Topic 2	VL VL
Topic 3	L QT
WEEK 2	
Topic 1	VL VL VL VL
Topic 2	VL VL QT
Topic 3	QP L QP L
WEEK 3	
Topic 1	VL VL VL QT
Topic 2	VL VL QT
Topic 3	QP L QP
WEEK 4	
Topic 1	VL VL VL QT
Topic 2	VL VL VL QT
Topic 3	QP L QP L QP L QP
WEEK 5	
Topic 1	VL VL VL QT
Topic 2	VL VL VL QT
Topic 3	QT L QP L QP
WEEK 6	
Topic 1	VL VL VL VL QT
Topic 2	QP L QP

Fig. 1. MOOC structure week by week

For the analysis, all students were considered, except those who did not report any activity, leaving a cohort of 27,922 students who registered about 3.5 million interactions in the course. 15% of registered students were between 18 and 24 years old, 50% were between 25 and 34 years old, and 22% were between 35 and 44 years old. 64% of the students reported being male and 34% female. 34% of the students come from Chile, 20% from Mexico, 13% from Peru, 12% from Colombia, 7% from Spain and 5% from Ecuador.

3.2 Behavioral Pattern Exploration

To explore the behavior patterns of students in the MOOC and answer the research questions, we use the Process Mining methodology called PM^2 [21]. PM^2 is a simplification and flexibility of the L* Life-cycle model [22] and it has been used in different disciplines such as health and business [23, 24]. The stages resulting from this adaptation are the following: 1) Extraction, 2) Generation of the Event Log, 3) Model Discovery, and 4) Model Analysis.

Extraction Stage. In this stage, the activity data or log files recorded by the platform were extracted. The platform generates a set of files in CSV format. This set of files consists of 86 files of which only 8 were selected (Users, Course grades, Course progress, Course items, Course item grades, Course item types, Course lesson, and Course module) to analyze student behavior based on student interactions with course resources. After this, a cleaning and transformation of the data was done.

Generation of the Event Log. In this stage, the event log is defined that will serve in the following stages to discover the process model that allows interpreting the behavior of students in the MOOC. The event log is a file that stores information about students' interactions with the digital resources of the course. The first step in generating the event log was to define two concepts to interpret the data traces of the interactions with the MOOC. Specifically, the concept of session and interaction were defined: ***(1) A study session*** is a period in which students interact with course resources and record continuous activity, with intervals of inactivity no longer than 30 min. It means; that if the student did not carry out any activity or interaction with the course, the platform will end the session and consider it as a new one [30]. ***(2) An interaction*** is an action that is stored in the data traces recorded by Coursera and that reflects a student's interaction with one of the MOOC's digital resources. For this work, 8 types of interactions that the student can register when interacting with video-lectures, assessments, and readings were defined. Table 1 presents the interactions and their meanings.

Table 1. Types of interaction

Resource	Interaction	Meaning
Video-lecture	VL-Begin	Video-lecture starts
	VL-Beginagain	Restart a video lecture that has not been completed
	VL-End	Complete a video-lecture
	VL-Repeat	Return to a video-lecture that you have already completed in the past to review part or all of it
Assessment	Eval-Begin	Assessment starts
	Eval-Beginagain	Restart an assessment that has not been completed
	Eval-End	Pass an assessment
	Eval-Repeat	Return to an assessment that you have already passed in the past to review part or all of it
Reading	Sup	Enter reading material

The resulting event log contains: (1) user id, (2) time stamp, (3) the interaction performed, (4) the session number in which the interaction with the MOOC resources occurs (Fig. 2).

	case_id	time-stamp	Actividad	Sesión	Estado
0	00032063f5c9d360e410e65732ead778cf5f64f2	2018-08-14 13:51:21.130	Video-Lectura	1	VL-Inicia
1	00032063f5c9d360e410e65732ead778cf5f64f2	2018-08-14 13:58:59.657	Video-Lectura	1	VL-Termina
2	00032063f5c9d360e410e65732ead778cf5f64f2	2018-08-14 13:59:16.640	Video-Lectura	1	VL-Inicia
3	00032063f5c9d360e410e65732ead778cf5f64f2	2018-08-14 14:02:58.905	Video-Lectura	1	VL-Termina

Fig. 2. Event log Example

Model Discovery: In this stage, a Process Mining discovery algorithm is applied. This algorithm allows us to extract a process model that models the behavior of students graphically. Specifically, the Disco software is used,[1] which implements a fuzzy algorithm (based on Fuzzy miner) [26].

Model Analysis: As a result of the previous stage, a process model is obtained for each Event Log as shown in Fig. 3. This model represents the behavior of students who do only video-lectures in the MOOC. Each box represents the activity carried out and the number inside it represents the number of times that activity is repeated by the students in the MOOC. The darkest blue box represents the activity that has been done the most times by students in the MOOC, in this case the activity "Video-lecture-Begin" has been done 7,678 times. On the other hand, the bows or arrows that join two activities (boxes) represent the transitions from one activity to another and the number above the bow represents the number of times they went from an activity "A" to an activity "B". For example, there is a path that goes from "Video-Lecture-Begin" to "Video-Lecture-End" and that path was performed 5,107 times. The highlighted black arrow represents the frequency of the transition from one activity to another and is proportional to the width of the activity.

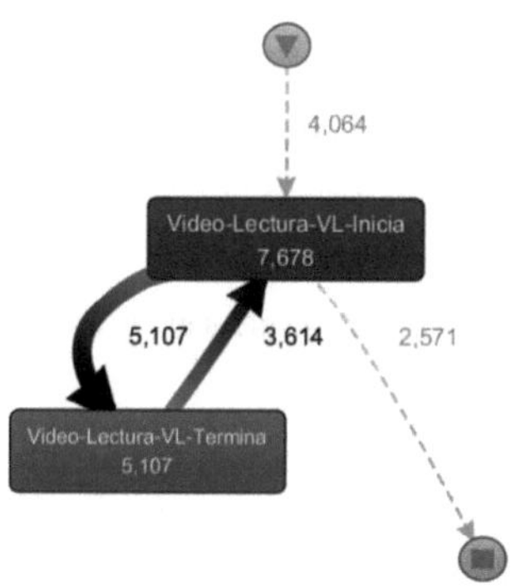

Fig. 3. Event log Example

[1] Disc Software: https://fluxicon.com/disco/.

4 Results

This section presents the results obtained from the analysis of the Event Logs. The results have been organized according to the research questions.

R.Q.1. What Learning Sequences Do Students Take During Their Study Sessions in a MOOC?

Based on the defined Event Log (Fig. 2), we generated the process model that contains the learning sequences of the students in the MOOC. Figure 4 shows the process model that contains the learning sequences that students carry out in the MOOC.

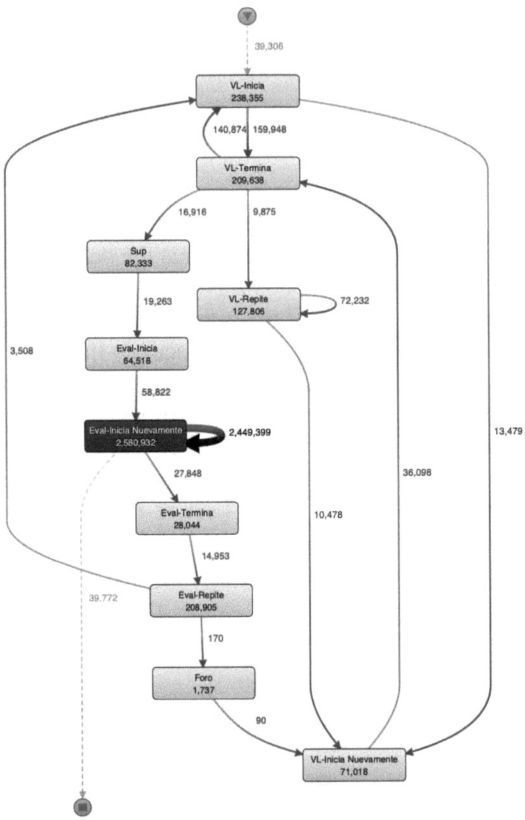

Fig. 4. Process model with the learning sequences that students carry out in the MOOC

From Fig. 4 it can be seen that: 1) the activity that is repeated the most times is "Eval-Start-Again" with 2,580,932 repetitions (representing 71.43% of the total repetitions) and the transition from this activity to it repeats 2,449,399 times, this being the most frequent activity and transition. This means that students repeatedly initiate an evaluation; 2) the next most frequent learning sequence is "VL-Begin → VL-End" repeating 159,948 times followed by the learning sequence "VL-End → VL-Begin" which is repeated 140,847 times. This means that students start and finish the video lectures proposed in the MOOC; 3) the learning sequence "Vl-End → Sup → Eval-Begin → Eval-Beginagain → Eval-Beginagain → Eval-End → Eval-Repeat → VL-Begin" is the most frequent route that students take and that adheres to the design of the MOOC. However, the sequence "Eval-End → Eval-Repeat → VL-Begin" indicates that students after finishing an assessment return to watch it in order to monitor their progress and then prepare to start a new video-lecture. Figure 5 presents the list of the 57,238 types of learning sessions (Variants) that the students undertook. Specifically, Fig. 5 shows session type 9 (Variant 9) in which the sequence of activities that a student performs in the MOOC in that type of session is graphically shown. This is starting and ending video lectures in the same session, where 1,728 student sessions have this type of behavior (5 events with a duration of 12 min).

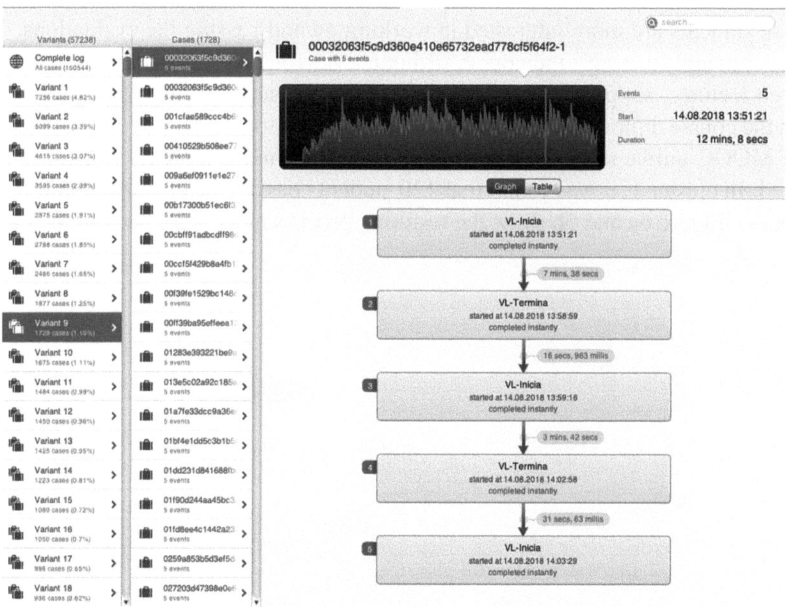

Fig. 5. List of the 57,238 types of learning sessions in the MOOC

R.Q.2. How Can Students Be Classified Based on the Learning Sequences Detected During a Study Session?

To group the students, the sequences of activities that the students perform in their study sessions in the MOOC were considered (see Fig. 5 - Variants). Additionally, the frequencies of interaction of the students with: 1) formative assessments, 2) summative assessments, 3) supplements, 4) Forum, 5) Video-lecture, 6) the duration of the sessions were used as grouping variables. The above indicators were considered regardless of whether they passed or failed the course, since it is desired to identify the learning patterns that students make when following the MOOC. Agglomerative hierarchical grouping based on Ward's method was used as a method. This clustering technique is recommended for detecting groups of students in online contexts [25]. To select the optimal number of clusters, the dendrogram was inspected to see the different ways of cutting the tree structure, in order to obtain a minimum interpretable number of clusters that explain the behavior of the users. However, in a complementary way, the silhouette score and the elbow technique were used as quantitative methods. Result obtained by the elbow method (k = 2), silhouette score (0.536).

Students in Cluster 0 or characterized as "Comprehensive" [3], perform sequences of activities (learning patterns) that students would be expected to perform in the MOOC. This is to work sequentially first with the Video-lectures, then the supplements as proposed in the course design. After this, they address the evaluation activities and finish them before starting a new Video-lecture. In this group, 353 students pass the course and 22,352 fail the course. In contrast, students in Cluster 1 or characterized as "Strategic" [3] work exclusively with the evaluations and to a lesser extent in the Video-lectures, so these students are more interested in working on and passing the evaluations. These students attempt to certify the course without reviewing supplementary materials such as video-lectures, supplements, or forums. This is an indicator that their purpose is to obtain the course diploma, regardless of achieving an in-depth knowledge of the content of the MOOC unlike students in cluster 0, with students in cluster 1 being more goal oriented. In cluster 1, it was found that 120 students passed the course and 5,097 failed the course. Figure 6a and 6b show the resulting process models for each of the clusters.

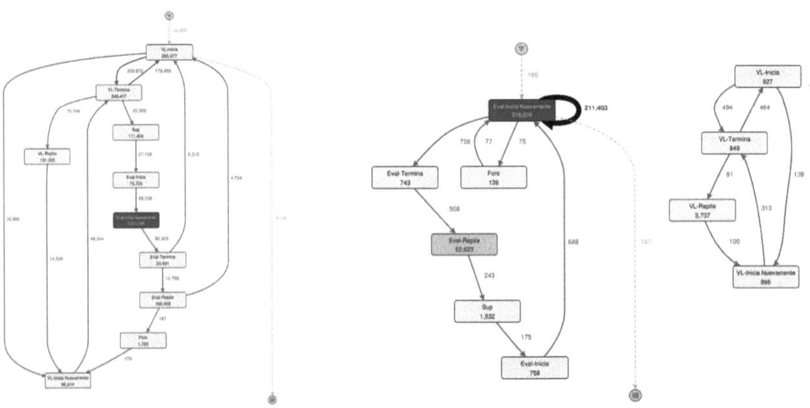

(a) (b)

Fig. 6. (a) Process Model Cluster 0. (b) Process Model Cluster 1

5 Discussion of the Results

To move beyond binary categorizations (completers vs. non-completers) and develop specific interventions or adaptive features, researchers [9, 10, 12, 15] began to develop classification schemes or typologies based on student behavior and engagement patterns. These classifications help to deconstruct the broad category of 'non-completers' and to understand the varied ways in which students interact with MOOC platforms and content. Through these works, common archetypes emerge, particularly those representing minimal engagement ("Sampling," "Observers," "Samplers," "Bystanders") and full engagement/completion ("Completing," "Active Participants," "Keen Completers," "All-rounders"). However, there is significant divergence in how intermediate levels of engagement are categorized. This variation is strongly influenced by the MOOC's pedagogical model (xMOOC vs. cMOOC vs. socioconstructivist) and the specific data analyzed (assessment/video logs, discussion activity, qualitative interviews, specific activity types). The differences between classifications derived from Coursera [4], cMOOCs [20], and FutureLearn [17] underscore the profound impact of pedagogical choices and platform design on student behavior patterns. Social features, networking expectations, and the structure of activities shape how students interact and, consequently, how they are classified.

While prior typologies have provided essential insights into the heterogeneity of learner behaviors in MOOCs—moving beyond binary metrics such as course completion—their methodological limitations constrain the depth and actionability of the resulting analyses. Studies based on clustering techniques (e.g., [12, 28]) rely on aggregated behavioral vectors, often losing the granularity and temporality of sequential actions. Other qualitative approaches, such as observational synthesis or thematic analysis of interviews [10], provide valuable contextual depth but lack scalability and objective event-driven traceability. Furthermore, classifications based solely on activity types [29] omit the sequencing of actions, a critical dimension for understanding learning flows. In contrast, our adoption of Educational Process Mining addresses these limitations by modeling complete behavioral trajectories across different resource types, capturing both the order and timing of student interactions. This allows not only for the visualization of learning pathways and the identification of bottlenecks, but also for the systematic evaluation of alignment with instructional designs and performance outcomes. As such, our approach offers a more holistic and data-driven lens for understanding engagement in MOOCs, bridging the gap between descriptive categorization and actionable learning process diagnostics.

A relevant line of research that relates to our work is presented by Mair [27], who analyzed behavioral patterns in quiz attempts within a mandatory MOOC in Austria. In their study, the authors classified learners based on the number of quiz attempts, identifying five distinct behavioral patterns (e.g., "10 points are enough", "training is more important than the score", "minimal effort", among others). Their approach focused exclusively on quiz repetitions as a proxy for engagement and learning strategies, using quantitative descriptive analysis supported by sequential visualizations. In contrast, our study adopts a Process Mining methodology, which enables us to capture and represent not only repetition patterns in assessments but also complete temporal learning sequences across multiple types of MOOC resources (video lectures, readings, formative and summative assessments). Unlike the approach by [27], our analysis covers full learning sessions and defines learning pathways at different levels of granularity (micro, meso, and macro), offering a more comprehensive view of student behavior throughout the course. Furthermore, while [27] focused on a mandatory MOOC with a relatively small cohort (N = 1,200), our study analyzes a large-scale open MOOC with a significantly larger cohort (N ≈ 28,000 active students, over 3.5 million interactions), enabling broader generalization of findings to diverse learning contexts. It is worth noting that although both studies identify types of students with strategic or thorough behaviors, our approach allows us to connect these strategies with the duration and frequency of study sessions and students' final performance, as well as their engagement over time. For example, we found that strategic learners tend to have shorter sessions focused on assessments, whereas comprehensive learners spend more time and follow sequences aligned with the course's instructional design. This extends the contributions of studies like [27] by showing how navigation strategies impact the overall learning experience beyond quiz outcomes. Finally, we believe that integrating techniques such as Educational Process Mining could complement future studies on quiz behavior, like that of Mair [27], by enhancing the clarity and interpretability of analyses related to student learning behaviors in massive online learning environments.

6 Conclusions and Limitations of the Study

This paper presents an exploratory study to characterize student behavior in online environments. This article contributes to the study and understanding of how students develop their learning sequences in their study sessions in a MOOC. Although there is previous work in the literature that has explored the learning trajectories that students make in a MOOC [3, 13], this work, in comparison with those mentioned above, analyzes the study trajectories that students make at the micro level, as a result of interactions with the course resources. In addition, it characterizes the students' study sessions throughout the 6 weeks of the course. This allows for advanced knowledge about how students use a MOOC, whether they take it to learn by working exhaustively with course resources, or whether it is to obtain a certificate or validate their knowledge by working solely with course assessments.

The main conclusions of this study are the following. ***First***, the greatest number of interactions throughout the 6 weeks occurs with summative assessments followed by video lectures. Students interact more with formative assessments than with course readings (supplements), with forums being the activity that records the fewest interactions throughout the 6 weeks. ***Second***, the students, based on their learning sequences, were classified into two groups: 1) students characterized as "Comprehensive" [3], perform sequences of activities that students would be expected to perform in the MOOC. This is to work sequentially first with the Video-lectures, then the supplements as proposed in the course design. Then they address the evaluation activities and finish them before starting a new Video-lecture again; 2) students characterized as "Strategic" [3], work exclusively with evaluations and to a lesser extent with Video lectures. These students are interested in working and passing the evaluations. These students attempt to certify the course without reviewing supplementary materials such as Video-lectures, supplements, or forums. ***Third***, "Understanding" students who pass the course work sessions that on average last longer during the 6 weeks of the course compared to students in this same group who fail the course. "Understanding" students work constantly and intensively with course materials. ***Fourth***, "Strategic" students who pass the course work sessions that on average last longer during the 6 weeks of the course compared to the same students in this group who fail the course. However, they work less intensely than the "Understanding" students who pass the course. This suggests that "Strategic" and course-passing students seek to certify the MOOC with no intention of working along the course route but rather focus on passing assessments.

The results of this study are subject to some limitations given by the nature of the data and the methodological choices made. First, the identification of the activities that are designed in a MOOC are limited by the technological platforms on which the courses are implemented and the interpretation of the observed actions that students perform when interacting with the course, by the quantity and quality of data that the platforms store. Second, the generalization of these results is subject to the limitations of the methodology used in this study, as well as the results obtained through the use of Process Mining techniques. Despite the aforementioned limitations, the article advances in the understanding of online learning. The findings complement previous work in the literature on other platforms for online courses such as Learning Management Systems. However, in a MOOC, students are heterogeneous and highly diverse, so the results found in this study enrich the current literature.

Acknowledgements. This work has been co-financed by the Vice-Rectorate for Research of the University of Cuenca (VIUC), Cuenca-Ecuador.

References

1. Shah, D.: By the Numbers: MOOCs in 2019. Cl. Cent. (2019)
2. Kizilcec, R.F., Cohen, G.L.: Eight-minute self-regulation intervention raises educational attainment at scale in individualist but not collectivist cultures. Proc. Natl. Acad. Sci. **114**(17), 4348–4353 (2017)
3. Maldonado-Mahauad, J., Pérez-Sanagustín, M., Kizilcec, R.F., Morales, N., Munoz-Gama, J.: Mining theory-based patterns from Big data: identifying self-regulated learning strategies in Massive Open Online Courses. Comput. Human Behav. (2018). https://doi.org/10.1016/j.chb.2017.11.011
4. Matcha, W., et al.: Detection of learning strategies: a comparison of process, sequence and network analytic approaches. In: European Conference on Technology Enhanced Learning, pp. 525–540 (2019)
5. Bogarín, A., Romero, C., Cerezo, R., Sánchez-Santillán, M.: Clustering for improving educational process mining. In: Proceedings of the Fourth International Conference on Learning Analytics And Knowledge, pp. 11–15 (2014)
6. Sonnenberg, C., Bannert, M.: Discovering the effects of metacognitive prompts on the sequential structure of srl-processes using process mining techniques. J. Learn. Anal. **2**(1), 72–100 (2015)
7. Guo, P.J., Kim, J., Rubin, R.: How video production affects student engagement: an empirical study of MOOC videos. In: Proceedings of the First ACM Conference on Learning@ Scale Conference, pp. 41–50 (2014)
8. Coates, H.: Student engagement in campus-based and online education: university connections. Routledge, London (2006)
9. Hew, K.F., Cheung, W.S.: Students' and instructors' use of massive open online courses (MOOCs): motivations and challenges. Educ. Res. Rev. **12**, 45–58 (2014). https://doi.org/10.1016/j.edurev.2014.05.001

10. Milligan, C., Littlejohn, A., Margaryan, A.: Patterns of engagement in connectivist MOOCs. J. Online Learn. Teach. **9**(2), 149–159 (2013)
11. Xiong, Y., Li, H., Kornhaber, M.L., Suen, H.K., Pursel, B., Goins, D.D.: Examining the relations among student motivation, engagement, and retention in a MOOC: a structural equation modeling approach. Glob. Educ. Rev. **2**(3), 23–33 (2015)
12. Kizilcec, R.F., Piech, C., Schneider, E.: Deconstructing disengagement: analyzing learner subpopulations in massive open online courses. In: Proceedings of the Third International Conference on Learning Analytics and Knowledge, pp. 170–179 (2013)
13. Hadwin, A., Nesbit, J., Jamieson-Noel, D., Code, J., Winne, P.: Examining trace data to explore self-regulated learning. Metacogn. Learn. **2**(2–3), 107–124 (2007)
14. Biswas, G., Jeong, H., Kinnebrew, J.S., Sulcer, B., Roscoe, R.O.D.: Measuring self-regulated learning skills through social interactions in a teachable agent environment. Res. Pract. Technol. Enhanc. Learn. **5**(2), 123–152 (2010)
15. Maldonado, J.J., Palta, R., Vázquez, J., Bermeo, J.L., Pérez-Sanagustín, M., Munoz-Gama, J.: Exploring differences in how learners navigate in MOOCs based on self-regulated learning and learning styles: a process mining approach. In: Computing Conference (CLEI), XLII Latin American, pp. 1–12 (2016)
16. de Barba, P.G., Malekian, D., Oliveira, E.A., Bailey, J., Ryan, T., Kennedy, G.: The importance and meaning of session behaviour in a MOOC. Comput. Educ. **146**, 103772 (2020). https://doi.org/10.1016/j.compedu.2019.103772
17. Romero, M., Usart, M.: The time factor in MOOCs: time-on-task, interaction temporal patterns, and time perspectives in a MOOC. In: CSEDU 2014 - Proceedings of the 6th International Conference on Computer Supported Education (2014)
18. Sapunar-Opazo, D., Pérez-Álvarez, R., Maldonado-Mahauad, J., Alario-Hoyos, C., Pérez-Sanagustín, M.: Analyzing learners' activity beyond the MOOC. In: CEUR Workshop Proceedings (2018)
19. Tough, A.: The adult's learning projects. a fresh approach to theory and practice in adult learning (1971)
20. Fincham, O.E., Gasevic, D.V., Jovanovic, J.M., Pardo, A.: From study tactics to learning strategies: an analytical method for extracting interpretable representations. IEEE Trans. Learn. Technol. (2018)
21. van Eck, M.L., Lu, X., Leemans, S.J.J., van der Aalst, W.M.P.: PM^2: a process mining project methodology. In: Advanced Information Systems Engineering, pp. 297–313 (2015)
22. van Der Aalst, W.: Process mining: discovery, conformance and enhancement of business processes. Springer Science & Business Media, Heidelberg (2011)
23. Rojas, E., Munoz-Gama, J., Sepúlveda, M., Capurro, D.: Process mining in healthcare: a literature review. J. Biomed. Inform. (2016)
24. Arias Chaves, M., Rojas Cordoba, E.: Deciphering event logs in SharePoint Server: a methodology based on process mining. In: Computing Conference (CLEI), XL Latin American, pp. 1–12 (2014)
25. Kovanović, V., Gašević, D., Dawson, S., Joksimović, S., Baker, R.S., Hatala, M.: Penetrating the black box of time-on-task estimation. In: ACM International Conference Proceeding Series (2015). https://doi.org/10.1145/2723576.2723623
26. Günther, C.W., Rozinat, A.: Disco: discover your processes. BPM **940**, 40–44 (2012)
27. Mair, B., et al.: Patterns of quiz attempts in a MOOC. The full-points-pattern and other patterns on the way to a successful MOOC in a lecture setting. In: Bastiaens, T. (ed.) Proceedings of EdMedia + Innovate Learning, pp. 1169–1179. Association for the Advancement of Computing in Education (AACE), New York (2022). https://www.learntechlib.org/primary/p/221430

28. Ferguson, R., Clow, D.: Examining engagement: analysing learner subpopulations in massive open online courses (MOOCs). In: Proceedings of the Fifth International Conference on Learning Analytics and Knowledge, pp. 51–58. ACM, New York (2015)
29. Anderson, A., Huttenlocher, D., Kleinberg, J., Leskovec, J.: Engaging with massive online courses. In: Proceedings of the 23rd International Conference on World Wide Web, pp. 687–698. ACM, New York (2014)
30. Kovanovic, V., Gaševic, D., Dawson, S., Joksimovic, S., Baker, R.S., Hatala, M.: Penetrating the black box of time-on-task estimation. In: ACM International Conference Proceeding Series (2015). https://doi.org/10.1145/2723576.2723623

How Can We Understand Students' Needs and Expectations in Online Courses to Improve Their Engagement and Learning Experience?

Kristian Stancin(✉), Danijela Jaksic, and Ana Petrovic

Faculty of Informatics and Digital Technologies, University of Rijeka, Radmile Matejcic 2, 51000 Rijeka, Croatia
kristian.stancin@inf.uniri.hr

Abstract. Understanding the needs and expectations of students in online courses is critical for improving satisfaction, fostering engagement, and increasing academic success. This paper explores these factors through empirical research. After reviewing existing literature on student needs and expectations in online learning, the paper examines key issues influencing student satisfaction, with a particular focus on Learning Management Systems (LMS). It identifies research gaps and highlights critical factors affecting student engagement. The paper presents the results of an empirical study conducted to collect data directly from computer science students about their needs and expectations of online courses. The research methodology includes a survey of 49 university students who participated in online courses. It includes questions about students' experiences with online courses, how they perceive the organization and implementation of online courses, which activities are most useful to them, and questions providing insight into students' expectations for future online courses. The study also explores the role of social and emotional aspects of online learning, such as the importance of building a community and interacting with peers, in shaping the overall learning experience and compares the results with previous related work that has examined the impact of integrating social networks into e-learning on student satisfaction. Findings highlight the need for a student-centered approach to online course design. This research lays the foundation for future work aimed at developing recommendations for managing student engagement and proposes a novel online course model. This model integrates features of both LMS and social media to enhance sustainability, inclusivity, and scalability in online education.

Keywords: Online Courses · Engagement · Students' Needs

1 Introduction

As online education becomes increasingly prevalent, especially in the wake of global disruptions like the COVID-19 pandemic, educators and institutions are striving to adapt to the unique challenges and opportunities presented by virtual learning environments. Central to this adaptation is the recognition that student satisfaction and

E. Hamonic and R. Sharrock (Eds.): EMOOCS 2025, LNCS 15733, pp. 60–71, 2026.
https://doi.org/10.1007/978-3-032-00056-9_6

engagement are pivotal components influencing academic outcomes in online settings. Student satisfaction in online learning is multifaceted, encompassing elements such as course design, instructor interaction, technological infrastructure, and the availability of support resources. Research indicates that when students perceive their online courses as well-structured and interactive, their satisfaction levels tend to increase, which in turn positively affects their academic performance [1–3]. Engagement in online learning environments is another critical factor that directly correlates with student success. Active engagement strategies, such as collaborative projects, interactive discussions, and real-time feedback, have been shown to enhance learning experiences and outcomes [4–6].

The integration of Learning Management Systems (LMS) plays a significant role in shaping both satisfaction and engagement in online education. LMS platforms provide a centralized hub for course materials, assessments, and communication, facilitating a structured and accessible learning experience [7–9]. Research has also explored the role of social media and social networking sites in education, particularly in online learning contexts. Studies indicate that integrating social media into learning environments can enhance student interaction, collaboration, and knowledge-sharing, leading to higher engagement and motivation [10–13]. Despite the benefits of both LMS and social media in online learning, there remains a significant gap in effectively integrating these systems into a unified digital learning environment. While LMS platforms offer structure, organization, and formal assessment tools, they often lack the dynamic and interactive elements of social media that foster student engagement. Conversely, social media platforms encourage participation and collaboration but may not provide the necessary framework for academic rigor and structured learning pathways. Addressing this gap presents an opportunity to create a hybrid model that incorporates the strengths of both systems.

The primary goal of this paper is to identify critical factors that influence student satisfaction and engagement, with a special focus on the role of LMS platforms. Insights from this study are expected to contribute to the design of student-centred model for online courses that not only enhance learning outcomes but also promote inclusivity and scalability in online education by leveraging the structured approach of LMS systems while incorporating the interactive and community-driven aspects of social media.

This paper is structured as follows: Sect. 2 gives a brief review of recent work on student satisfaction, engagement, and the use of LMS in online learning environments; Sect. 3 outlines the research design, including participant selection, data collection methods, and analytical approaches; Sect. 4 presents the results of the empirical study; Sect. 5 gives some discussion on the findings and research limitations; and finally Sect. 6 summarizes main conclusions and gives some considerations for future research.

2 Related Work

Student satisfaction in online learning is influenced by multiple interrelated factors, each playing a crucial role in shaping the overall learning experience. One of the most significant predictors of satisfaction is learner-content interaction, where engaging and well-structured materials enhance perceived course value and foster deeper learning [14,

15]. Instructor presence also plays a crucial role, as students report higher satisfaction when instructors provide continuous support and meaningful interactions [14, 16, 17]. Course structure and design significantly influence satisfaction, with well-organized content, clear objectives, and intuitive navigation improving students' perceptions of course quality [18, 19]. Engagement, both cognitive and emotional, further mediates satisfaction, as active participation in discussions and assignments fosters a sense of connection and motivation [16, 20]. Technological reliability is another critical factor. Seamless, user-friendly platforms enhance the learning experience, while technical issues can lead to frustration and disengagement [16, 21]. Lastly, self-efficacy and autonomy contribute positively to satisfaction, as students who feel confident and capable of managing their own learning tend to be more motivated and successful [14, 22]. Student engagement in online learning is influenced by social, technological, pedagogical, and motivational factors. A strong sense of community and social support from instructors enhance participation by increasing students' confidence in their academic abilities [23]. Instructor engagement, reflected in responsiveness and active participation, directly influences student motivation and interaction as well [24].

The integration of LMS plays a crucial role in shaping student satisfaction and engagement in online education. Key functionalities such as ease of use, communication tools, and personalized learning paths significantly influence learning experiences. Students' perception of LMS ease of use and usefulness is a major determinant of satisfaction. System characteristics, well-structured course design, and instructor support all contribute to a seamless learning experience [25, 26]. Communication and interaction within LMS platforms further enhance engagement, as effective feedback mechanisms and interactive course structures foster meaningful connections between students and instructors [27]. Integrating social media features into LMS is known to help improve usability, communication, and personalization, thereby enhancing student engagement and satisfaction. Regarding the usability enhancements, familiar interfaces, such as those resembling Facebook, are preferred by students for communication, making LMS more user-friendly [28]. Additionally, the ease of use of social media platforms can be transferred to LMS, improving overall user experience [11, 29]. Social media also facilitates better communication and interaction between students and instructors, with students more likely to engage in these environments [10, 28, 30]. By aligning with students' preferred communication styles and fostering a sense of community, integrating social media features creates a more student-centered LMS that boosts engagement and promotes collaborative learning, which is linked to improved academic performance and satisfaction.

3 Methodology

Students' attitudes and opinions on their needs and expectations of online courses and the impact of using LMS on their satisfaction in the e-learning environment were tested using a questionnaire survey. A survey was distributed via Google Forms and a Moodle-based LMS to students in all three years of a bachelor's degree program in computer science, as well as both years of a master's degree program. Students from different academic years took part in a survey in the winter semester of the academic year 2024/2025. Since the survey was open for two weeks, completely anonymous, voluntary, and posed no risk to participants, formal informed consent was not required. Students were free to decide whether or not to participate. Prior to completing the survey, participants were provided with detailed information regarding the research context, its purpose, the procedures involved, the anonymity of responses, and the potential benefits of participation. The number of participating students was 49 (out of a total of 414 students enrolled in all study programs).

The survey consisted of 14 questions, including 3 open-ended and 11 closed-ended questions. The closed-ended items comprised yes/no questions (e.g. *Do you consider the course materials understandable, interactive, multimedia enriched and available on time?*), multiple-response options (e.g. *What activities do you consider the best for learning?*, or How often would you participate in interactive activities?), and items measured on a 5-point Likert scale (e.g. *Determine to what extent, in your experience, the listed elements were achieved through e-courses.*). The survey is available in Croatian language on this link. The survey questions were used to test the main research questions, which were: "*How does the integration of specific LMS functionalities play a role in shaping engagement and better learning experience in online education?*" (RQ1), and "*What are students' perceptions on the ways LMS features could be optimized for improving their learning experience and engagement?*" (RQ2).

The questionnaire was divided into 6 main areas of interest: 1) general characteristics, 2) experiences with online courses, 3) organization of online courses, 4) activities in online courses, 5) implementation of online courses, and 6) functionalities of LMS. The survey results were recorded and semi-automatically processed using both Google Forms and the statistical tool IBM SPSS Statistics Version 29. Closed questions were processed automatically by the system, but the open questions were processed manually by the authors by sorting the answers into relevant categories using Microsoft Office Excel 2021.

4 Results

A total of 49 participants took part in the study, 40 of them are at the undergraduate level of study and 9 at the graduate level. All faculty's courses are delivered in a hybrid format, combining face-to-face lectures in the classroom with online learning, which may be conducted synchronously or asynchronously. Each course includes a total of 30 h of lectures and 30 h of practical exercises per semester. The maximum proportion of online lectures per course is limited to 40%. The online component is delivered primarily in an asynchronous format, in accordance with university guidelines, and includes a variety of teaching materials, interactive lessons, discussion forums, and self-assessment activities within the LMS. A smaller portion of the online instruction is conducted synchronously, typically for activities such as project presentations or laboratory exercises. In accordance with this approach, all students are required to utilize a Moodle-based LMS platform for each course they are enrolled in.

Participants were asked how they would rate their overall experience with online courses so far, and 41 out of 49 students (84%) state that they are satisfied or fully satisfied with the overall experience. Only one student is not satisfied, and 7 are neither satisfied nor unsatisfied. When asked about the importance of various elements of online course organization, **participants agree that regular and timely communication with teachers is the most important, followed by the quality and clarity of teaching materials, the alignment of activities with assessment requirements and the technical simplicity and user-friendliness of the e-learning platform**. On the other hand, access to additional resources (recommended books, articles, video materials) received the lowest rating. Details are presented in Table 1.

Table 1. Mean values for elements of online course organization

Elements of online course organization	Means (1-5)	Std. dev.
Clearly defined learning objectives and outcomes	4.39	1.10
Course structure (weekly plans, modules)	4.35	0.88
Regular and timely communication with teachers	4.78	0.51
Teacher availability for questions and support	4.27	0.95
Quality and clarity of teaching materials	4.63	0.64
Flexibility of schedules for students with diverse commitments	4.12	1.01
Access to additional resources (books, articles, video materials)	3.43	1.12
Frequency and quality of feedback on assignments and activities	4.22	0.85
Alignment of activities with assessment requirements	4.45	0.82
Integration of digital tools (e.g., interactive platforms, simulations)	3.88	1.03
Technical simplicity and user-friendliness of the e-learning platform	4.45	0.82

Furthermore, the study also examined the quality of the online course materials. Most participants perceive the materials as sufficiently comprehensible, adequately interactive, and enriched with multimedia. Additionally, they agree that all materials are made available on time. Detailed findings are presented in Fig. 1.

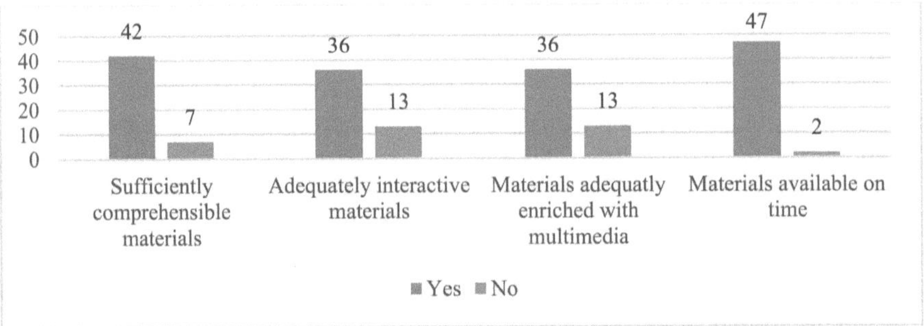

Fig. 1. Student' perceptions of online course materials

Regarding the types of activities (Fig. 2), participants consider **online tests and quizzes to be the most useful for their learning (67%), followed by video lectures (51%) and interactive exercises (45%)**. The least useful activities, according to the participants, are forum discussions (4%) and the writing of essays and papers (14%).

When participants were asked how frequently they would like to engage in interactive activities such as discussions or group tasks, only 3 participants expressed a

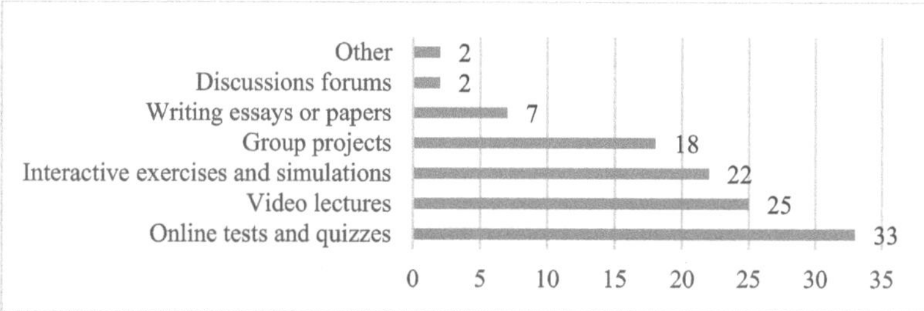

Fig. 2. Perception of most useful activities for learning

preference for weekly participation, 11 preferred every two weeks, 19 once a month, and 14 would prefer less frequently than that. This indicates that **over 70% of participants would engage in interactive activities once a month or less**, which is surprising given that approximately 45% of participants consider interactive tasks and simulations to be among the most important activities for learning.

To answer the **RQ1 about the role of LMS functionalities in shaping engagement and better learning experience**, participants rated the elements of online course implementation based on their own experiences. Figure 3 illustrates the perceived extent of achievement for each element, with a rating of 1 indicating that the element was not achieved at all in the online courses, and a rating of 5 indicating that it was fully achieved. Participants believe that nearly all elements were successfully implemented in the online courses (more than 50% of participants consider elements to be achieved or fully achieved), **except for the ability to communicate in real-time and the possibility of informal communication with teachers, which received ratings lower than 50%.** The highest-rated element is the accessibility of materials and activities, with 90% of participants considering it to be achieved or fully achieved. This is followed by the flexibility in organizing one's own time, with 82% agreement.

Participants were also asked to rate the functionalities of the LMS, with 1 representing "very poor" and 5 representing "very good." Table 2 presents the mean values of the participants' answers along with the corresponding standard deviations. From this data, it can be concluded that the **highest-rated functionalities are the ease of navigation and content discovery and the integration of additional tools** (e.g., quizzes, forums, assignments, video content, games, wikis, webinars, etc.), both with a mean value of 4.18. This is followed by the loading speed of materials and activities with a mean value of 4.10. The **lowest-rated functionality is enjoyable activities for study breaks**, with an average score of 2.53, but majority of other functionalities, such as **user experience on mobile devices, availability of real-time communication, informal learning and additional resources, ability to engage in informal communication with peers and professors, and opportunity to create and participate in virtual communities or groups, also scored low** (below 3.80).

To answer the **RQ2 about students' perceptions on the ways LMS features could be optimized for improving their learning experience and engagement**, it was necessary to qualitatively analyse the open-end questions from the survey. The qualitative results indicate that the most frequently mentioned advantage of online and hybrid

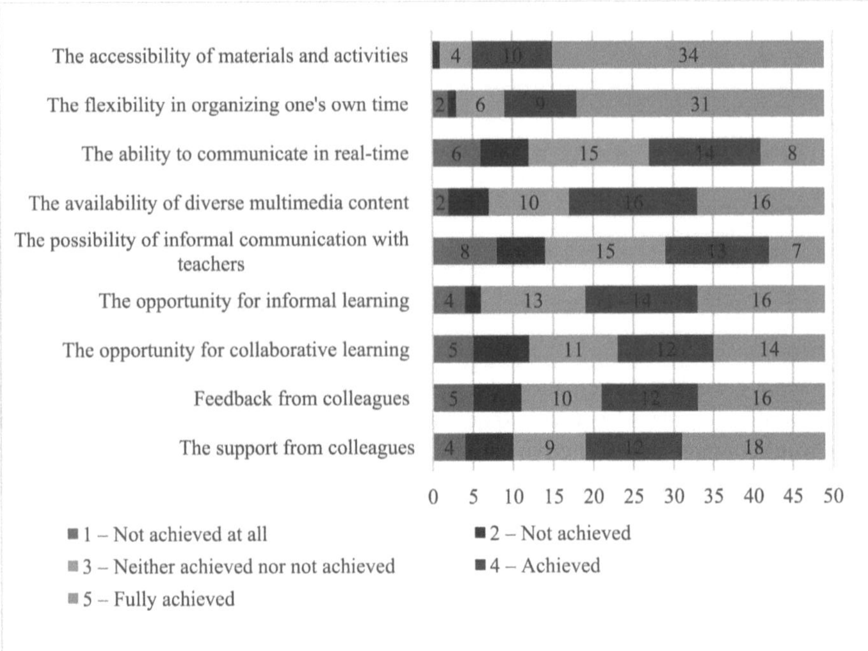

Fig. 3. Ratings of the elements of online course implementation

Table 2. Mean values for LMS functionalities

LMS functionalities	Means (1-5)	Std. dev.
Ease of navigation and content discovery	4,18	0,95
System stability (free from technical issues and interruptions)	4,04	0,98
Loading speed of materials and activities	4,10	1,07
Integration of additional tools (e.g., quizzes, video, games, wikis, etc.)	4,18	1,05
User experience on mobile devices	3,35	1,11
Availability of real-time communication	3,51	1,02
Informal learning and additional resources	3,78	1,09
Ability to engage in informal communication with peers and professors	3,39	1,20
Opportunity to create and participate in virtual communities or groups	3,41	1,02
Enjoyable activities for study breaks	2,53	1,21

courses is **flexibility**, with participants emphasizing the ability to manage their own time and study at their own pace. Participants also value the option to revisit video lectures and explanations, which supports individualized learning. Access to materials is another key benefit, as participants highlighted the ease of obtaining essential resources, the ability to review content multiple times, and the availability of recorded lectures for complex topics. Regarding challenges in online and hybrid courses, participants identified issues with locating and organizing learning resources, particularly when materials are not clearly structured. Some participants mentioned concerns about the reliability of task submissions and the accumulation of coursework if regular assessments are not conducted. Additionally, participants highlighted problems with understanding complex topics without direct guidance and the difficulty of managing deadlines, especially when multiple important tasks converge within the same period. Despite these challenges, 33% of participants reported no significant difficulties, emphasizing that they find the online environment manageable with proper organization and accessible resources.

The results regarding participants' emotional responses when accessing online course platforms reveal a spectrum of feelings, with satisfaction being the most prevalent. Participants reported **feeling satisfied due to the accessibility of materials and the organized structure of the platform**. Some participants expressed **feelings of motivation**, particularly when the course content was well-structured and engaging. However, some participants indicated feelings of uncertainty, often linked to doubts about task completion and the accuracy of their submissions. Frustration was also mentioned, especially regarding **unclear instructions and the lack of immediate feedback** from teachers. Few participants reported feelings of concern or anxiety, particularly when accessing grades or managing deadlines. Neutral responses were also common, with several participants stating that their emotional reaction depended on the specific course or task. Overall, **57% of participants state a positive emotional response, 20% a neutral emotional response, and 23% state a negative emotional response**.

Regarding the functionalities lacking in the current LMS platform, a recurring concern was the **inconsistent structure across different courses**, which complicates navigation. Participants suggested improvements to **mobile accessibility and enhanced calendar features**, such as the ability to export deadlines to external calendars (e.g., iCal files). Other requested functionalities included **group communication spaces for informal student interaction, improved feedback systems where teachers could leave comments on submitted assignments, and public grade tables to foster competition and motivation**.

When asked for concrete suggestions to improve their satisfaction and experience with the LMS platform, participants mentioned again **enhancing the mobile version to align with the desktop experience**. Several participants suggested the addition of **more interactive learning materials**, such as self-assessment quizzes and video content, to facilitate knowledge retention. Improved communication tools were also a recurring theme, with requests for **better chat spaces** that support multimedia attachments and clearer teacher contact information, including office hours.

5 Discussion and Limitations

The integration of specific LMS functionalities is crucial in enhancing engagement and fostering an improved learning experience in online education. The findings of this study indicate the need for further enhancement of functionalities that facilitate real-time communication and enjoyable activities for study breaks, which aligns more closely with the communication patterns commonly found in social media environments. This result is in line with an earlier study that investigated the effects of integrating social networks into e-learning [10] which found that real-time communication significantly impacts student satisfaction. In their research, 68% of participants indicated that real-time communication would positively influence their studies, yet less than half felt this was adequately achieved in their online courses. Similarly, informal communication with teachers via social networks was positively received by 45% of students, though only 41% felt this was sufficiently implemented.

The findings highlight the potential benefits of incorporating social media characteristics into LMS platforms. Features such as real-time communication, informal interaction with peers and instructors, enjoyable activities for study breaks and multimedia-rich content can emulate the dynamic and engaging environment of social networks. This approach can foster a sense of community, enhance student engagement, and improve the overall learning experience by making it more interactive and responsive to students' needs.

Like any study, this research has certain limitations. It was conducted within a specific timeframe and among a limited sample of students, which may affect the generalizability of the findings to other populations or educational settings. Expanding the research over a longer period and across multiple faculties could offer deeper insights and more reliable conclusions. Additionally, as the study focused on students from a single faculty, the results may not fully capture the diversity of experiences across different disciplines where online learning dynamics can vary significantly. Finally, while survey anonymity ensured honest feedback, it also limited the ability to follow up on specific responses for further clarification.

6 Conclusions and Future Work

This paper highlights key factors affecting student engagement and the learning experience, with a particular emphasis on the role of LMS platforms. The results from the study reveal significant insights into students' perceptions of online courses, emphasizing both advantages and challenges. Flexibility, access to materials, and the ability to revisit lectures were highlighted as key benefits, while issues with organizing resources, reliability of submissions, and managing deadlines were notable challenges. Participants' emotional responses indicated a generally positive experience, though uncertainty and frustration were also present. The findings suggest that while online learning offers substantial benefits, improvements in LMS structure, mobile accessibility, and communication tools are crucial for enhancing student engagement and learning experience. The study underscores the importance of enhancing features that support real-time communication and provide enjoyable study break activities, reflecting the interactive nature of social media environments. Integrating these specific functionalities is essential for increasing student engagement and improving the online learning experience. The findings advocate for a student-centred approach to online course design that balances structured content delivery with interactive, community-driven engagement. Future research will focus on further refining recommendations for managing student satisfaction in online environments, with an emphasis on the development of a comprehensive e-learning model. This includes designing and testing a novel online course framework that merges LMS functionalities with social media elements to create an engaging, interactive, and structured learning space. Ultimately, these efforts will contribute to the conceptualization and development of a unified platform aimed at improving student engagement, fostering a sense of community, and supporting academic success through a holistic and adaptive online learning experience.

Acknowledgments. The research has been co-funded by "uniri-iskusni-drustv-23-209 (3203)" under the project "Development of an e-learning course design model based on recommendations for managing student satisfaction in higher education".

Disclosure of Interests. The authors have no competing interests to declare that are relevant to the content of this article.

References

1. Johar, N.A., Kew, S.N., Tasir, Z., Koh, E.: Learning analytics on student engagement to enhance students' learning performance: a systematic review, MDPI (2023). https://doi.org/10.3390/su15107849
2. Galal, S., Vyas, D., Ndung'u, M., Wu, G., Webber, M.: Assessing learner engagement and the impact on academic performance within a virtual learning environment. Pharmacy **11**(1), 36 (2023). https://doi.org/10.3390/pharmacy11010036
3. Sahni, J.: Is learning analytics the future of online education? assessing student engagement and academic performance in the online learning environment. Int. J. Emerg. Technol. Learn. **18**(2), 33–49 (2023). https://doi.org/10.3991/ijet.v18i02.32167
4. Moubayed, A., Injadat, M., Shami, A., Lutfiyya, H.: Relationship between student engagement and performance in e-learning environment using association rules. In: 2018 IEEE World Engineering Education Conference (EDUNINE), pp. 1–6. IEEE (2018). https://doi.org/10.1109/EDUNINE.2018.8451005
5. Almusaed, A., Almssad, A., Yitmen, I., Homod, R.Z.: Enhancing student engagement: harnessing 'AIED''s power in hybrid education—a review analysis. Multidisciplinary Digital Publishing Institute (MDPI) (2023). https://doi.org/10.3390/educsci13070632
6. Singh, A., Singh, D., Chhikara, S.: Online learning: Challenges and suggestions to enhance student engagement in higher education institutions. In: Reshaping Entrepreneurial Education Within an Industry 4.0 Context, pp. 59–80. IGI Global (2024). https://doi.org/10.4018/979-8-3693-0409-9.ch004
7. Abaricia, C., Delos Santos, M.L.: Enhancing e-learning system through Learning Management System (LMS) technologies: reshape the learner experience. Int. J. Comput. Sci. Res. **7**, 2066–2079 (2023). https://doi.org/10.25147/ijcsr.2017.001.1.152
8. Hernández-García, Á., Cuenca-Enrique, C., Del-Río-Carazo, L., Iglesias-Pradas, S.: Exploring the relationship between LMS interactions and academic performance: a learning cycle approach. Comput. Human Behav. **155**(2024). https://doi.org/10.1016/j.chb.2024.108183
9. Sappaile, B.I., Donna, E., Lasinggaru, F., Mokodenseho, S.: Analyzing the influence of digital learning platforms on student engagement and academic performance (2023)
10. Jaksic, D., Stancin, K.: The impact of social network integration in e-learning on student satisfaction: an empirical study, pp. 324–336 (2024). https://doi.org/10.1007/978-3-031-73427-4_32
11. Al-Rahmi, A.M., Shamsuddin, A., Wahab, E., Al-Rahmi, W.M., Alyoussef, I.Y., Crawford, J.: Social media use in higher education: building a structural equation model for student satisfaction and performance. Front Public Health, vol. 10 (2022). https://doi.org/10.3389/fpubh.2022.1003007
12. Turnbull, D., Chugh, R., Luck, J.: Learning management systems and social media: a case for their integration in higher education institutions,. Res. Learn. Technol. **31** (2023). https://doi.org/10.25304/rlt.v31.2814

13. Oroni, C.Z., Xianping, F.: Modelling the mediation role of digital learning platforms on social media capability and students' academic performance. Educ. Inf. Technol. (Dordr) **29**(10), 11979–12000 (2024). https://doi.org/10.1007/s10639-023-12360-w
14. Alqurashi, E.: Predicting student satisfaction and perceived learning within online learning environments. Distan. Educ. **40**, 133–148 (2018). https://doi.org/10.1080/01587919.2018.1553562
15. Zhang, Y., Lin, C.: Student interaction and the role of the teacher in a state virtual high school: what predicts online learning satisfaction? Technol. Pedagog. Educ. **29**, 57–71 (2020). https://doi.org/10.1080/1475939X.2019.1694061
16. Nagaratnam, S., Sim, T.Y., Tan, S.F., Leong, H.: Online learning engagement factors of undergraduate students' learning outcomes: effects on learning satisfaction and performance. Int. J. Emerg. Technol. Learn. **18**, 39–58 (2023). https://doi.org/10.3991/ijet.v18i23.38745
17. Kim, S.-H., Park, S.: What contributed to students' online learning satisfaction during the pandemic? Distan. Educ. **44**, 6–23 (2022). https://doi.org/10.1080/01587919.2022.2150147
18. Kim, S., Kim, D.-J.: Structural relationship of key factors for student satisfaction and achievement in asynchronous online learning. Sustainability (2021). https://doi.org/10.3390/SU13126734
19. Kauffman, H.: A review of predictive factors of student success in and satisfaction with online learning. Res. Learn. Technol. **23**, 1–13 (2015). https://doi.org/10.3402/RLT.V23.26507
20. Nia, H.S., et al.: Student satisfaction and academic efficacy during online learning with the mediating effect of student engagement: a multi-country study. PLoS One **18** (2023). https://doi.org/10.1371/journal.pone.0285315
21. Elshami, W., Taha, M., Abuzaid, M., Saravanan, C., Al Kawas, S., Abdalla, M.: Satisfaction with online learning in the new normal: perspective of students and faculty at medical and health sciences colleges. Med. Educ. Online **26** (2021). https://doi.org/10.1080/10872981.2021.1920090
22. Abuhassna, H., Al-Rahmi, W., Yahya, N., Zakaria, M., Kosnin, A., Darwish, M.: Development of a new model on utilizing online learning platforms to improve students' academic achievements and satisfaction. Int. J. Educ. Technol. High. Educ. **17** (2020). https://doi.org/10.1186/s41239-020-00216-z
23. Vayre, E., Vonthron, A.-M.: Psychological engagement of students in distance and online learning. J. Educ. Comput. Res. **55**, 197–218 (2017). https://doi.org/10.1177/0735633116656849
24. Dwivedi, A., Dwivedi, P., Bobek, S., Zabukovšek, S.S.: Factors affecting students' engagement with online content in blended learning. Kybernetes **48**, 1500–1515 (2019). https://doi.org/10.1108/K-10-2018-0559
25. Ghazal, S., Al-Samarraie, H., Aldowah, H.: 'I am still learning': modeling LMS critical success factors for promoting students' experience and satisfaction in a blended learning environment. IEEE Access **6**, 77179–77201 (2018). https://doi.org/10.1109/ACCESS.2018.2879677
26. Alturki, U., Aldraiweesh, A.: Application of Learning Management System (LMS) during the COVID-19 pandemic: a sustainable acceptance model of the expansion technology approach. Sustainability (2021). https://doi.org/10.3390/su131910991
27. Rubin, B., Fernandes, R., Avgerinou, M.: The effects of technology on the Community of Inquiry and satisfaction with online courses. Internet High. Educ. **17**, 48–57 (2013). https://doi.org/10.1016/J.IHEDUC.2012.09.006
28. Maneewongvatana, S., Maneewongvatana, S.: Can Facebook be a New Communicative Channel in a Student-Centered LMS? (2012). https://consensus.app/papers/can-facebook-be-a-new-communicative-channel-in-a-maneewongvatana-maneewongvatana/b47ab31ebe0a561aa6a1f3278cfd1d2e/

29. Al-Maatouk, Q., Othman, M., Aldraiweesh, A., Alturki, U., Al-Rahmi, W., Aljeraiwi, A.: Task-technology fit and technology acceptance model application to structure and evaluate the adoption of social media in academia. IEEE Access **8**, 78427–78440 (2020). https://doi.org/10.1109/ACCESS.2020.2990420
30. Alamri, M., Almaiah, M.A., Al-Rahmi, W.: Social media applications affecting students' academic performance: a model developed for sustainability in higher education. Sustainability (2020). https://doi.org/10.3390/su12166471

Empowering Non-specialist Teachers and Students in Coding: A Case Study of a Python MOOC in an Austrian High School

Daniela Wolf[1](✉) and Martin Ebner[2]

[1] Ferdinand Porsche FernFH, Ferdinand Porsche Ring 3, 2700 Wr. Neustadt, Austria
daniela.wolf@fernfh.ac.at
[2] Technische Universität Graz, Rechbauerstraße 12, 8010 Graz, Austria
martin.ebner@tugraz.at

Abstract. This paper explores the integration of a Massive Open Online Course (MOOC) into the computer science curriculum of fifth-grade classes at an Austrian high school (so called "Gymnasium") to introduce students to Python programming. A total of 42 students were surveyed, and two non-specialist teachers with no to little programming experience were interviewed to assess the MOOC's impact and practical feasibility. While the MOOC provided a valuable entry point for many students in programming and online learning, the results also highlighted several challenges. Although over half of the students (57%) rated the MOOC as 'very useful' or 'useful', motivation for further self-learning was moderate, and only a subset expressed interest in continuing coding independently. Teachers appreciated the structured content and expert-led videos, which enabled them to facilitate programming instruction despite their limited technical background. However, they also reported difficulties in meeting the diverse pacing needs of students. These findings indicate that while MOOCs can offer accessible resources for both students and non-specialist teachers, their effectiveness depends on thoughtful integration and scaffolding. The study offers insights into the conditions under which MOOCs may support secondary level coding education, particularly in contexts with limited access to qualified computer science educators.

Keywords: MOOCs · Non-specialist Teachers · Programming Instruction

1 Introduction

In Austria, many high schools are experiencing a shortage of adequately trained computer science teachers, leading to non-specialist educators being assigned to teach the subject. As a result, computer science instruction is often limited to basic software applications like Microsoft Word, Excel, and PowerPoint, rather than introducing students to the fundamental principles of programming. Considering this, Massive Open Online Courses (MOOCs) present a promising alternative that could not only provide students with up-to-date content and a self-paced learning environment, which is especially valuable in rapidly evolving fields like coding and technology but also enable non-specialist

E. Hamonic and R. Sharrock (Eds.): EMOOCS 2025, LNCS 15733, pp. 72–85, 2026.
https://doi.org/10.1007/978-3-032-00056-9_7

teachers to effectively facilitate programming instruction. Therefore, this study explores the potential of MOOCs to enhance coding education in schools, specifically through the integration of a Python programming MOOC into a 5th-grade high school. The study focuses on examining students' perceptions of the MOOC overall, as well as its perceived contribution to the development of their programming competencies. The research also explores the challenges faced by non-specialist teachers, with limited formal training in computer science, and the potential benefits they see in using the MOOC as a tool to facilitate coding instruction. The central research question is: *How can MOOCs be implemented to enhance students' coding skills in secondary education, particularly when non-specialist teachers, with limited formal training in computer science, are responsible for teaching the subject?* By examining this, the study aims to shed light on how MOOCs can help non-specialist educators teach programming, offering a potential solution to the shortage of qualified computer science teachers in schools and improving access to quality coding education for secondary students.

2 Prior Work

While much of the research has focused on MOOCs in higher education, their application in secondary schools (age 10 to 18), particularly for teaching coding, remains underexplored [4, 8, 11]. In Finland, Kurhila and Vivahainen [10] reported that several high schools incorporated a MOOC corresponding to the University of Helsinki's Computer Science 1 course, offering formal credits in programming upon completion. In Austria, Khalil and Ebner [8] examined the "Mechanics in Everyday Life" MOOC for high school students using learning analytics. Although many participants perceived the course more as an additional homework assignment, the findings indicated that MOOCs have potential when they are meaningfully integrated into the classroom and accompanied by teacher guidance [8]. In Germany [2, 11, 14], as well as in countries such as the United States, Thailand, and Israel [3, 5, 12, 13], research has also examined the potential of MOOCs to support the development of technical skills, particularly programming and coding, among younger students. This highlights the increasing recognition of MOOCs as valuable tool for developing essential skills in secondary education. In an era of rapid technological change, understanding how these systems function is increasingly critical for both academic success and future career development. Moreover, MOOCs provide students with the opportunity to familiarize themselves with digital tools and learning platforms, boosting their digital readiness and information literacy [4]. Additionally, MOOCs present a scalable solution for schools dealing with resource constraints or a shortage of specialized teaching staff as they are offering ready-made, pedagogically structured and excellent resource materials [7]. By providing up-to-date content, MOOCs can fill gaps that traditional curricula may lack [2]. However, there is little to no research on how MOOCs can specifically support non-specialist teachers in secondary education, where teacher shortages in subjects like computer science are common. Furthermore, a consistent challenge with MOOCs is that self-paced learning environments require strong self-regulation skills and motivation [9]. Secondary school students often struggle with the autonomy required by MOOCs. As a result, it has been suggested that MOOCs for this age group should incorporate support mechanisms, such as blended learning, to maintain engagement and motivation [8]. Yet, empirical evidence on how online and face-to-face components should be integrated remains limited [15, 16]. One possible approach is to leverage well-developed and content-rich MOOCs while providing accompanying in-person sessions to offer structure and support to learners. Specifically, this could involve integrating live or archived MOOCs into an existing computer science course in a hybrid format [1], or adopting a flipped classroom model, where the MOOC enables students to review relevant material in advance, preparing them for in-class discussions [15]. This combination of online and face-to-face learning can create a balanced environment that meets the needs of diverse learners. In previous studies, students also reported a positive experience, highlighting that the face-to-face classes helped them stay on track with the self-paced MOOC component [1].

3 Method

This study used a mixed-methods approach, combining quantitative surveys and qualitative interviews to evaluate the impact of the Python MOOC. Participants included 42 students (aged 14–15) and two non-specialist teachers. The students completed the MOOC as part of their mandatory computer science course in the summer semester of 2023 (3 classes, including one all-girls class), and in the winter semester of 2023/24 (2 classes), while the teachers facilitated the course with the help of solution guides and the support of a professionally qualified computer science teacher. The evaluation included post-MOOC surveys assessing students' engagement, motivation, and skills, along with interviews with the teachers about their experiences. The student questionnaire consisted of 24 questions: 18 closed-ended questions with a single response option, 4 multiple-choice questions, and 2 open-ended questions. For closed-ended questions, participants selected for example responses such as 'Very useful', 'Useful', 'Moderately useful', or 'Less useful' regarding the MOOC's impact on learning programming skills. Open-ended questions allowed for detailed reflections on improvements and challenges. The two teachers were interviewed orally without a structured interview guide, allowing for flexible and reflective conversations. Based on these interviews, a more structured teacher questionnaire was developed, consisting of 22 questions: 15 requiring a single answer, 4 with multiple responses, and 3 open-ended questions on improvements and challenges. Both teachers completed the questionnaire following the interview, and their responses were included in the analysis of the results.

4 MOOC Integration

The live Python programming MOOC, *Programmieren lernen mit Python - Schulversion*[1], offered through the HPI Open School and designed for beginners with no prior knowledge, was integrated into the classroom setting. Unlike many MOOCs that are primarily designed for adults or higher education contexts, this course is tailored to meet the needs of school students to close the gap in computer science education in German

[1] https://open.hpi.de/courses/pythonjunior-schule2024.

schools [14]. The availability of the MOOC in German - a rarity within the predominantly English-speaking MOOC landscape - combined with its synchronous format and timely release at a pedagogically advantageous point in the school year, were additional factors that significantly influenced its selection. Moreover, the MOOC was chosen for its combination of video tutorials, interactive exercises, and continuous support from the providers, creating a well-balanced approach between self-directed learning and guided assistance. This didactic design not only promotes the understanding of programming concepts but also boosts student motivation and engagement, making it an ideal tool for both students and teachers in secondary education.

Furthermore, the installation of programming environments is often a significant challenge in computer science classroom. It can be time-consuming and technically demanding, especially for teachers without a computer science background. The MOOC addresses this issue by allowing students to program directly in the browser, eliminating the need for additional software installation [11, 14]. This feature simplifies the learning process and ensures that students and teachers can focus on coding rather than the technical setup. In addition, the tool automatically grades students' work by running tests to verify if their solutions meet the specified requirements, providing immediate feedback [14]. This automated grading system not only enhances the learning experience for students but also offers valuable support to teachers.

The implementation of the MOOC in the classroom was carried out in stages to ensure a smooth adaptation for both students and teachers. In the initial lesson, teachers provided an overview of the MOOC's objectives and guided students through the platform. After this introduction, the class collectively watched the first video, which introduced the first programming example, "Hello World." Following the video, students completed the first of three exercises in collaboration with the teacher, while the second and third exercise was intended for independent completion. Following this approach, each topic (such as variables, strings, data types, etc.) was progressively covered. This collaborative approach ensured that students developed a thorough understanding of the material before transitioning to more independent work. Each class started with a Kahoot quiz, created by the computer science teacher, to review the key points from the previous MOOC content, and to ensure that students had a solid grasp of the foundational concepts before progressing to new content. This structure facilitated a continuous cycle of learning, gradually increasing students' independence.

5 Results

A total of 42 students, including 28 females, participated in the questionnaire. Although engineering MOOCs report a low registration and participation rate of female students [6] the relatively high number of 27 women in our study can be attributed to the fact that we worked with one all-girls class and four mixed-gender classes, which likely contributed to the higher female participation in our study.

The interviews with the teachers (one male and one female) were also conducted after the implementation of the MOOC, in order to capture their experiences and insights regarding the integration of the course into the classroom.

5.1 Previous Knowledge of MOOCs (n = 42)

The evaluation results revealed that a significant majority of students, 86% (36 students), had no prior experience with MOOCs, marking this as their first interaction with this type of learning format. Additionally, 12% (5 students) had heard of MOOCs but had not directly engaged with one, while only 2% (1 student) had occasionally used MOOCs before (Table 1).

Table 1. Previous Experience with MOOCs (n = 42).

Response	Total	Male	Female	Percentage
No, I didn't know what a Massive Open Online Course (MOOC) was before the MOOC	36	11	25	86%
No, I had heard of MOOCs but had no direct experience with them	5	3	2	12%
Yes, I occassionally use MOOCs in my free time	1	0	1	2%

5.2 Previous Programming Experience (n = 42)

The data on previous programming experience showed that 64% (27 students) had no programming background. 24% (10 students) had some experience from previous school, while 12% (5 students) engaged in programming occasionally in their free time (Table 2).

Table 2. Previous Experience with Programming (n = 42).

Response	Total	Male	Female	Percentage
Yes, I ocassionally program in my free time	5	3	2	12%
No, I had never programmed before the MOOC	27	9	18	64%
Yes, I had programmed before the MOOC in class	10	2	8	24%

5.3 Python Experience (n = 15)

The results indicated that most students had minimal exposure to Python. Specifically, 47% (7 students) had no experience. This corresponds to 17% of the total 42 students. Additionally, 20% (3 students) had basic experience in Python. 20% (3 students) were familiar with Python but lacked hands-on experience. Only 13% (2 students) possessed advanced Python skills. 27 participants did not provide an answer (Table 3).

Table 3. Previous Experience with Python (n = 15).

Response	Total	Male	Female	Percentage
Yes, I have worked a lot with Python and can develop larger programs	2	2	0	13%
Yes, I have written some small programs in Python	3	0	3	20%
Yes, I have seen Python code but have never programmed myself	3	2	1	20%
No, I have never worked with Python	7	1	6	47%

5.4 Ease of Navigation in the MOOC (n = 15)

The findings show that 53% (8 students) found the MOOC platform to be user-friendly and intuitive, allowing them to navigate it with ease. This corresponds to 19% of the total 42 students. Another 33% (5 students) needed a brief adjustment period but ultimately adapted to the platform without significant issues, which represents 12% of the total 42 students. Meanwhile, 14% (2 student) encountered challenges with navigation, finding some aspects of the course setup confusing. 27 participants did not provide an answer (Table 4).

Table 4. Ease of Navigation on the MOOC Platform (n = 15).

Response	Total	Male	Female	Percentage
Yes, I quickly got used to the MOOC. The platform was user-friendly and intiutively designed, allowing me to navigate the course easily	8	3	5	53%
Yes, I found my way around the MOOC relatively quickly. Although it took some time to get used to the interface, I was able to orient myself well after a short time	5	2	3	33%
No, it took me a while to get used to the MOOC. The navigation and use of the platform were confusing at first, but I got better over time	1	0	1	7%
No, at first, I had trouble navigating the MOOC. The platform was complex, and it took a while to familiarize myself with the features	1	0	1	7%

5.5 Difficulty Level of the MOOC (n = 15)

The difficulty level of the MOOC was generally considered appropriate by 33% (5 students) and well-balanced by 40% (6 students). 27% (4 students) found the difficulty level of the MOOC too high. Out of the total of 42 students, 14% considered the MOOC well-balanced, 12% found it appropriate, 10% found it difficult, and 27 students did not provide an answer (Table 5).

Table 5. Perceived Difficulty Level of the MOOC (n = 15).

Response	Total	Male	Female	Percentage
The difficulty of the MOOC was well-balanced. The course presented challenges but was still achievable and motivated me to give my best	6	3	3	40%
The difficulty of the MOOC was too high for me. The content was demanding and required a lot of background knowledge that I didn't always have	4	0	4	27%
I found the difficulty level of the MOOC appropriate. The content was well-structured and built on itself, allowing me to continuously expand my knowledge	5	2	3	33%

5.6 Enjoyment of the MOOC (n = 15)

60% (9 students) liked the MOOC overall, while 40% (6 students) did not find it as appealing. Out of the total of 42 students, 21% liked the MOOC, 14% did not find it as appealing, and 27 students provided no answer (Table 6).

Table 6. Overall Enjoyment of the MOOC (n = 15).

Response	Total	Male	Female	Percentage
The MOOC did not appeal to me particularly	6	2	4	40%
I really liked the MOOC	1	1	0	7%
I mostly liked the MOOC	8	2	6	53%

The results of the questionnaire revealed that the most enjoyed aspects of the MOOC were the ability to control the learning pace and the improvement in programming skills, with ten students mentioning both. Eight students appreciated the flexibility to choose their learning location. Additionally, five students found the ability to effectively apply what they learned to be particularly valuable. Two students highlighted the positive impact the MOOC had on their learning curve, due to its well-structured content and clear learning objectives.

5.7 Strengths and Challenges (n = 15)

The most frequently mentioned advantage, cited by eleven participants, was the ability to learn at their own pace. Six participants highlighted the flexibility of the course, particularly the ability to adapt learning time and location. Two students appreciated the self-directed learning aspect, while one participant noted the benefits of collaborative learning and increased interactivity. The most frequent issue was *"less interaction with other students in the classroom"*, mentioned by three participants. Other concerns included *"motivation difficulties"*, *"lack of individual customization"*, and *"lack of direct feedback"* each noted by two participants. The challenges they encountered while using the MOOC included technical issues such as server overload and problems with account details, like username deletion. Some students found it difficult to follow the videos and retain all the information, while others noted that the system only accepted one solution path, even when their answers were correct. There were also cases where the system incorrectly marked answers as wrong despite them being correct.

Students felt that the videos were either too boring or lacked excitement, and they suggested making the videos more interesting and engaging. Specific suggestions included adding more dynamic elements to the videos, improving their clarity, and providing better explanations for the steps involved. A few participants also mentioned the need for more variety in the solutions presented in the exercises, as well as clearer instructions and additional support when encountering difficulties. Some also requested better feedback from the instructors and the ability to ask questions directly to the teachers, rather than relying on peers.

5.8 Perceived Usefulness of the MOOC for Learning Programming Skills (n = 42)

The evaluation results for the perceived usefulness of the MOOC in learning programming skills reveal that 14% (6 students) considered it very useful, while 43% (18 students) found it useful. Additionally, 38% (16 students) rated its usefulness as average, with 5% (2 students) finding it less useful (Table 7).

Table 7. Perceived Usefulness of the MOOC for Learning Programming Skills (n = 42).

Response	Total	Male	Female	Percentage
Very useful: The MOOC was extremely useful for learning programming skills	6	5	1	14%
Useful: The MOOC was useful for learning programming skills	18	5	13	43%
Average useful: The MOOC was moderately useful for learning programming skills	16	4	12	38%
Less useful: The MOOC was less useful for learning programming skills	2	0	2	5%

5.9 Recommendation of the MOOC to Other Students (n = 42)

The survey results on whether students would recommend the MOOC to others show a range of opinions. About 16% (7 students) indicated they would for sure recommend, while 24% (10 students) would likely recommend it. 50% (21 students) responded with "maybe". Meanwhile, 10% (4 students) were not likely to recommend the course (Table 8).

Table 8. Likelihood of Recommending the MOOC to Others (n = 42).

Response	Total	Male	Female	Percentage
Yes, definitely	7	4	3	16%
Yes, probably	10	4	6	24%
Maybe	21	6	15	50%
No, rather not	4	0	4	10%

5.10 Interest in Using MOOCs in Other Subjects (n = 42)

The survey results on students' interest in using MOOCs for other subjects reveal moderate enthusiasm. About 64% (27 students) indicated they might consider using MOOCs in other subjects. About 19% (8 students) indicated they might not consider. 12% (5 students) saw potential benefits in integrating MOOCs into different areas of study, and 5% (2 students) were interested in this expansion (Table 9).

Table 9. Students' Interest in Using MOOCs for Other Subjects (n = 42).

Response	Total	Male	Female	Percentage
Yes, definitely	2	2	0	5%
Yes, probably	5	3	2	12%
Maybe	27	8	19	64%
No, rather not	8	1	7	19%

5.11 Motivation for Continued Self-learning (n = 42)

The evaluation results regarding motivation indicate that 48% (20 students) felt a moderate level of motivation from participating in the MOOC. Meanwhile, 26% (11 students) reported feeling less motivated, and 26% (11 students) felt encouraged by the MOOC to pursue further self-directed learning (Table 10).

Table 10. Motivation Levels from Participation in the MOOC (n = 42).

Response	Total	Male	Female	Percentage
Motivated	11	7	4	26%
Less motivated	11	4	7	26%
Average motivated	20	3	17	48%

5.12 Teacher Feedback (n = 2)

Both teachers had basic programming knowledge, mostly gained through Scratch or as part of professional development courses. One teacher had some little experience with Python, while the other had never worked with it before.

Neither of the teachers had previous experience using MOOCs, either as participants or in classroom settings. While they were familiar with the term "MOOC" and had heard of MOOCs, they had no direct experience with them. Despite this lack of experience, both teachers found their way around the MOOC quickly. The platform was user-friendly and intuitively designed, allowing them to navigate the course without any difficulties. They also observed that the students adapted to the platform just as quickly. The teachers rated the quality of the videos and other learning resources highly, noting that they were well-suited to engage students and facilitate understanding. They did not encounter any technical issues, suggesting that the MOOC platform was stable and accessible. The teachers also noted that it was extremely helpful to receive the solutions to exercises in advance from the professionally qualified computer science teacher. For students who progressed quickly through the MOOC, they distributed the example solutions and encouraged the students to independently identify errors. This approach proved valuable, especially for the non-specialist computer science teachers, who often face difficulties in providing further support when students move beyond the material. By giving students the solutions, they could work through the problems themselves and find solutions independently, which also fostered problem-solving skills and deeper engagement with the content. The teachers considered the MOOC "*very useful*" for teaching programming skills, appreciating its structured and clear content, which supported student comprehension. They expressed in general, that the quotes "*The MOOC was somewhat monotonous, but it was fun and something different. We really learned programming. It was meaningful*" were frequently mentioned from the students in the classroom. The teachers also expressed confidence in recommending the MOOC to other educators, especially those who may need additional structure and support to teach programming. The experience also inspired the teachers to consider using MOOCs for their own professional development, recognizing the platform's potential as a valuable learning tool for both students and teachers. Given the limited number of teachers involved in this research study, it is not intended to inform future decisions or provide a comprehensive overview. Instead, we aim to present a new study that also explores the use of MOOCs by non-specialist teachers.

6 Discussion

The results from this study highlight both the strengths and challenges of integrating a Python programming MOOC into secondary education. The majority of students (86%) had no prior experience with MOOCs, making this their first exposure to such a learning format. This is significant because it underscores the MOOC's potential in reaching students who are new to MOOC learning environments. Additionally, the students' previous programming experience was largely limited, with 64% having no background in coding, suggesting that the MOOC served as an introductory tool for many. In terms of navigation, most students found the MOOC platform to be user-friendly, with 53% reporting a seamless experience. This aligns with findings from Staubitz et al. [14], where a positive user experience with the MOOC platform was observed despite initial challenges. However, some students expressed difficulties, with 14% struggling with navigation. This disparity between ease of use and difficulties could reflect differences in digital readiness among students, as MOOCs often demand a higher level of autonomy compared to traditional learning formats. As the study by Grella et al. [2], has shown, a lack of teacher guidance in the absence of in-person interactions can lead to frustration among students, affecting their engagement and satisfaction with the platform. When asked about the difficulty level of the course, 26% of the total 42 students considered the MOOC to be appropriate and well-balanced, while 10% found it too challenging. This suggests that while the MOOC was generally effective for a wide range of learners, some students might need additional scaffolding or support to succeed. These findings resonate with Grover et al. [3], where the combination of traditional teaching and MOOC content in a Blended Learning environment was found to be beneficial in improving understanding, particularly for students with less prior knowledge. The integration of face-to-face interactions may have helped address challenges related to the difficulty and engagement of the content. The enjoyment of the course was relatively high for $n = 15$, with 60% of students expressing enjoyment. However, when considering the total of 42 students, only 21% rated the MOOC as overall enjoyable, while 64% (27 students) did not provide an answer. The higher levels of enjoyment reported by a subset of students align with other studies, such as Panyajamorn et al. [12], which highlighted the positive impact of MOOCs on student engagement, particularly when students felt motivated and were able to progress at their own pace. However, the 50% lower satisfaction among all students in this study suggests that personalization and engagement need further improvement. Specifically, students cited a lack of interaction with other students and the teacher, which echoes findings from Grella et al. [2], where the limited interaction with instructors and peers was considered a major challenge. This calls for MOOCs to incorporate more interactive elements and community-building opportunities for the class itself. Students also reported technical difficulties, such as server overload and errors marking correct answers as incorrect. These challenges mirror the findings of Hermans & Aivaloglou [5], where technical issues and system reliability were identified as key barriers to students' learning experiences in MOOC environments. Improving system stability and interactive video formats could address some of these concerns, as suggested by students who asked for clearer explanations and more engaging videos. Interestingly, the study also showed moderate interest in extending the use of MOOCs to other subjects, though it was not overwhelming. This suggests that broader adoption across different subjects in secondary schools may require further investigation into content suitability and student interest. This reflects the need for content adaptation identified in Staubitz et al. [14], where content for MOOCs needs to be tailored more specifically to both the subject matter and student needs to maximize effectiveness.

The feedback from the teachers was also insightful. Despite having limited experience with MOOCs, both teachers found the course to be user-friendly and appreciated the clarity of the videos and learning resources. This feedback aligns with the findings of Sharkia and Kohen [13], which indicate that MOOCs, particularly when taught by university-level experts and integrated into hybrid learning environments, might serve as a particularly valuable tool for non-specialist teachers. By providing access to expert instruction and well-structured content, MOOCs can complement or extend teachers' own subject knowledge, thereby enhancing their ability to support student learning. In your study, the teachers emphasized that the MOOC allowed them to guide students more effectively. However, they also mentioned the challenge of providing adequate support for students progressing faster than others. This reflects the importance of providing additional resources, such as solutions and teaching guides, which was also observed in other studies like Grella et al. [2]. Teachers found the MOOC to be a valuable tool for teaching programming and expressed confidence in recommending it to other educators, further supporting the idea that MOOCs, when well-integrated, can bridge the gap in teaching resources, especially in subjects facing teacher shortages.

7 Conclusion and Future Steps

This study presents initial findings, though not representative, suggesting that MOOCs, particularly in subjects such as computer science, hold significant potential by offering flexibility, structured, engaging instruction; help to bridge the CS teacher gap; enable scalable, accessible integration of programming in schools, and support long-term improvement of digital education in secondary schools. However, challenges such as technical difficulties, motivation issues, and the need for more interactive and personalized support highlight areas for improvement. These findings underscore the importance of designing MOOCs that ensure sustained engagement, particularly in self-paced learning environments. As MOOCs continue to gain traction in secondary education, further research and development are needed to refine their design and optimize their impact.

Limitation

This study has several limitations: the small overall sample size - particularly among teachers - limits the generalizability of the findings; the absence of additional indicators such as student learning outcomes restricts the evaluation of the MOOC's overall effectiveness; and the optional nature of questionnaire items led to varying response rates (e.g., n = 15 vs. n = 42), affecting the comparability of specific results.

References

1. Bruff, D.O., Fisher, D.H., McEwen, K.E., Smith, B.E.: Wrapping a MOOC: student perceptions of an experiment in blended learning. MERLOT J. Online Learn. Teach. **9**(2), 187–199 (2013). http://jolt.merlot.org/vol9no2/bruff_0613.htm
2. Grella, C.T., Staubitz, T., Teusner, R., Meinel, C.: Can MOOCs support secondary education in computer science?. In: Auer, M., Guralnick, D., Uhomoibhi, J. (eds.) ICL 2016. AISC, vol. 544, pp. 478–493. Springer, Cham (2017). https://doi.org/10.1007/978-3-319-50337-0_45
3. Grover, S., Pea, R., Cooper, S.: Designing for deeper learning in a blended computer science course for middle school students. Comput. Sci. Educ. **25**(2), 199–237 (2015). https://doi.org/10.1080/08993408.2015.1033142
4. Guggemos, J., Moser, L., Seufert, S.: Learners don't know best: shedding light on the phenomenon of the K-12 MOOC in the context of information literacy. Comput. Educ. **188**, 104552 (2022). https://doi.org/10.1016/j.compedu.2022.104552
5. Hermans, F., Aivaloglou, E.: Teaching software engineering principles to K-12 students: a MOOC on scratch. In: Proceedings of the 2017 IEEE/ACM 39th International Conference on Software Engineering: Software Engineering Education and Training Track (ICSE-SEET), pp. 13–22. IEEE (2017). https://doi.org/10.1109/ICSE-SEET.2017.13
6. Ihsen, S., Jeanrenaud, Y., de Vries, P.: Gender and diversity in engineering MOOCs: a first appraisal. In: Proceedings of the 43rd Annual SEFI Conference, pp. 1–10. SEFI (2015)
7. Israel, M.J.: Effectiveness of integrating MOOCs in traditional classrooms for undergraduate students. Int. Rev. Res. Open Distrib. Learn. **16**(5), 102–119 (2015)
8. Khalil, M., Ebner, M.: A STEM MOOC for school children: what does learning analytics tell us? In: 2015 International Conference on Interactive Collaborative Learning (ICL), pp. 1217–1221. IEEE (2015)
9. Kizilcec, R.F., Schneider, E.: Motivation as a lens to understand online learners: toward data-driven design with the OLEI scale. ACM Trans. Comput. Hum. Interact. (TOCHI) **22**(2), 6–23 (2015)
10. Kurhila, J., Vihavainen, A.: A purposeful MOOC to alleviate insufficient CS education in Finnish schools. ACM Trans. Comput. Educ. **15**(2), 10:1–10:18 (2015)
11. Löwis, M., Staubitz, T., Teusner, R., Renz, J., Meinel, C.: Scaling youth development training in IT using an xMOOC-platform. In: 2015 IEEE Frontiers in Education Conference (FIE), pp. 1–6. IEEE (2015)
12. Panyajamorn, T., Kohda, Y., Chongphaisal, P., Supnithi, T.: The effectiveness and suitability of MOOCs hybrid learning: a case study of public schools in Thai rural area. In: 11th International Conference on Knowledge, Information and Creativity Support Systems (KICSS), pp. 1–6. IEEE (2016). https://doi.org/10.1109/KICSS.2016.7951449
13. Sharkia, H., Kohen, Z.: "Simply math"—a hybrid MOOC supporting advanced mathematics learning in Israeli secondary schools. Educ. Sci. **15**(3), 271 (2025). https://doi.org/10.3390/educsci15030271
14. Staubitz, T., Teusner, R., Meinel, C.: MOOCs in secondary education – experiments and observations from German classrooms. In: 2019 IEEE Global Engineering Education Conference (EDUCON), pp. 173–182. IEEE (2019). https://doi.org/10.1109/EDUCON.2019.8725193
15. Thai, T.T.N., De Wever, B., Valcke, M.: The impact of a flipped classroom design on learning performance in higher education: looking for the best "blend" of lectures and guiding questions with feedback. Comput. Educ. **107**, 113–126 (2017). https://doi.org/10.1016/j.compedu.2017.01.003
16. Vo, H.M., Zhu, C., Diep, N.A.: The effect of blended learning on student performance at course-level in higher education: a meta-analysis. Stud. Educ. Eval. **53**, 17–28 (2017). https://doi.org/10.1016/j.stueduc.2017.01.002

Rethinking Online Community Beyond Self-paced MOOCs

Simona Ferrari[1] and Annarita Merigo[2](✉)

[1] Cremit, Catholic University of the Sacred Heart, Milan, Italy
simona.ferrari@unicatt.it

[2] Ilab, Catholic University of the Sacred Heart, Milan, Italy
annarita.merigo1@unicatt.it

Abstract. The rapid acceleration in the use of digital tools and platforms in education, driven by the COVID-19 pandemic, has also impacted Massive Open Online Courses (MOOCs), which are now available globally in various formats. An increasing number of individuals engage with these courses to enhance their knowledge, skills, and competencies for personal and professional development, benefiting from their free and easily accessible nature. This trend is also evident in our country, despite the absence of a definitive stance from European institutions regarding the accreditation and legal recognition of this type of education.

Contemporary MOOCs increasingly emphasize brevity, conciseness, and reusability in their content design, prioritizing audiovisual materials over text-based resources.

This shift aligns with an increasingly fast-paced, flexible, and personalized approach to digital learning. Consequently, training providers face the challenge of ensuring the sustainability of these courses, as they must continuously produce and update materials that rapidly evolve.

In this context of fast, flexible, and at times consumer-driven self-directed learning, it becomes particularly relevant to reintroduce the value of socially oriented learning within MOOCs. This necessitates a critical examination of sustainable engagement and participation strategies.

This study, conducted by CREMIT (Research Center on Media Education, Innovation, and Technology) and ILAB (Center for Innovation and Development of University Teaching and Technology) at Università Cattolica del Sacro Cuore, aims to:

1. Compare the instructional models of pre-COVID (tutored) and post-COVID (self-paced) MOOCs, highlighting changes and challenges related to the social dimension of learning;

2. Identify signs of community formation within self-paced MOOCs;

3. Identify key conditions for fostering and sustaining a learning community that extends beyond the conventional MOOC lifecycle.

To achieve these objectives, the study collected and analyzed monitoring data from 33 MOOCs delivered between 2014 and January 2025. The dataset includes both quantitative data (initial and final questionnaires, learning analytics, and retention metrics) and qualitative data (analysis of forum messaging).

A. Merigo—This article has been developed jointly by the authors. Simona Ferrari wrote § 1 and 3. Annarita Merigo wrote § 2. Section 4 has been written jointly.

E. Hamonic and R. Sharrock (Eds.): EMOOCS 2025, LNCS 15733, pp. 86–97, 2026.
https://doi.org/10.1007/978-3-032-00056-9_8

The contribution concludes with two forward-looking proposals: a hypothesis for the redesign of MOOCs, incorporating support tools for learner guidance and self-regulation; and the presentation of a new collaborative space dedicated to MOOC-related themes, envisioned as a platform for dialogue, reflection, and the co-design of new educational materials.

Keywords: Online Community · Community Development · Self-regulated learning

1 Introduction

Since 2014, Cremit (Research Centre on Media Education, Innovation and Technology), in collaboration with Ilab (Innovation for Digital Didactics) of the Università Cattolica del Sacro Cuore, has been producing and delivering MOOCs as part of the University's Third Mission. These MOOCs focus specifically on prevention and digital media education to support a 'digital culture' [1].

The pedagogical model guiding these MOOCs is rooted in three key principles: the social dimension of learning, the knowledge-building approach [2, 3], and relational pedagogy [4]. These pillars drive MOOCs in a participatory direction, fostering communication and collaboration among participants [5].

However, the COVID-19 pandemic and subsequent lockdowns have significantly altered digital consumption patterns, both quantitatively and qualitatively. Education has seen a shift toward micro-learning (brevity and speed), ubiquitous learning (independent of spatial constraints, balancing synchronous and asynchronous elements), learner-centered approaches (catering to individual interests and needs), and the development of dynamic literacies [6]. This shift is also evident in MOOCs. When comparing pre-COVID and post-COVID MOOCs, we observe changes in time structures, an increase in self-paced learning, reduced feedback mechanisms, and fewer dedicated communication spaces. These adjustments, often responding to user requests rather than massive enrollment numbers, risk fostering self-learning processes with low participation density.

This shift necessitates an in-depth reflection on the pedagogical value of community, which remains a crucial element for learning. Designing MOOCs to encourage peer interaction, the sharing of best practices, and mutual support is essential [7]. This study explores sustainable engagement and participation strategies in self-paced MOOCs and examines how to extend the community beyond the course lifecycle. It does so through three key steps:

- comparing pre-COVID and post-COVID MOOC models, focusing on changes in social learning processes;
- identifying signs of community in post-COVID MOOCs;
- determining requirements for sustaining a learning community beyond a MOOC's cycle.

2 Impact of the "COVID-19" Scenario on Cremit's MOOCs

From the inception of MOOCs at Università Cattolica, enhancing the social dimension has been a fundamental design principle [5], even within the light educational framework of MOOCs [8, 9]. The post-COVID redesign of MOOCs has aimed to support new forms of presence and participation. These dimensions have been systematically monitored through evaluation plans accompanying MOOC delivery since 2014. Monitoring includes participant feedback through final questionnaires, tracking data (a standard component of MOOC evaluation), forum message analysis, focus groups, and interviews conducted in various research projects.

In order to understand the changes in the social dimension, it is necessary to start by analysing the two MOOC models, with a few glances at the data.

2.1 The Pre-COVID Model

Between 2014 and 2021, Università Cattolica delivered 22 MOOCs via Blackboard's Open Education platform. These courses supported social learning through [5, 10, 11]:

- tutor facilitation and moderation;
- communication spaces (forums) for discussion and sharing;
- a communication plan designed to attract and engage learners actively;
- gradual content release to create an inclusive learning experience and mitigate dropouts typical of online courses. Table 1 summarises the design elements.

Table 1. Cremit – MOOCs Model from 2014 to 2021

Platform	Open Education by Blackboard
Orientation	FAQ
Materials	Videolessons + materials + e-tivity
Timing	Timed: weekly release (1 week socialisation + weekly module release + 1 week catch-up)
Duration	3 months
Tutoring	Asynchronous + synchronous
Communication	Alerts, e-mail, 6 threads in forum (Let's introduce ourselves, Reflections on the Honor Code, Doubts and difficulties with the platform, Let's discuss together, Questions on content, Assessment of the experience)
Assessment	Test at the end of each module
Certification	Certificate
Monitoring	Initial and final questionnaire

Tracking data indicates that this model was effective. Table 2 presents general tracking data on 20.987 enrolled participants. Of these, on average only 6.84% dropped out after the first week and 62.2% downloaded the course certificate, showing a very high completion rate compared to the 5–10% documented in the literature [12].

Table 2. Pre-Covid MOOCs

Learning Platform	No. Courses	No. Participants	No. Early drop-out (after 1 week)	No. Certificates	No. Final Q
Open Education	22	20.987	1.435 (6,84%)	13.048 (62, 2%)	9.637 (45,9%)

The second element is satisfaction: in the final questionnaires (N = 9.637), 49% of the users were completely satisfied, and 36.5% were very satisfied (using a 6-point scale, from 1 = not at all satisfied to 6 = completely).

A third element is related to student involvement. More than 95% viewed all the proposed content (with a functionalist-instrumental engagement) and 85% of forum messages were participant-generated, averaging 0.6 messages per participant (Table 6). About a quarter (24.91%) are 'communicative' participants in MOOCs. Furthermore, the final questionnaires show that:

- 12.2% identified as participative learners, 14% enthusiastic, 4.6% enterprising, 3.9% altruistic, 27% diligent, 1.3% lazy, 34% silent, 0.6% talkative, 0.5% pessimistic, 0.5% opportunistic, 0.6% dispersed/drop-out;
- tutoring scored 62% satisfaction and forum discussions scored 32% satisfaction;
- 31% felt involved in a learning community, with community members perceived as colleagues providing insights (27%), discussion partners (21%), sources of help (18%), professional contacts (32%), professionals in order to co-design resources and activities (27%).

Finally, the comparative analysis of messaging in the forums of 3 MOOCs, based on Gilly Salmon's *Five Step Model* [13], made it possible to observe a good qualitative level in the communicative exchange between e-tutors and students [14].

2.2 The Post-COVID Model

In the post-COVID period, from 2021 to the present, the design model of MOOCs has undergone several changes. One structural change was driven by the transition to a new platform introduced by the University, EduOpen, which conceptualizes communication spaces in a way that is more oriented toward courseware and less toward community engagement.

A second change concerns a shorter MOOC lifecycle, not only in terms of micro-MOOCs—characterized by a reduced overall duration, shorter modules, and more concise content—but also in terms of course sustainability, with fewer editions and less frequent content updates.

A third change has been driven by the economic sustainability of tutoring services, prompting a reconsideration of lighter forms of a role considered strategic [15], particularly in light of self-paced MOOCs. These MOOCs, in turn, challenge the existing model with the following demands: the ability to progress at one's own pace, necessitating the immediate and simultaneous availability of all materials; shorter course durations; a growing preference for synchronous over asynchronous interactions, both among students and with tutors; reduced participation; and a tendency for students to produce and share content only when it contributes to workload assessment.

In this context, the post-COVID MOOC design (Table 3) seeks to preserve the social dimension of learning.

Table 3. Cremit – MOOCs Model from 2021 to 2025

Platform	EduOpen
Orientation	FAQ + minitutorial
Resources	Videolessons + materials + e-tivity
Timing	Open
Duration	10/12 months
Tutoring	Light tutoring Asynchronous
Communication	1 thread in forum
Assessment	End of module Test
Certification	Certificate
Monitoring	Final questionnaire

Since 2021, 11 MOOCs have been delivered, reaching 4.916 participants (Table 4).

Table 4. Cremit Light tutored + Self paced MOOCs 2021–2025*

Learning Platform	No. Courses	No. Participants	No. Certificates	No. Final Q
EduOpen	11	4.916	1.743 (35,5%)	2.919 (59,6%)

*Last updated date: January 14, 2025.

Final satisfaction surveys (N = 2.919) reported a general satisfaction level of 52% (completely satisfied) and 30% (very satisfied). Additionally, 79% of participants engaged with all the MOOC content.

Despite the stability of the MOOC offering, participation patterns indicate significant shifts. Forum activity has notably declined, with an 81% share of messages generated by learners but at an average rate of only 0.1 message per participant.

Regarding discussion engagement, 47% of respondents rated forum discussions at level 6 on a satisfaction scale, while 44% reported feeling part of a learning community. This aligns with self-perceptions of participation: 14% identified as participatory, 17% as enthusiastic, 9% as proactive, 7% as altruistic, 21% as diligent, 1% as passive, 28% as silent, 2% as talkative, 1% as pessimistic, 1% as opportunistic, and 0.2% as disengaged/dropout. Participants perceived their peers in various ways:

- 34% saw them as colleagues who shared useful content;
- 33% viewed them as discussion partners on course topics;
- 30% considered them a resource for understanding complex concepts;
- 48% regarded them as potential professional contacts;
- 42% saw them as collaborators for co-developing activities, materials, and learning pathways.

In light of the relatively lukewarm participation data, this shift towards a lighter engagement approach appears to be the new lens through which learners interpret their participation, as reflected in the reported satisfaction levels. The social dimension is not being eliminated; rather, it is still sought and enacted by participants, albeit at a different level.

3 Signs of Community in Self-paced MOOCs

To explore the persistence of community engagement in self-paced MOOCs, data collection focused on:

- Retention data: examining user loyalty and enrollment in multiple MOOCs.
- Final questionnaires: assessing satisfaction with learning community involvement.
- Forum exchanges: conducting qualitative analysis of discussions.

Retention Data. Table 5 presents the percentages of learners who, out of the total 4.916 enrolled in the 11 post-COVID MOOCs, chose to enroll in more than one of the courses offered. The data analysis suggests the presence of a critical mass of users interested in topics related to "digital culture", who maintain their engagement and construct their own learning pathways independently, without these being explicitly proposed by the University. This group represents fertile ground for the emergence of a community driven by such participation.

Table 5. Retention

No partecipants	Enrolled in 2 MOOCs	Enrolled in 3 MOOCs	Enrolled in 4 MOOCs	Enrolled in 5 MOOCs	Enrolled in 6 MOOCs	Enrolled in 7 MOOCs	Enrolled in 8 MOOCs
4.916	601 12,22%	119 2,42%	42 0,85%	21 0,42%	8 0,16%	5 0,10%	1 0,02%

Final Questionnaires. The comparison between the answers to the final questionnaire of the pre-covid and post-covid MOOCs (Table 6) allows us to confirm the choices in the change of model, towards a dimension that accepts and welcomes lighter forms of participation in the training organisation. These results also tell of a pre-disposition of students to this dimension and not its "cancellation" for more self-instructive forms.

Table 6. Comparison of Pre-Covid and Post-Covid

	Pre-Covid	Post-Covid
Final questionnaire	9.637	2.919
Overall Satisfaction	49% completely satisfied	52% completely satisfied
	36,5% very satisfied	30% very satisfied
Forum satisfaction	32%	47%
Involvement in community	31%	44%
Collegues perceived as:		
• source of content	27%	34%
• possibility of comparison	21%	33%
• help in understanding contents	18%	30%
• professional contacts	32%	48%
• co-designer	27%	42%
Completion of activities	95%	79%
Forum		
• overall messages	14.732	670
• n° messages partecipants	12.491	541
• n° messagges tutor	1.792	129
Type of participant		
• participative	12,2%	14%
• enthusiastic	14%	17%
• enterprising	4,6%	9%
• altruistic	3,9%	7%
• diligent	27%	21%
• lazy	1,3%	1%
• silence	34%	28%
• chattering	0,6%	2%
• pessimistic	0,5%	1%
• opportunistic	0,5%	1%
• drop-out	0,6%	0,2%

Qualitative Analysis of Forums. The qualitative analysis of forums reveals participants' willingness to share a common interest within a perspective of learning and personal growth. These are signs of a community that emerges organically from participant interaction rather than being tutor-driven. This community engagement reflects an interest in course topics framed within a dynamic of exchange and relationship-building among peers. The types of contributions were classified as follows:

- Requests for discussion;
- Appreciation for course content;
- Personal reflections.

Similarly, the types of feedback observed included:

- Personal reworking of course topics;
- Sharing of resources;
- References to course materials.

Below are some qualitative examples of these messages:

Personal reflections: "[...] An increasingly common phenomenon is child influencers who, often pressured by their parents, are exposed on social media and lead highly stressful lives without the possibility of a normal childhood". "There are laws and regulations, such as the Italian law on the protection of minors in television (e.g., the self-regulation code for television), aimed at shielding children from harmful content. However, the complexity of modern media makes it difficult to enforce these regulations consistently". "What are your thoughts on digital media use for preschool children?" *[MOOC Infanzia Onlife: Gli adulti nell'educazione digitale].*

"This type of project should be strengthened to provide real employment opportunities for professionals in this field across the national territory, wherever interventions are needed to support the increasing fragility of the elderly, who are often overlooked". *[MOOC Tutor di comunità].*

Requests for discussion: "I would like to ask what types of stories are most suitable for children—should they include rules, and can they address themes of loss?" *[MOOC Infanzia Onlife: Gli adulti nell'educazione digitale].*

"Being a caregiver is an act of love that is both deeply engaging and demanding. I feel that in terms of caregiver support, we are still far behind in meeting actual needs. Is this just my impression? Does anyone else share similar or completely different views?" *[MOOC Per una cultura delle cure palliative].*

Appreciation for course content: "This course is very interesting because it presents possible pathways and tools to be implemented locally, even in small communities."

"I appreciated the videos featuring real-life testimonies". *[MOOC Tutor di comunità].*

Sharing of resources: "Books: *Il sentiero* by M. Dubuc; *Perché piangiamo?* by F. Pintadera and A. Sender; *L'anatra, la morte e il tulipano* by W. Erlbruch; *L'albero dei ricordi* by B. Teckentrup." *[MOOC Infanzia Onlife: Gli adulti nell'educazione digitale].*

References to course materials: "I believe it is crucial to focus on Tisseron's 3A approach—Accompaniment, Alternation, and Self-Regulation—so that digital proposals can be properly received and processed by children". *[MOOC Infanzia Onlife: Gli adulti nell'educazione digitale].*

4 Community as a Developed MOOC?

The analysis confirms the well-established importance of social interaction, even in MOOCs that are primarily designed for self-paced learning. We could suggest that the fifth step in Salmon's model for online course development [13]—the development phase—represents the outcome of MOOCs, at least for some participants. This phase lays the foundation for the concept of a post-MOOC that nurtures an active community. If we consider that MOOCs can serve as the catalyst for activating communities that can fully leverage the social dimension [16], we must then examine the conditions that make the community the final stage in a MOOC's life cycle. We identify three key conditions.

Identifying the Target Audience: Who should be engaged in the community-building process. Not all participants reach the fifth stage of Salmon's model. Many drop out early, while others may only engage at the initial stages, where the experience is limited to information exchange (Salmon's step 3).

Analyzing MOOC monitoring data allows us to identify participants who are most likely to thrive in a community setting—those who are open to building relationships, communicative, and deeply engaged with the topic. These 'profile' data help pinpoint the right audience for future proposals. Specifically, tracking participants who enroll in multiple MOOCs (retention) reveals a group with a deeper interest in digital topics, as well as a shared approach to understanding this phenomenon, including common themes, reflections, and language over time.

Through a targeted questionnaire administered to participants across at least three MOOCs, we aim to stimulate reflection on the community as a formative space for collective growth. The goal is to lay the groundwork for more direct involvement, turning the community into a purposeful entity that enhances the practices exchanged within it. Ultimately, this leads to the proposal of co-designing new MOOCs, ensuring the university's engagement with stakeholders [17], and securing funding for their development.

Identifying the Form of Community: A community as a space for sharing and reflection, existing externally and post-MOOC, but preserving the memory of the course. The community becomes a way for course producers and providers to capitalize on the MOOC experience, making sense of its increasingly short but costly (both economically and educationally) lifecycle. Capitalizing means enhancing:

- Materials produced over time that are prone to obsolescence. Knowledge maps and the ways in which knowledge is mediated (such as the archaeology and history of knowledge) form a crucial archive for understanding the relevance of knowledge, maps, and methods—especially when knowledge pertains to the digital world. Making such content available in a community space serves as a memory of that community, creating an archive of work that allows future participants to align themselves with the community, foster reflexivity, and identify new training needs to address.

- Human capital of tutors and MOOC participants who have invested in the course. Their forms of participation will continue to benefit from the relational space within the community, where the return on their investment is seen in a more focused group than the original course participants.
- Forms of restitution. Exploring how the 'gratuitousness' of the MOOC can lead to generative processes on the part of the learner—asking, "What can I offer to others?"—within contexts that encourage and protect such sharing. This could sustainably generate collective benefits. However, this process is challenging in mass contexts where participation varies widely.

The proposal is to initiate a co-design phase for the community, involving some MOOC staff members and more active participants, as identified through monitoring. This will include a webinar for presenting the idea, two focus groups for comparing co-design phases (such as user involvement methods, community types, moderation styles, communication plans, monitoring strategies, and design repositories), and an evaluation of the sustainability of the proposed approach, which will be assessed through a questionnaire given to MOOC participants.

Supporting the Value of the Community: Enhance the attention to and value of the community dimension for all participants in Cremit MOOCs. While it's true that not all participants in a MOOC are ready for community engagement, this doesn't mean that the community aspect shouldn't be a focal point of reflection and support, especially with an eye toward future participation. Respecting each participant's individual learning path is essential, but MOOCs should be seen as spaces that reinforce this outward-facing dimension.

To this end, work is underway to redesign MOOCs to incorporate strategies that better support participants' self-regulation [18, 19]. Besides enhancing the formative aspect of the MOOC itself, self-regulation is crucial for participants to successfully engage in the social and community dimensions of the course. Therefore, the proposal is to:

- Include a module common to all MOOCs that addresses self-regulated learning, which is a critical aspect of online education. The module will begin with a questionnaire to help participants assess their current learning habits and reflect on the various dimensions of regulation. Additional in-depth materials will be provided to support learners in effectively planning, monitoring, and evaluating their own learning progress.
- Revise the forums to optimize the tutor's role in promoting awareness of the significance of participation, using a 4-stage framework (Cluster, Orient, Focus, and Network) that has already been documented in the literature [20].

Each of these development proposals will be monitored to assess their impact on the community dimension, viewed as the outcome of a MOOC that doesn't end but rather regenerates throughout its lifecycle.

5 Conclusions

Community could ensure continuity to the social capital generated by MOOCs. To implement the project described in § 4, it will be necessary to revisit the community models proposed by literature to identify the one that best fits the identified needs, in order to initiate a pilot experiment.

This must be sustainable both for the organization activating the community and for the potential participating learners.

Regarding the moderation of the future community, it is necessary to better understand which actions to undertake to support it, also attempting to train AI-based interaction systems. In this regard, the categorization work carried out on the analysis of forum messaging (§ 3) will be useful. Shifting from a qualitative to a quantitative approach in communication analyses could also solve a limitation of the study.

References

1. Ferrari, S.: Alleanze digitali: i media oggi da problema a risorsa per la corresponsabilità scuola-famiglia. In: Comunità e corresponsabilità educativa. Soggetti, compiti e strategie, pp. 29–38. Pensa Multimedia Editore, Lecce (2019)
2. Laurillard, D.: Rethinking University Teaching: A Conversational Framework for the Effective Use of Learning Technologies, 2nd edn. RoutledgeFalmer, London (2002)
3. Gibbs, G., Jenkins, A.: Teaching Large Classes in Higher Education: How to Maintain Quality with Reduced Resources. Routledge, London (1992)
4. Gravett, K., Taylor, A.C., Fairchild, N.: Pedagogies of mattering: re-conceptualising relational pedagogies in higher education. Teach. High. Educ., 1–16 (2021)
5. Ferrari, S., Rivoltella, P.C., Rizzi, C., Scott, F.: Designing MOOCs in higher education. Outcomes of an experimentation at the Catholic University of Milan. REM **7**(1), 1–10 (2015)
6. Potter, J., McDougall, J.: Digital Media, Culture and Education: Theorising Third Space Literacies, pp.1–205. Palgrave Macmillan, London (2017)
7. Gamage, D., Whitting, M.: Together we Learn Better: Leveraging Communities of Practice for MOOC Learners. Association for Computing Machinery, New York (2021)
8. Ferrari, S., Rizzi, C., Rivoltella, P.G.: La formazione leggera. I MOOC per lo sviluppo di competenze nella Media Education. In: Media education in Italia. Oggetti e ambiti della formazione, pp. 176–195. Franco Angeli, Milano (2019)
9. Ferrari, S., Triacca, S., Braga, G.: Design for learning in the third space: opportunities and challenges. REM, 1–10 (2021)
10. Ferrari, S., Piccardi, L.: Studiare la CMC: i forum di discussione. In: Cattaneo, A., Rivoltella, P.C. (eds.) Tecnologie, formazione, professioni. Idee e tecniche per l'innovazione Edizioni Unicopli, Milano, pp. 185–204 (2010)
11. Ferrari, S., Garavaglia, A.: Io scrivo, tu mi leggi? qualcuno risponderà... lurking e partecipazione nei gruppi di apprendimento on line. Inf. Sci. Decis. Mak. **39**, 417–429 (2010)
12. Goopio, J., Cheung, C.: The MOOC dropout phenomenon and retention strategies. J. Teach. Travel Tour. **21**(2), 177–197 (2021)
13. Salmon, G.: Computer mediated conferencing for management learning at the open university. Manag. Learn. **31**(4), 491–502 (2000)
14. Merigo, A.: Formazione a distanza (FAD) e MOOC, un'analisi durante il tirocinio in Media Education (2020). https://www.cremit.it/formazione-a-distanza-fad-e-mooc-unanalisi-durante-il-tirocinio-in-media-education/. Accessed 17 Apr 2025

15. Ferrari, S., Triacca, S.: The strategic role of the e-tutor in new learning contexts. In: Agrati, L.S., et al. (eds.) HELMeTO 2020. CCIS, vol. 1344, pp. 300–314. Springer, Cham (2021). https://doi.org/10.1007/978-3-030-67435-9_23
16. Shepherd, C.E., Bolliger, D.U.: Extending Online Community Beyond Courses: Making the Case for Program Community. Routledge (2022)
17. Kennedy, E., Laurillard, D., Zeitoun, S.: The CoMOOC model for global professional collaboration on sustainability. In: Proceedings of the EMOOCs 2023: Post-Covid Prospects for Massive Open Online Courses – Boost or Backlash?, pp. 291–303. Universitätsverlag Potsdam, Potsdam, Germany (2023)
18. Dinh, T., Phuong, H.Y.: MOOC learners' perspectives of the effects of self-regulated learning strategy intervention on their self-regulation and speaking performance. Cogent Educ. **11**(1), 1–24 (2024)
19. Onah, D., Pang, E., Sinclair, J., Uhomoibhi, J.: An innovative MOOC platform: the implications of self-directed learning abilities to improve motivation in learning and to support self-regulation. Int. J. Inf. Learn. Technol. (2021)
20. Gamage, D.: Scaffolding social presence in MOOCs (2021)

Insights on Teaching AI at Scale: Data-Driven Feedback for Learner-Centered Improvement

Zuhra Sofyan(✉) and Christoph Meinel

Hasso-Plattner Institute, Potsdam, Germany
zuhra.sofyan@hpi.de

Abstract. Teaching Artificial Intelligence (AI) at scale presents unique challenges in designing effective, learner-centered educational experiences. This paper explores how data-driven feedback from learners in a wide-scale platform is used as a reference in mapping the strengths and weaknesses perceived by learners in Massive Open Online Courses (MOOCs) on AI. Using responses based on post-course surveys, we use statistics and Latent Dirichlet Allocation (LDA) to uncover recurring themes in learners' choices and open-ended comments. The findings reveal that different demographics have different course perceptions, and in general, integrating interactive content is one of the attractions to increase learners' engagement in completing their courses. These insights offer the opportunities to refine MOOC structure and content for a more inclusive and engaging learning environment. This study contributes to the growing body of research in AI education, especially in large-scale online formats, by demonstrating how analysis of user feedback can pinpoint actionable insights. The results of this exploratory study can provide recommendations to course designers for preparing AI education content across different user segment profiles to continuously improve AI-focused MOOCs and better meet the evolving needs of learners.

Keywords: MOOCs · Artificial Intelligence Education · Latent Dirichlet Allocation · Topic Modelling · Interactive Content · Learning Analytics

1 Introduction

Artificial Intelligence (AI) is rapidly expanding and being applied across various fields. As a result, there is a growing demand for educational platforms that can provide AI education at scale. Massive Open Online Courses (MOOCs) have become a key medium for meeting this need. With their flexibility and accessibility, MOOCs make quality AI education widely available by lowering barriers to entry for learners worldwide.

Despite the advantages offered by MOOCs, they also face a major challenge common to online course providers: low participation rates among enrolled

E. Hamonic and R. Sharrock (Eds.): EMOOCS 2025, LNCS 15733, pp. 98–107, 2026.
https://doi.org/10.1007/978-3-032-00056-9_9

learners. High dropout rates remain a common issue, especially when strong conceptual understanding is involved, such as in AI courses. Unlike traditional classroom settings or small-scale e-learning environments where instructors can adapt in real-time to learners' needs, MOOCs rely heavily on pre-designed content and offer limited interaction with instructors, usually through forums and Q&A sessions. To bridge this gap, instructors often integrate interactive content (IC) such as quizzes, coding exercises, and interactive videos to improve learner engagement and comprehension.

Even with the adoption of interactive content, its actual impact on learner experience, particularly in AI-focused MOOCs, remains under-researched. While previous studies have examined engagement metrics related to interactive videos [5,10,12,16], as well as other interactive elements [2,4,13], learner perception is an area that requires further exploration. Insights from open-ended survey responses can reveal nuances that predefined survey feedback might overlook. However, processing large-scale responses poses another significant challenge.

This study aims to uncover how learners perceive IC in AI-focused MOOCs on KI-Campus by applying topic modeling techniques to large-scale learner feedback. We use Latent Dirichlet Allocation (LDA) to extract key themes from post-course survey responses across multiple AI courses. By analyzing topics emerging from positive feedback and comparing them across learner demographics, such as gender and age, which have been previously associated with different engagement, motivation, and preferences [3,6,7], we identify aspects of IC that enhance the learning experience and suggest improvements for instructors, for more inclusive courses.

Our research provides data-driven insights to support designing more effective AI MOOC content. Using topic modeling, we highlight learners' priorities while addressing their needs. This is particularly valuable for course creators, instructors, and MOOC providers seeking to optimize AI course design to better align with learner expectations. We hope our findings deepen our understanding of learner needs and offer practical recommendations to improve online AI education at scale.

2 Related Work

2.1 Interactive Content in AI-Education MOOCs

In its development, interactive content such as interactive videos, various interactive quizzes, and coding exercises are adopted by AI-focused MOOCs and have been proven to increase learner engagement in large-scale online education settings [5]. By actively involving learners in the learning process to replace interaction in real-world classroom settings, this element helps bridge the gap between theoretical concepts and practical applications [2,4].

On the KI-Campus platform, IC has been used extensively and has become one of the important points in the guide for instructors to design a course. Previous research on KI-Campus shows how courses that use IC have higher engagement rates than those that do not [15]. Other study also shows how the benefits of strategically placing IC as a self-assessment tool embedded directly into course materials significantly impact users [14].

As an evaluation and process to improve the quality of content, especially related to the use of IC provided in delivering teaching about AI, it is important to explore user feedback in a user-centered learning experience approach, which requires a special approach to get good insight in large-scale text feedback analysis [9].

2.2 Text Analysis and Topic Modelling in Educational Context

Natural Language Processing (NLP) techniques have been found to be effective for analyzing educational data, especially in understanding the learner experience from feedback [9]. LDA, which is a topic modeling NLP technique, is able to explore latent themes in large text datasets [1,8]. As an unsupervised learning method, LDA is suitable for this case, where we cluster themes from an unlabeled dataset derived from open-ended questions in a survey. With the use of this LDA technique, it is expected that data-driven insights will provide themes to be used as evaluation materials for instructors in designing courses or improving existing content within the framework of AI-Education MOOC.

3 Methodology

In this section, we describe the data used, the LDA topic modeling, and the qualitative analysis used to generate the information that will be discussed in the results section.

3.1 Data Collection and Preprocessing

The data was collected from responses taken from the post-course survey, focusing on 40 courses that used interactive elements extensively as part of the course content as well as a tool for self-assessment tests.

The open-ended question from the said post-course survey is intended to evaluate the course from the learner's point of view; it serves to evaluate the positive aspects of the course, especially from the integration of interactive elements in course content.

The selected courses are based on several categories, such as AI in Education, Data Literacy, AI in Medicine, Foundation of AI, Machine Learning, and Societal Aspect of AI.

The dataset consists of textual feedback, which will then be paired with statistical data from the same survey to provide a comprehensive overview. It will also be viewed based on the age and gender demographics of the survey participants for comparison. These responses are then collected in CSV and combined into a single dataset for analysis. Prior to analysis, missing responses were removed to ensure data integrity.

To prepare the textual data for analysis, we applied Natural Language Processing (NLP) techniques using NLTK and Gensim libraries by executing several steps, including lowercasing, tokenization, stopword removal, punctuation, and number removal, and converting into bag-of-words representation, before being ready to be consumed in the LDA process.

3.2 Latent Dirichlet Allocation Topic Modelling

To identify key themes from course participants' responses, we employ LDA, which is a topic modeling method that assumes each document (user response) consists of a mixture of topics, and each topic is represented by a distribution of words.

Due to the nature of LDA, which is an unsupervised method, the measure is done by testing the model on several configurations to see the optimal results. Several key parameters are considered in the LDA model configuration, including adjusting the topic numbers and the number of iterations until we get the highest topic coherence score, following the method applied in previous research by Rödel et al. (2015) [11]. A relevance threshold is also applied when interpreting topic proportions. We use a threshold weight equal to 0.05, which means a topic is only considered to exist in a document if its probability of occurrence is above 5%. This is done to avoid the presence of unrepresentative topics and improve the accuracy of the presence of topics in the dataset. Then, using pyLDAvis, these results will be re-evaluated manually to see the distance relationship between each topic cluster created.

3.3 Data Analysis

To explore the emerging themes, in addition to directly analyzing the themes generated from the LDA modeling process, the resulting themes are also viewed in terms of demographics, in this case, in terms of gender and age group. This is to analyze the differences and similarities of the themes that appear in each user group. With the application of LDA and going deeper into different demographic user groups, a broader understanding of the interactivity role in MOOCs will be obtained.

4 Results

4.1 Overall Theme

When running LDA in the post-course survey on the positive response section of the question "What did you particularly like about the course?", we analyzed 1,312 responses after cleaning and preprocessing the data. This resulted in several dominant theme clusters, as shown in Table 1. The most common opinion highlights content variety and interactive videos as the most preferred interactive elements, particularly as test aids.

Interactive videos in this context refer to video content created using H5P, enriched with embedded interactive features such as quizzes, clickable hotspots, and pop-up text. These elements act as self-assessment tools, allowing learners to reinforce key concepts as they watch and interact with the video.

Other key themes related to interactive content include positive user experiences with various interactive elements (topics 2, 3, 5, 8, and 9), as well as the importance of course structure, content quality, and best practices in mastering AI concepts (topics 4, 6, 7, and 10).

Table 1. Overall Theme Feedback

Topic	Top Words	Theme	Prop.
1	everything, topics, easy, well, variety	General positive feedback and topic variety	34.32
2	videos, tasks, interactive, short, video	Interactive video and task-based learning	32.54
3	tests, self, quiz, time, informative	Self-assessment and informative quizzes	14.19
4	well, structured, information, course, explanations	Course structure and explanation quality	14.12
5	good, structure, videos, course, quizzes	Course design and assessment format	13.74
6	content, good, language, learning, course	Learning content and language clarity	12.63
7	short, examples, exercises, application, units	Concise examples and applied exercises	11.89
8	questions, good, videos, interviews, ai	Interview content and AI topics	11.89
9	graphics, examples, clear, applications, jupyter	Visual examples and practical tools	11.74
10	understandable, comprehensive, topics, course, overview	Topic overview and comprehensibility	9.21

4.2 Themes Based on Demographics

From the next two tables (Table 2 and Table 3), we gain insight into several similar positive themes among both male and female users. The topic structure has the biggest proportion for both groups. Self-testing and interactive elements are frequently mentioned as valuable tools (topics 1, 2, 4, 5, 9, and 10 for males, topic 1, 2, 4,5, 6, and 8 for females). Specifically, videos are seen as an effective learning medium by both. Both male and female learners also gave positive feedback on the clear structure and well-organized content. However, there are subtle differences in preferences, most notably in the learning approach. Male learners have a higher proportion of preference for structured assessment and content overview, while females prefer variety, depth, and clarity.

Table 2. Male Response

Topic	Top Words	Theme	Prop.
1	structure, self, tests, clear, good	Structured self-assessment	19.63
2	videos, good, course, interviews, questions	Video content and interactive elements	18.21
3	easy, understand, tasks, ai, video	Ease of understanding and AI content	14.51
4	well, graphics, examples, topics, course	Visual and well-presented content	14.08
5	good, quizzes, learning, comprehensive, many	Good quizzes and comprehensive learning	12.52
6	structured, well, topic, presentation, understandable	Structured presentation and clarity	12.52
7	content, learning, time, topics, online	Learning content and time management	12.23
8	everything, informative, practical, good, overview	Informative and practical overview	12.23
9	topics, good, lecturers, presented, variety	Variety in lecture presentation	12.09
10	ai, short, learning, video, design	Short AI videos and design focus	9.82

Table 3. Female Response

Topic	Top Words	Theme	Prop.
1	everything, examples, structure, different, application	Examples and structural variety	16.40
2	self, tests, videos, liked, way	Self-tests and video engagement	14.59
3	well, content, structured, course, explanations	Well-structured and explained content	14.23
4	topics, videos, variety, short, topic	Topic diversity and short videos	13.69
5	videos, quizzes, material, course, good	Video and quiz-based materials	13.15
6	questions, quiz, video, detailed, tests	Detailed quizzes and video tests	12.25
7	explained, ai, many, good, understandable	Clear explanations and AI-related topics	12.25
8	well, knowledge, programming, interactive, structure	Programming knowledge and interactivity	10.99
9	structure, graphics, well, easy, understand	Visual structure and ease of understanding	10.63
10	varied, learning, design, yes, elements	Varied learning elements and design	9.91

5 Theme in Different Age Groups

From Tables 4, 5, and 6, we can infer some similarities across the three age groups, as all of them agree that video is the most useful medium, with all of them having a positive experience with the interactive and engaging video content. In addition, the interactive elements that served as tools for self-test assessment were considered very valuable, and they also appreciated the well-structured course content and sufficient practical exercises in the AI course they attended.

Interestingly, there are key differences in the perceptions of each age group. Young learners prefer short, engaging videos, varied interactive quizzes, and example-based learning. Mid-career learners focus on structured content, practical learning, and comprehensive explanations. Meanwhile, older learners value easy-to-follow, well-timed content, structured progression, and diverse explanation.

Table 4. Theme for Age Group 18–30 Years Old

Topic	Top Words	Theme	Prop.
1	videos, information, simple, well, structure	Informative and well-structured videos	18.63
2	everything, liked, learning, different, many	General appreciation and learning variety	15.21
3	self, tests, videos, test, quiz	Self-testing and assessment content	13.88
4	videos, short, good, well, quizzes	Short and effective video content	13.50
5	interactive, graphics, videos, explanation, elements	Interactive elements and visual explanations	12.74
6	examples, video, application, design, varied	Practical examples and varied design	12.17
7	content, information, knowledge, course, easy	Accessible and informative content	11.60
8	topics, material, programming, well, overview	Programming topics and course overview	11.41
9	videos, learning, short, ai, different	Short videos and AI learning	8.56
10	learning, structure, course, good, clear	Course structure and learning clarity	8.37

Table 5. Theme for Age Group 30–50 Years Old

Topic	Top Words	Theme	Prop.
1	well, structured, tasks, presented, understandable	Well-structured tasks and clear presentation	16.98
2	structure, clear, good, language, broad	Clear structure and language diversity	15.73
3	topics, easy, variety, understand, speakers	Topic variety and ease of understanding	15.11
4	self, practical, tests, quiz, structure	Practical self-tests and structure	15.11
5	overview, good, examples, comprehensive, videos	Comprehensive overviews and examples	13.46
6	videos, content, topics, examples, liked	Engaging content with examples	12.84
7	videos, well, knowledge, course, explanations	Video explanations and course knowledge	12.01
8	well, ai, knowledge, content, course	AI knowledge and well-prepared content	10.77
9	everything, quizzes, course, topics, good	General positive feedback and quizzes	10.77
10	learning, structure, study, interactive, easy	Structured and interactive learning	8.28

Table 6. Theme for Age Group Above 50 Years Old

Topic	Top Words	Theme	Prop.
1	structure, clear, understandable, good, information	Clear structure and understandable information	16.33
3	well, varied, structured, course, questions	Well-structured and varied course content	15.99
2	good, presentation, course, videos, different	Good presentations and diverse course materials	13.95
4	videos, good, time, modules, texts	Video-based learning and modular content	13.61
9	easy, good, course, language, elements	Ease of understanding and language clarity	12.59
8	everything, structure, great, compact, units	Compact structure and overall satisfaction	10.20
5	short, content, video, learning, skills	Short video content for skill development	9.86
6	good, well, important, level, structuring	Important structural aspects and quality	8.50
7	examples, ai, helpful, supplement, application	AI examples and helpful supplements	8.50
10	well, videos, different, explanations, speakers	Different speakers and video explanations	7.48

6 Conclusion and Future Work

6.1 Conclusion

This study analyzed post-course survey responses to evaluate learner engagement with interactive content in AI-related MOOCs. The results indicated that interactive videos, particularly those enriched with self-testing features, were highly valued by learners. Another dominant theme that emerged showed that users valued well-structured courses, clear explanations, engaging multimedia elements, and tests significantly contributed to the positive learning experience.

Demographic analysis showed commonalities and differences across gender and age groups. While both male and female learners found interactive videos and self-testing beneficial, males preferred structured content and clarity, whereas females valued varied, engaging video content. Age-based analysis highlighted that younger learners favored short, engaging videos, mid-career learners preferred structured and practical content, and older learners appreciated easy-to-follow, well-paced learning materials, being the most dominant theme among others.

As an exploratory study, this finding emphasizes that even in a large-scale setup, it is important for content creators to consider user perception to differentiate learning approaches based on the target demographics they want to reach to obtain optimal engagement.

6.2 Future Work

Future research should focus on other user groups to see the different themes that emerge, as well as explore other open-ended questions to enrich our understanding of user needs in the context of AI-focused MOOCs. Additionally, research towards usability and accessibility improvement, especially on interactive content that is based on user preference, such as interactive video, can be prioritized and adjusted to the profile of most users enrolled in the course. This will certainly make MOOCs more inclusive and effective for a wider audience.

Acknowledgments. The Germany Federal Ministry of Education and Research (*Bundesministerium fur Bildung und Forschung*) supported the work to produce this research.

References

1. Du, W., Zhu, H., Saeheaw, T.: Application of the LDA model to semantic annotation of web-based English educational resources. J. Web Eng. **20**(4), 1113–1136 (2021)
2. Grünewald, F., Meinel, C., Totschnig, M., Willems, C.: Designing MOOCs for the support of multiple learning styles. In: Hernández-Leo, D., Ley, T., Klamma, R., Harrer, A. (eds.) EC-TEL 2013. LNCS, vol. 8095, pp. 371–382. Springer, Heidelberg (2013). https://doi.org/10.1007/978-3-642-40814-4_29
3. Guajardo Leal, B.E., Valenzuela González, J.R., Scott, J.: Student engagement as predictor of xMOOC completion: an analysis from five courses on energy sustainability. Online Learn. **23**(2) (2019). https://doi.org/10.24059/olj.v23i2.1523
4. Hsu, W.C., Garimella, V.B., Lee, L.: Examining the factors that affect online learning engagement: a micro-qualitative approach. In: Mishra, D., Chuang, Y. (eds.) Learning How to Learn Using Multimedia. LNET, pp. 11–22. Springer, Singapore (2021). https://doi.org/10.1007/978-981-16-1784-3_2

5. Kolas, L., Nordseth, H., Hoem, J.: Interactive modules in a MOOC. In: 2016 15th International Conference on Information Technology Based Higher Education and Training (ITHET), pp. 1–8. IEEE, Istanbul, Turkey (2016). https://doi.org/10.1109/ITHET.2016.7760707
6. Li, K.: MOOC learners' demographics, self-regulated learning strategy, perceived learning and satisfaction: a structural equation modeling approach. Comput. Educ. **132**, 16–30 (2019). https://doi.org/10.1016/j.compedu.2019.01.003
7. Moore, R.L., Wang, C.: Influence of learner motivational dispositions on MOOC completion. J. Comput. High. Educ. **33**(1), 121–134 (2020). https://doi.org/10.1007/s12528-020-09258-8
8. Nabor, Z.B., Onesa, R.O., Pandes, T.L.O., Oñate, J.J.S.: Thematic analysis of students' perception and attitudes towards online class using latent Dirichlet allocation. In: 2024 Artificial Intelligence x Humanities, Education, and Art (AIxHEART), pp. 64–69. IEEE, Laguna Hills, CA, USA (2024). https://doi.org/10.1109/AIxHeart62327.2024.00019
9. Nanda, G., Douglas, K.A., Waller, D.R., Merzdorf, H.E., Goldwasser, D.: Analyzing large collections of open-ended feedback from MOOC learners using LDA topic modeling and qualitative analysis. IEEE Trans. Learn. Technol. **14**(2), 146–160 (2021). https://doi.org/10.1109/TLT.2021.3064798
10. Petan, S., Mocofan, M., Vasiu, R.: Enhancing learning in massive open online courses through interactive video. In: eLSE 2014, pp. 291–297. Bucharest, RO (2014). https://doi.org/10.12753/2066-026X-14-042
11. Röder, M., Both, A., Hinneburg, A.: Exploring the space of topic coherence measures. In: Proceedings of the Eighth ACM International Conference on Web Search and Data Mining, pp. 399–408. ACM, Shanghai, China (2015). https://doi.org/10.1145/2684822.2685324
12. Seckman, C.: Impact of interactive video communication versus text-based feedback on teaching, social, and cognitive presence in online learning communities. Nurse Educ. **43**(1), 18–22 (2018). https://doi.org/10.1097/NNE.0000000000000448
13. Serth, S., Teusner, R., Renz, J., Uflacker, M.: Evaluating digital worksheets with interactive programming exercises for K-12 education. In: 2019 IEEE Frontiers in Education Conference (FIE), pp. 1–9. IEEE, Covington, KY, USA (2019). https://doi.org/10.1109/FIE43999.2019.9028680
14. Sofyan, Z., Meinel, C.: Exploring interactive content in MOOCs for training educators in AI education. In: International Conference on Electrical Engineering and Informatics (2024)
15. Sofyan, Z., Meinel, C.: Should we use it or not? Insights into utilizing interactive content in AI-teaching MOOCs platform. In: 2024 IEEE Digital Education and MOOCS Conference (DEMOcon), pp. 1–6. IEEE, Atlanta, GA, USA (2024). https://doi.org/10.1109/DEMOcon63027.2024.10748215
16. Weinert, T., Benner, D., Dickhaut, E., Janson, A., Schöbel, S., Leimeister, J.M.: Engaging students through interactive learning videos in higher education: developing a creation process and design patterns for interactive learning videos. Commun. Assoc. Inf. Syst. **55**, 475–506 (2024). https://doi.org/10.17705/1CAIS.05519

Leveraging Graph Retrieval-Augmented Generation to Support Learners' Understanding of Knowledge Concepts in MOOCs

Mohamed Abdelmagied(✉), Mohamed Amine Chatti, Shoeb Joarder, Qurat Ul Ain, and Rawaa Alatrash

Social Computing Group, Faculty of Computer Science, University of Duisburg-Essen, Duisburg, Germany
mohamed.abdelmagied@stud.uni-due.de, mohamed.chatti@uni-due.de
https://www.uni-due.de/soco/

Abstract. Massive Open Online Courses (MOOCs) lack direct interaction between learners and instructors, making it challenging for learners to understand new knowledge concepts. Recently, learners have increasingly used Large Language Models (LLMs) to support them in acquiring new knowledge. However, LLMs are prone to hallucinations which limits their reliability. Retrieval-Augmented Generation (RAG) addresses this issue by retrieving relevant documents before generating a response. However, the application of RAG across different MOOCs is limited by unstructured learning material. Furthermore, current RAG systems do not actively guide learners toward their learning needs. To address these challenges, we propose a Graph RAG pipeline that leverages Educational Knowledge Graphs (EduKGs) and Personal Knowledge Graphs (PKGs) to guide learners to understand knowledge concepts in the MOOC platform CourseMapper. Specifically, we implement (1) a PKG-based Question Generation method to recommend personalized questions for learners in context, and (2) an EduKG-based Question Answering method that leverages the relationships between knowledge concepts in the EduKG to answer learner selected questions. To evaluate both methods, we conducted a study with 3 expert instructors on 3 different MOOCs in the MOOC platform CourseMapper. The results of the evaluation show the potential of Graph RAG to empower learners to understand new knowledge concepts in a personalized learning experience.

Keywords: Educational Knowledge Graphs · Personal Knowledge Graphs · Graph Retrieval-Augmented Generation · Large Language Models

1 Introduction

Massive Open Online Course (MOOC) platforms have emerged as a key digital technology driving the change in the educational landscape in the last decade,

E. Hamonic and R. Sharrock (Eds.): EMOOCS 2025, LNCS 15733, pp. 108–118, 2026.
https://doi.org/10.1007/978-3-032-00056-9_10

as they promote self-regulated and lifelong learning [7]. However, MOOC platforms present learners with new challenges due to lack of interaction with their instructors. Therefore, learners might find it difficult to acquire new knowledge that helps them achieve their goals [8]. Recently, Large Language Models (LLMs) have shown remarkable performances in numerous Natural Language Processing (NLP) tasks such as Question Answering [11]. Their ability to answer general knowledge questions led to extensive use by learners to answer their questions in education. However, there is concern about the unsystematic use of these models, as it has several practical issues, such as hallucinations [13]. Hallucinations lead LLMs to generate context-unaware or even false content, which can have negative effects on learners. Therefore, several educational systems have emerged that try to mitigate these issues using methodologies such as Retrieval-Augmented Generation (RAG). RAG aims to reduce hallucinations by retrieving relevant documents from a knowledge base and providing them to the LLM before generating a response [5,9,10].

However, the complex structure and relationships between different concepts in knowledge bases can represent a challenge for RAG systems. Graph RAG [12] can address this challenge by its ability to capture complex relationships between different concepts and establishing links between different documents in Knowledge Graphs (KGs) to retrieve more relevant and personalized information. Graph RAG can be divided into three main steps, which are *graph-based indexing*, *graph-guided retrieval* and *graph-enhanced generation* [12]. *Graph-based indexing* stores KG data in a manner that allows efficient traversal of graph information, which enhances retrieval quality. *Graph-guided retrieval* leverages structural information in a KG to retrieve more accurate results. *Graph-enhanced generation* uses the information provided from the KG to generate a response with better reasoning.

Another limitation of RAG that causes its application to be limited to specific courses is that it requires the creation of knowledge bases from course materials that are specifically curated for retrieval. However, this is not always the case in MOOCs, where instructors often upload unstructured materials such as lecture slides that may lack the necessary structure for effective knowledge retrieval. Moreover, this constraint limits learners from accessing additional resources that could provide deeper insights beyond the content presented in the MOOC. Educational Knowledge Graphs (EduKGs) can be an effective tool to extract structured knowledge concepts from learning material and linking to external learning resources that can be used as a supporting data source in RAG [1].

RAG systems in education have an additional limitation in that they require learners to pro-actively formulate questions according to their learning needs [5,9,10]. However, they do not actively guide learners in identifying the specific knowledge or questions required to achieve their learning goals and do not direct them in learning the essential knowledge concepts necessary for their educational progress. This can cause learners to diverge from their learning goals or ask off-topic questions that would cause the system to hallucinate. Therefore, it is essential for such systems to guide learners by indicating what knowledge concepts they need to learn and providing personalized recommendations of questions that would help them understand the knowledge concepts. Asking the right questions requires an effective modeling of the learners' needs. Recently, Personal Knowledge Graphs (PKGs) have been proposed to model learners in a MOOC context, based on the knowledge concepts that they did not understand [4]. These PKGs can help learners identify knowledge concepts they need to learn to achieve their goals. Moreover, PKGs can be leveraged to generate personalized questions that can help learners understand new knowledge concepts.

In this paper, we leverage EduKGs and PKGs to implement a Graph RAG pipeline that can guide learners in understanding new knowledge concepts in the MOOC platform CourseMapper [3]. Specifically, we propose (1) a PKG-based Question Generation method to recommend personalized questions for each learner according to the knowledge concepts that they do not understand, and (2) an EduKG-based Question Answering method to answer user-selected questions by leveraging the relationships between knowledge concepts in the EduKG. Furthermore, we evaluated the two proposed methods in our Graph RAG pipeline with three expert instructors on three different MOOCs to assess the linguistic and task-oriented qualities of the generated questions and answers. Our study demonstrates the potential of our proposed Graph RAG pipeline to empower learners to control the Question Generation and Answering processes in MOOCs, according to their learning needs and goals. In particular, leveraging PKGs to guide learners to ask questions that help them understand the knowledge concepts was perceived as effective to help learners ask the right questions in context.

2 EduKG and PKG Construction in CourseMapper

In general, a KG is a graph in which the nodes are knowledge entities and the edges are relationships between them. An EduKG can represent any type of entities in educational systems. These entities can be knowledge concepts, instructors, courses, or even universities [2]. In CourseMapper, instructors can upload Learning Materials (LM) to the MOOC platform. For every LM, an EduKG is automatically constructed, where the EduKG includes further entities such as Slides (S), Main Concepts (MC), Related Concepts (RC) and Learners (L), as shown in Fig. 1. Each LM contains a set of S. Then, each S consists of a set of MCs extracted using a keyphrase extraction algorithm. These MCs are tagged with Wikipedia articles that discuss the concept. The EduKG is expanded by extracting other Wikipedia articles referenced in the MC and adding them as RCs. Furthermore, learners can update their knowledge states by identifying MCs as "Did Not Understand" (DNU). By allowing learners to update their states, learners can personalize the EduKG to produce their PKG. Both the EduKG and PKG information are stored in a Neo4j graph database. The EduKG and PKG give learners a structured overview of what concepts should be learned to achieve their learning goals.

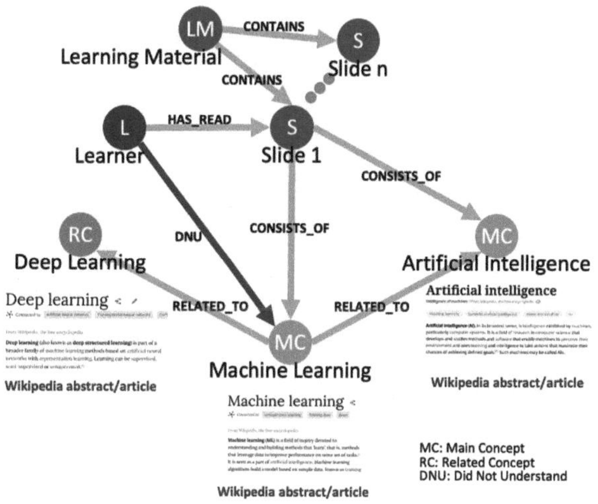

Fig. 1. An overview of an example EduKG in CourseMapper: Each Learning Material (LM) contains Slides (S), Each Slide consists of Main Concepts (MCs) which also correspond to Wikipedia Articles. Each MC is related to Related Concepts (RCs) which are further concepts extracted from the MC article on Wikipedia.

3 Methodology

In this section, we present our approach to achieve personalized Question Generation and Question Answering using Graph RAG to support learners' understanding of new knowledge concepts in CourseMapper. Firstly, we present the abstract pipeline by referring to a user scenario. Then, we dive into the technical aspects of the pipeline by discussing our workflows for implementing PKG-based Question Generation and EduKG-based Question Answering.

3.1 User Scenario

Farah is a university student who is enrolled as a learner in the MOOC 'Learning Analytics' delivered through CourseMapper. The instructor of the MOOC uploaded a new LM titled 'Introduction to Machine Learning'. While navigating the slides in the LM, she recognizes that she is unable to understand 'Slide 4', which mentions the definition of Machine Learning (Fig. 2,**a**). Therefore, she views her PKG for that slide. She notices several MCs for 'Slide 4' (Fig. 2,**b**). She realizes that she still does not fully understand the concept of 'Artificial Intelligence', which is a broader field than Machine Learning. She selects the concept and clicks on 'MARK AS NOT UNDERSTOOD'. Afterward, she sees a dialog open with some suggested questions that can help her understand the concept of 'Artificial Intelligence' as shown in Fig. 2 **c**. Therefore, she selects the third question 'What are some applications of artificial intelligence'. Finally, she receives answers Fig. 2 **d**, which are supported by evidence from a Wikipedia article in the EduKG. Now, Farah understands more about 'Artificial Intelligence' and is motivated to explore more about this concept by selecting other generated questions.

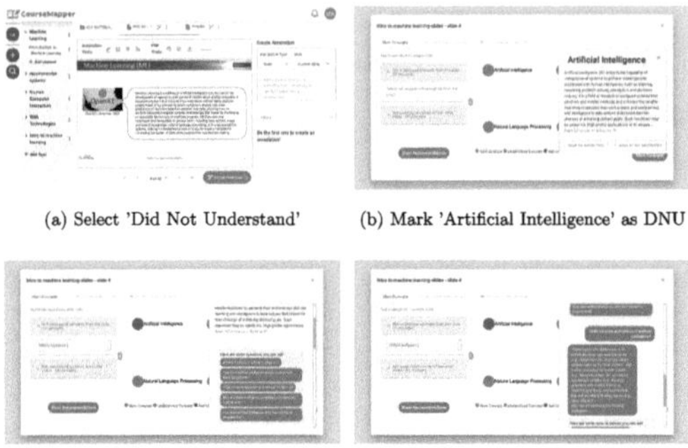

(a) Select 'Did Not Understand' (b) Mark 'Artificial Intelligence' as DNU

(c) Question Generation for DNU Concept (d) Question Answering and Citation

Fig. 2. A user scenario of the PKG-based Question Generation and EduKG-based Question Answering in CourseMapper.

3.2 PKG-Based Question Generation

To generate questions that address individual learner's needs in context, we leverage their PKG to provide the LLM with a model of the learner. To ensure a PKG-based Question Generation that generates questions that are relevant to the current learner's context, we carefully designed a prompt such that the LLM generates questions about the DNU concepts that are only based on the text provided from the current slide or the MCs contained in the slide. When a learner marks a concept as DNU, the system triggers a *graph-guided retrieval* function that retrieves information from the learner's PKG stored in the Neo4j database, including the DNU concept, the slide text (slide_text) that contains the DNU concept, and other MCs that the slide contains (slide_concepts), as shown in Fig. 3 (**A**). This knowledge is provided in a zero-shot Question Generation prompt template for a GPT 3.5-turbo LLM model (Fig. 3, **P1**). To overcome challenges associated with Question Generation using LLMs, the prompt template is designed to follow some rules (qg_rules), such as not to repeat questions that are semantically similar. To ensure that learners interact with the questions based on their importance to the slide, we developed *graph-based re-ranking* of the questions by computing their embeddings using a sentence-transformer model and ranking them based on the similarity of their embeddings to the embedding of the slide text (Fig. 3, **B**).

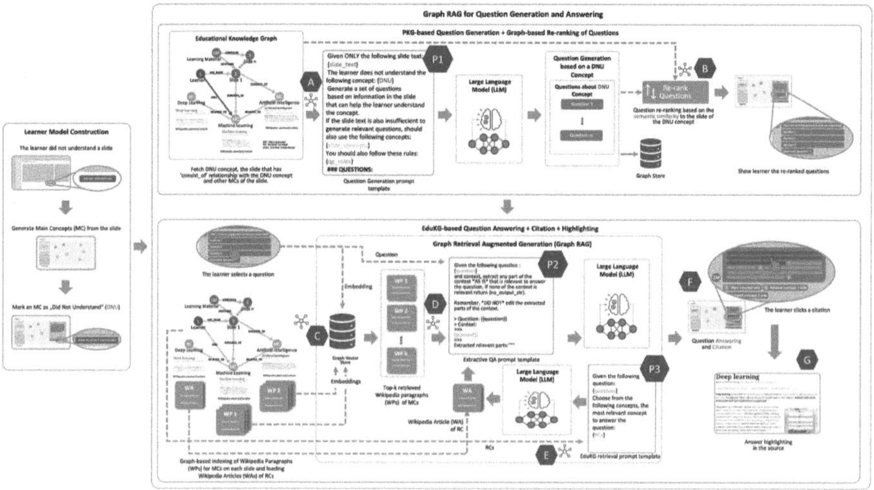

Fig. 3. An overview of the pipeline for implementing PKG-based Question Generation and EduKG-based Question Answering with the steps: (**A**) *graph-guided retrieval* for Question Generation, (**P1**) Question Generation prompt template, (**B**) *graph-based re-ranking*, (**C**) *graph-based indexing*, (**D**) and (**E**) *graph-guided retrieval* for Question Answering, (**P2**) Extractive Question Answering prompt template, (**P3**) EduKG retrieval prompt template, (**F**) Answers with citations, (**G**) Highlighted answers.

3.3 EduKG-Based Question Answering

To answer a learner's selected question, we perform *graph-guided retrieval* using the EduKG. To this end, the Wikipedia articles of the MCs in the current slide are chunked into a set of paragraphs and each Wikipedia Paragraph (WP) is indexed as a node in the graph vector store set up in Neo4j. The *graph-based indexing* process takes place by calculating the vector embedding of each paragraph using a sentence-transformers language model. When the learner selects a question, the question is also transformed to a vector embedding and the most similar WPs to the questions are retrieved based on the cosine similarity, as shown in Fig. 3 (**C**). After retrieving the most relevant Wikipedia contexts to the question (Fig. 3, **D**), they are injected into the Extracive QA prompt template shown in Fig. 3 (**P2**). This prompt should cause the LLM's answer to be strictly based on extracted Wikipedia contexts, thus reducing hallucinations. In case that the LLM does not generate answers (i.e., the MC WPs do not contain an answer to the selected question), we leverage the EduKG to get the RCs to the MCs in the slide. For example, the answer to a question such as 'What is parameter tuning in Machine Learning?' might not be in the WPs of the MC 'Machine Learning', however, it can be found in an RC of 'Machine Learning', such as 'Hyperparameter Optimization' because it is a more specialized topic that addresses this question. To achieve this, we load the full Wikipedia Articles (WA) of the RCs but without embedding. We avoid indexing the WAs of

RCs in the graph vector store as each MC might have hundreds of RCs which would cause the *graph-based indexing* to be slower. To retrieve answers from WAs of RCs, we employ an LLM retriever that is prompted using the EduKG retrieval prompt template (Fig. 3, **P3**) to perform *graph-guided retrieval* by traversing the EduKG and reasoning which RCs might contain an answer to the question (Fig. 3, **E**). The WA of the retrieved RC is then provided back to the Extractive QA prompt template **P2** to extract answers from them. After extracting the answers from the given contexts, the answers are provided to the learners along with citations of the resources (Fig. 3, **F**). By clicking on the answer, the learner is redirected to the source with the answer highlighted as illustrated in Fig. 3 (**G**). This can ensure that learners explore beyond the answers provided to them by the LLM.

4 Evaluation

In this section, we present the results of the human evaluation for the PKG-based Question Generation and EduKG-based Question Answering pipelines, in terms of linguistic and task-oriented dimensions.

4.1 PKG-Based Question Generation Evaluation

We asked 3 instructors who deliver MOOCs through CourseMapper to evaluate the PKG-based Question Generation pipeline according to linguistic and task-oriented criteria. The evaluators are a Professor and two Teaching Assistants at the local university. The evaluation was carried out over three different MOOCs according to the instructor's area of expertise. The topics of the MOOCs were Learning Analytics (LA), Human-Computer Interaction (HCI) and Web Technologies (WT). Each instructor was asked to interact with the pipeline, in which they would select an LM from their MOOC. Then, they were asked to find slides that learners would find challenging. Then, they were asked to select any MC as DNU. For every DNU concept, they were asked to evaluate all recommended questions. The process was repeated for several DNU concepts in every MOOC. For LA and WT, 6 DNU concepts and 30 Question-Answer pairs were evaluated for each. For HCI, 8 DNU concepts and 40 Question-Answer pairs were evaluated.

We follow an evaluation framework similar to Fu et al. [6]. The framework provides seven dimensions for evaluating Question Generation models. The dimensions are divided into linguistic and task-oriented dimensions. Linguistic dimensions are Fluency (Flu.), Clarity (Clar.), and Conciseness (Conc.). The task-oriented dimensions are Relevance (Rel.), Consistency (Cons.), Answerability (Ans.), and Answer Consistency (AnsC.). Relevance is the most prevalent metric in evaluating Question Generation [6]. In the context of our pipeline, Relevance plays an important role since the main purpose of PKG-based Question Generation is to personalize the learning experience for every learner. This can be validated by measuring the relevance of the question to the chosen slide

(Rel_{slide}) and DNU concept ($Rel_{dnuconcept}$). The other task-oriented dimensions are all particularly defined to address challenges in Question Generation for reading comprehension tasks, which is not the focus of this work; therefore, we refrain from evaluating questions according to them. The five dimensions that we used, namely Flu., Clar., Conc., Rel_{slide}, and $Rel_{dnuconcept}$ are evaluated on a scale 1 to 3, the higher being better. Table 1 shows the results of the evaluation of the PKG-based Question Generation for the three different MOOCs. The evaluation shows very promising results with regards to both linguistic aspects and relevance. Our results show that the pipeline does not face linguistic challenges. In terms of relevance, the pipeline scores in general high, which is very promising as it shows that it can effectively support learners to ask the right questions in context, according to their needs. Furthermore, the instructors were very impressed with the level of detail in the questions and the level of relevance provided with regard to every slide and every DNU concept, and they showed an interest in deploying the feature into their MOOCs in the future.

Table 1. Comparison of PKG-based Question Generation on linguistic and relevance evaluation dimensions across different MOOCs

MOOCs	Flu.	Clar.	Conc.	$\mathrm{Rel}_{\mathrm{slide}}$	$\mathrm{Rel}_{\mathrm{dnuconcept}}$	Avg.
Learning Analytics	2.967	2.867	2.967	3.000	3.000	2.961
Human-Computer Interaction	3.000	2.875	3.000	2.725	2.55	2.83
Web Technologies	2.969	2.750	2.943	2.875	2.496	2.806
Weighted Avg.	2.981	2.835	2.973	2.853	2.668	2.862

4.2 EduKG-Based Question Answering Evaluation

We asked the instructors to review the accuracy of the responses they receive on each question they select. While, there are other metrics to evaluate Question Answering, we choose accuracy in order to align with the evaluations of other RAG systems used in education [9,10], which define accuracy as either correct or incorrect. Table 2 presents the results of the perceived accuracy of EduKG-based Question Answering for the three different MOOCs. These results show the challenging aspect of EduKG-based Question Answering. According to the instructors, most answers were considered too abstract or not directly to the point which leads them to being identified as incorrect. By reviewing the data, we find several possible reasons for this. The EduKG is constructed of Wikipedia articles and the LLM is prompted to extract the most relevant information from the retrieved Wikipedia articles as it is with no further reasoning. While this might lead to higher levels of trust, as the retrieved text is exactly as in Wikipedia, it leads the LLM to generate responses that are abstract. Another reason could be the lack of disambiguation capabilities of the retrieval process. For example, in the MOOC HCI, one of the evaluated DNU concepts was ‘Emergency

Exit' in reference to a concept in User Experience (UX). However, the retriever was incapable to distinguish it from the 'Emergency Exit' for buildings. In general, the instructors found the pipeline to be highly interactive. According to their comments, they believe that with further modifications to the EduKG-based Question Answering, the pipeline can be an essential tool for learners and instructors to have a more structured and personalized learning experience in MOOCs.

Table 2. Accuracy of responses of the EduKG-based Question Answering in MOOCs

MOOCs	Accuracy (%)	Number of Correct Answers/Total Number of Answers
Learning Analytics	56.67	17/30
Human-Computer Interaction	45.00	18/40
Web Technologies	33.33	10/30
Weighted Average	45.00	45/100

5 Conclusion and Future Work

In this paper, we presented an innovative approach that leverages Educational Knowledge Graphs (EduKGs) and Personal Knowledge Graphs (PKGs) to implement a Graph RAG pipeline that can guide learners in understanding new knowledge concepts in the MOOC platform CourseMapper. The evaluation results show the potential of in-context Question Generation and Answering using Graph RAG in MOOCs. In particular, PKG-based Question Generation was perceived as effective to guide learners to learn new concepts in context. However, EduKG-based Question Answering still requires further enhancements to improve its accuracy and reliability. In this aspect, the first modification could be constructing the EduKG using further external learning resources that might hold more details to knowledge concepts than Wikipedia articles such as the learning material of other MOOCs, scientific literature or even recommended videos about the concepts. The second modification could be to review further methods that would allow the LLMs to use the provided resources as evidence but still give it room to perform reasoning and provide further explanations. For example, the chain-of-thought method can allow the LLM to leverage an EduKG as a structured data source to perform advanced reasoning that is still relevant to the content of the MOOC and supported by evidence from the EduKG.

Disclosure of Interests. The authors have no competing interests to declare that are relevant to the content of this article.

References

1. Abu-Rasheed, H., et al.: LLM-assisted knowledge graph completion for curriculum and domain modelling in personalized higher education recommendations. arXiv preprint arXiv:2501.12300 (2025)
2. Ain, Q.U., Chatti, M.A., Bakar, K.G.C., Joarder, S., Alatrash, R.: Automatic construction of educational knowledge graphs: a word embedding-based approach. Information **14**(10), 526 (2023)
3. Ain, Q.U., et al.: Learning channels to support interaction and collaboration in coursemapper. In: Proceedings of the 14th International Conference on Education Technology and Computers, pp. 252–260 (2022)
4. Ain, Q.U., Chatti, M.A., Meteng Kamdem, P.A., Alatrash, R., Joarder, S., Siepmann, C.: Learner modeling and recommendation of learning resources using personal knowledge graphs. In: Proceedings of the 14th Learning Analytics and Knowledge Conference, pp. 273–283 (2024)
5. Dan, Y., et al.: EduChat: a large-scale language model-based chatbot system for intelligent education. arXiv preprint arXiv:2308.02773 (2023)
6. Fu, W., Wei, B., Hu, J., Cai, Z., Liu, J.: Qgeval: benchmarking multi-dimensional evaluation for question generation. arXiv preprint arXiv:2406.05707 (2024)
7. Haleem, A., Javaid, M., Qadri, M.A., Suman, R.: Understanding the role of digital technologies in education: A review. Sustain. Oper. Comput. **3**, 275–285 (2022)
8. Henderikx, M., Kreijns, K., Xu, K.M., Kalz, M.: Making barriers to learning in MOOCs visible. a factor analytical approach. Open Praxis **13**(2), 143–159 (2021)
9. Liu, C., Hoang, L., Stolman, A., Wu, B.: HiTA: a RAG-based educational platform that centers educators in the instructional loop. In: Olney, A.M., Chounta, I.A., Liu, Z., Santos, O.C., Bittencourt, I.I. (eds.) AIED 2024. LNCS, vol. 14830, pp. 405–412. Springer, Cham (2024). https://doi.org/10.1007/978-3-031-64299-9_37
10. Liu, R., Zenke, C., Liu, C., Holmes, A., Thornton, P., Malan, D.J.: Teaching CS50 with AI: leveraging generative artificial intelligence in computer science education. In: Proceedings of the 55th ACM Technical Symposium on Computer Science Education, vol. 1, pp. 750–756 (2024)
11. Naveed, H., et al.: A comprehensive overview of large language models. arXiv preprint arXiv:2307.06435 (2023)
12. Peng, B., et al.: Graph retrieval-augmented generation: a survey (2024). https://arxiv.org/abs/2408.08921
13. Wang, S., et al.: Large language models for education: a survey and outlook. arXiv preprint arXiv:2403.18105 (2024)

Top-Down vs. Bottom-Up Approaches for Automatic Educational Knowledge Graph Construction in CourseMapper

Qurat Ul Ain(✉), Mohamed Amine Chatti, Amr Shakhshir, Jean Qussa, Rawaa Alatrash, and Shoeb Joarder

Social Computing Group, Faculty of Computer Science, University of Duisburg-Essen, Duisburg, Germany
qurat.ain@stud.uni-due.de

Abstract. The automatic construction of Educational Knowledge Graphs (EduKGs) is crucial for modeling domain knowledge in digital learning environments, particularly in Massive Open Online Courses (MOOCs). However, identifying the most effective approach for constructing accurate EduKGs remains a challenge. This study compares Top-down and Bottom-up approaches for automatic EduKG construction, evaluating their effectiveness in capturing and structuring knowledge concepts from learning materials in our MOOC platform CourseMapper. Through a user study and expert validation using Simple Random Sampling (SRS), results indicate that the Bottom-up approach outperforms the Top-down approach in accurately identifying and mapping key knowledge concepts. To further enhance EduKG accuracy, we integrate a Human-in-the-Loop approach, allowing course moderators to review and refine the EduKG before publication. This structured comparison provides a scalable framework for improving knowledge representation in MOOCs, ultimately supporting more personalized and adaptive learning experiences.

Keywords: Massive Open Online Courses · Educational Knowledge Graphs · Top-down vs. Bottom-up Approaches · Human-in-the-Loop

1 Introduction

The rapid growth of online education has led to the widespread adoption of Massive Open Online Courses (MOOCs), offering learners open access to high-quality education at scale and fostering lifelong learning opportunities [1,10]. As MOOCs continue to evolve, Artificial Intelligence (AI) is playing a transformative role in enhancing their effectiveness. Among the various AI-driven innovations in education, Knowledge Graphs (KGs) have emerged as a powerful tool for structuring and organizing knowledge, and enabling personalized and interconnected learning experiences. Their application in education, referred

E. Hamonic and R. Sharrock (Eds.): EMOOCS 2025, LNCS 15733, pp. 119–129, 2026.
https://doi.org/10.1007/978-3-032-00056-9_11

to as Educational Knowledge Graphs (EduKGs), is revolutionizing how knowledge is organized, represented, and applied, ultimately enriching the learning experiences [1].

EduKGs are increasingly being integrated into MOOCs for various purposes, e.g. optimizing learning resource utilization [6], predicting learning behavior [19], recommending knowledge concepts and courses [10,12], and many more. Despite their benefits, constructing accurate EduKGs remains a significant challenge. Traditional methods depend on domain experts, making EduKGs construction time-consuming and resource-intensive [2]. Moreover, the increasing volume of educational data has driven the need for automated EduKG construction, yet existing approaches often struggle with accuracy and performance [2,13]. Recent advancements in Large Language Models (LLMs) have driven research into enhancing EduKG generation with LLM-based approaches as well [9]. However, there is currently no standard approach for constructing EduKGs in MOOCs, particularly in terms of evaluating different methodologies such as Top-down and Bottom-up. Identifying the most effective strategy is crucial, as the accuracy of EduKGs directly impacts their usefulness in MOOCs. Moreover, given that MOOCs consist of multiple materials structured into pages, it is essential to explore whether EduKGs should be constructed holistically from entire materials or incrementally page-by-page. To address this gap, in this paper, we experiment with two pipelines of automatic EduKG construction, namely Top-down and Bottom-up approaches in our MOOC platform CourseMapper [3]. Our findings indicate that the Bottom-up approach achieves the highest accuracy, demonstrating its effectiveness in constructing reliable EduKGs for MOOCs. Additionally, acknowledging the importance of human involvement in EduKG construction, we integrate a Human-in-the-Loop approach in our pipeline, enabling course experts to review and refine the automatically generated EduKGs before publication. This balances automation with human expertise, ensuring quality while minimizing manual effort.

2 CourseMapper

Our MOOC platform CourseMapper consists of a range of unique features designed to enhance the online learning experience by addressing various learner needs. These features set our platform apart from existing MOOC platforms by offering innovative functionalities that improve interaction and communication in online learning, foster learner engagement, enhance personalization, and support learning analytics (see Fig. 1).

Learning Channels: Each course in CourseMapper includes multiple learning channels, which serve as collaborative spaces within the MOOC platform. These learning channels (Fig. 1a, L1) are created for each course topic (Fig. 1a, L2), enabling learners to engage with PDF and video learning materials (Fig. 1a , L3), discuss concepts with peers and instructors, and share relevant resources within the designated space. The concept of learning channels provides a more

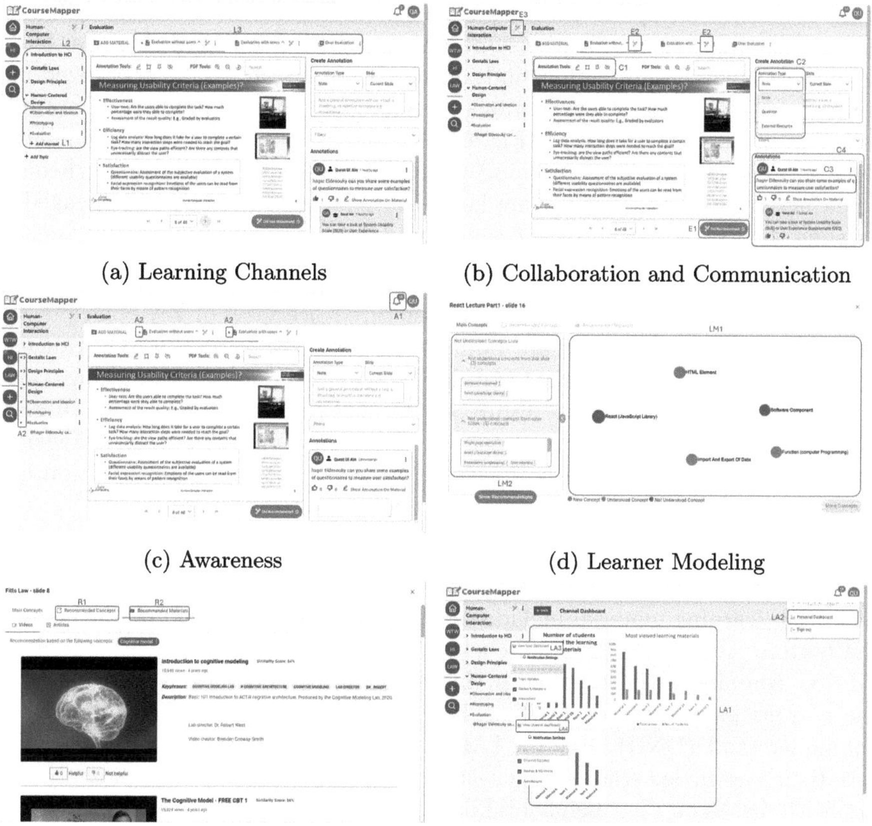

(a) Learning Channels (b) Collaboration and Communication

(c) Awareness (d) Learner Modeling

(e) Recommendation (f) Learning Analytics

Fig. 1. An overview of UI of CourseMapper demonstrating different features.

organized and interactive way to structure courses, fostering deeper engagement and knowledge sharing among learners.

Collaboration and Communication: Learners can collaborate on PDF and video learning materials using three different annotation tools (i.e., highlight, draw, pinpoint) (Fig. 1b, C1) to mark specific parts of a learning material and add a note, question, or external resource link, referred to as annotation types (Fig. 1b, C2). Additionally, the mention feature (using @) (Fig. 1b, C3), allows learners to tag others by name, enabling direct interaction. All annotations appear in the discussion panel (Fig. 1b, C4) alongside the learning material, where learners can view, respond to, or like/dislike them. Using shared annotations, learners can engage in deeper discussions on learning materials, enhance collaboration, and improve communication with both peers and instructors.

Awareness: CourseMapper includes a notification system to enhance awareness of course activities among course participants. Learner's activities (e.g., annotations, replies etc.) are logged as xAPI statements and then used to generate relevant notifications. Based on their personalized settings, learners receive tailored notifications in their newsfeed (Fig. 1c, A1), categorized into course updates, replies and mentions, and annotations. In addition to notifications, an orange dot indicator (Fig. 1c, A2) serves as a visual cue, highlighting the respective course, topic, learning channel, and/or learning material whenever a new activity occurs. This feature helps learners stay informed and engaged by drawing their attention to recent course updates.

Educational Knowledge Graphs: In CourseMapper, Educational Knowledge Graphs (EduKGs) provide learners a structured overview of key concepts and their relationships. EduKGs are built at three levels: Slide-EduKG (concepts within a slide) (Fig. 1b, E1), LM-EduKG (concepts across a learning material) (Fig. 1b, E2), and Course-EduKG (concepts throughout a course) (Fig. 1b, E3). Stored in a Neo4j graph database, nodes represent concepts, categories, slides, and learning materials, connected by edges representing the relationships between them. EduKGs construction details are discussed in Sect. 4.

Learner Modeling: Learner modeling plays a crucial role in enhancing personalization, engagement, and learning effectiveness in MOOCs. In CourseMapper, each PDF learning material includes a "Did Not Understand (DNU)" button at the bottom (Fig. 1b, E1). When clicked, learners are presented with the Slide-EduKG containing the top five main concepts extracted from the content of the current page (Fig. 1d, LM1). They can then mark the concepts they do not understand (DNU) (Fig. 1d, LM2), allowing them to explicitly communicate their knowledge state to the system rather than having the system infer it implicitly based on their behavioral data. These DNU concepts are linked to the learner to formulate their Personal Knowledge Graph (PKG), creating a structured representation of the learner. This PKG-based learner model is further leveraged to provide personalized recommendations.

Recommendation: PKG-based learner models are further used to generate personalized recommendations of related knowledge concepts (Fig. 1e, R1), using Graph Convolutional Networks (GCNs) and pre-trained transformer language model encoders. To increase transparency, explanations of the recommended concepts are provided using the structural and semantic information in the EduKG [5]. Moreover, the learners are provided personalized recommendations of external learning resources (Fig. 1e, R2) including YouTube videos and Wikipedia articles [4], using both PKG-based and content-based recommendation algorithms.

Learning Analytics: In CourseMapper, learners' activity data collected as xAPI statements, is used to analyze user engagement patterns and generate meaningful learning insights through an external open Learning Analytics (LA) platform, OpenLAP [11]. OpenLAP supports self-service LA by empowering end-users to take control of the LA indicator design process, through intuitive user interfaces. Using OpenLAP, various LA indicators are generated from the xAPI data (Fig. 1f, LA1) and visually represented in dashboards at different levels

(Fig. 1f, LA2-3-4) within CourseMapper through iframes. These analytics enable learners and educators to track progress, identify learning patterns, and make informed decisions to improve the learning experience.

3 EduKG Construction Phases

EduKG construction is a multi-phase process involving several key steps described below.

Text Extraction: This phase extracts text from PDF learning materials while preserving document structure. Standard extraction methods often overlook layout variations, so we use a simplified layout-aware approach. It involves: (1) identifying contiguous text blocks, (2) categorizing them using rules, and (3) merging them in sequence. We used PDFMiner [18] that retrieves character positions, grouping them into structured text blocks based on coordinate proximity.

Keyphrase Extraction: After extracting text, we apply keyphrase extraction as a pre-step for entity linking to Wikipedia. This approach improves efficiency by reducing the volume of text sent to the entity-linking service. For keyphrase extraction algorithm, we used $SIFRank_{SqueezeBERT}$ [2] chosen based on its accuracy and performance results [2].

Concept Identification: Extracted keyphrases are mapped to relevant concepts from external knowledge base DBpedia. Following [13], we use DBpedia Spotlight [16] to link keyphrases to DBpedia concepts through spotting, candidate selection, and disambiguation, with the support value set to 5 and the confidence threshold to 0.35 [8]. However, entity-linking tools like DBpedia Spotlight can produce incorrect annotations due to automatic processing without manual verification. To mitigate this, we apply a weighting strategy to assess semantic similarity between identified concepts and learning materials, described later.

Concept Expansion: To improve EduKG coverage, diversity, and knowledge exploration, we expand identified concepts, as keyphrase extraction and concept identification may miss some relevant concepts [15]. This expansion follows two approaches: related concept expansion, which enriches EduKG with semantically related DBpedia concepts (e.g., linking "Natural language processing" to "Natural language understanding" via dbo:wikiPageWikiLink), and category-based expansion, which associates concepts with their DBpedia categories (e.g., linking "Natural language processing" to "Category:Computational linguistics" via dct:subject) using SPARQL queries, providing hierarchical context and facilitate broader concept discovery.

Concept Weighting: While concept expansion enriches the EduKG, it may introduce noise by adding irrelevant concepts [14]. To address this, we apply a concept-weighting strategy that prioritizes contextually and semantically relevant concepts while minimizing noise. Building upon the strategy by Manrique et al. [13], we propose a transformer-based weighting approach using SBERT [17] for embedding generation. Our approach (w_{SBERT}) assigns weights based on cosine similarity between embeddings of learning material content and Wikipedia article text of the concept, retrieved via the Wikipedia API. The same method is used for related concepts, while Wikipedia categories lacking descriptive text are weighted based on similarity between the learning material content embedding and the category name embedding. This ensures only the most contextually relevant concepts, related concepts, and categories are included in the EduKG.

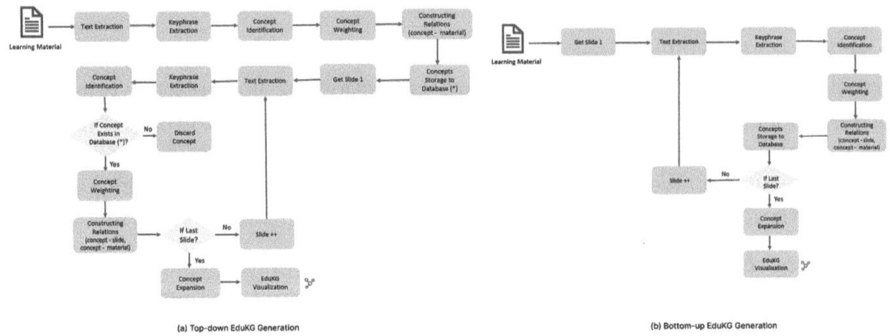

Fig. 2. A comparison of Top-down vs. Bottom-up Pipelines.

4 EduKG Construction Pipelines

We propose and experiment with two pipelines for EduKG construction in MOOCs, namely Top-down and Bottom-up, discussed below (Fig. 2).

4.1 Top-Down EduKG Construction

The Top-down approach (Fig. 2a) starts by extracting text from the entire PDF learning material, which is passed to the keyphrase extraction module. The keyphrase extractor identifies n keyphrases from the learning material, where n=15*the number of slides in the material, as this formula proved to cover all the possible keyphrases based on experiment. These keyphrases are annotated with DBpedia Spotlight to identify Main Concepts (MCs), which are then weighted by computing the cosine similarity between the MC's Wikipedia article embedding and the learning material's text embedding. Relationships between the MCs and the learning material are stored in a Neo4j database. This method generates a single EduKG for the entire learning material (LM-EduKG). To provide more granular views, the approach is extended to generate EduKGs for individual slides (Slide-EduKG). Text is extracted from each slide, keyphrases are identified, and the corresponding MCs are checked against the LM-EduKG. If the concept already exists, it is weighted, and relationships are created; otherwise, it is discarded. After covering all slides, concept expansion is applied on the whole EduKG to include related concepts and categories from Wikipedia.

4.2 Bottom-Up EduKG Construction

The Bottom-up approach (Fig. 2b) constructs the EduKG starting from each slide/PDF page of the learning material, with the text extracted from each slide as the initial reference. From each slide, 15 keyphrases are extracted, as more than 95% of slides contain fewer than 15 keyphrases. These keyphrases are linked to MCs via DBpedia Spotlight, and each concept's weight is calculated based on the cosine similarity between the SBERT embedding of the concept's Wikipedia abstract and the SBERT embedding of the learning material text (w_{LM}). Additionally, a slide similarity score (w_{Slide}) is calculated based on the cosine similarity between the SBERT embedding of the concept's Wikipedia abstract and the SBERT embedding of the slide text. The final importance of the concept per slide is determined by the sum of the slide similarity score (w_{Slide}) and the concept weight (w_{LM}). Relations are established between the MCs and both the slide and the learning material. After annotating each slide, the data is stored in the Neo4j database for immediate access, allowing users to explore the Slide-EduKG even before the entire LM-EduKG is completed. This ensures that users can access partial results while the construction continues. Once all slides are annotated, concept expansion is performed. Lastly, the EduKGs for each slide are aggregated into a comprehensive LM-EduKG. This approach ensures that concepts related to a slide are accurately represented, and any concepts at the slide level are carried over to the learning material level.

5 Evaluation

For the evaluation, using our MOOC platform CourseMapper, we conducted an online user study followed by a human annotation study to assess which pipeline produces the most accurate and performant EduKG.

5.1 Evaluation of EduKG Performance

To evaluate the performance of Top-down vs. Bottom-up pipelines, a user study was conducted with 19 participants (11M, 8F) from three different courses taught in our chair. Invitations were sent to 47 individuals, with 19 responding to evaluate 34 learning materials in total. EduKGs were constructed for different learning materials using both the Top-down and Bottom-up pipelines in CourseMapper. The evaluation involved assessing Precision(P), Mean Reciprocal Rank (MRR), and Mean Average Precision (MAP) for top-k results based on participants' feedback. Participants were introduced to the platform, the research goals, and the evaluation task. They randomly selected a learning material that they were most familiar with, and the corresponding EduKG (consisting of Top-15 MCs) was shown to them. Afterwards, they completed a questionnaire for each Top-down and Bottom-up EduKG. The questionnaire included questions on: 1) Familiarity with the topic (1: Not familiar, 5: Expert), 2) Relevance of concepts to the material (1 to 15 concepts), 3) Expected concepts not included in the list, and 4) Ranking the concepts from most to least relevant. In addition, users provided feedback on whether the EduKG covered important content, helped them form an understanding of the material, and overall satisfaction with the results. The results (Table 1) showed similar performance between both models. However, the bottom-up approach showed slightly better precision at higher k-values and MAP, suggesting that it retrieved more effective information. A T-test revealed no significant differences between the models. In terms of user experience, the bottom-up EduKG was rated more favorably by the participants.

Table 1. Results of the evaluation of Top-down vs. Bottom-up approaches

Pipeline	User study			SRS evaluation	
	P@15	MRR	MAP	Mean Value μ_s	Normal Approximation Value $\mu_s \pm \sigma$
Top-down	0.807	0.941	0.807	0.38	0.38 ± 0.048
Bottom-up	**0.812**	0.941	**0.812**	**0.40**	$\mathbf{0.4 \pm 0.049}$

5.2 Evaluation of EduKG Accuracy

To assess the accuracy of EduKGs generated using the Top-down and Bottom-up approaches, we employed the Simple Random Sampling (SRS) method by Gao et al. [7]. This method evaluates the correctness of knowledge graph (KG) triples (subject, predicate, object) through two key tasks: *entity identification* (verifying node meanings using contextual information) and *relationship validation* (ensuring correct links between nodes). In this way, accuracy is calculated as the mean of sample judgments. If the margin of error (MoE) exceeds a predefined threshold, additional samples are evaluated until accuracy stabilizes. There are several matrices involved in the calculation of accuracy. The *mean accuracy* (μ_s) of a sample set with (n_s) samples in SRS is computed as:

$$\mu_s = \frac{1}{n_s} \sum\nolimits_{i=1}^{n_s} f(t_i)$$

where $f(t_i)$ is 1 for accurate samples and 0 otherwise. The *normal approximation* estimates the accuracy range:

$$\mu_s \pm z_{\alpha/2} \sqrt{\frac{\mu_s(1-\mu_s)}{n_s}}$$

where $z_{\alpha/2}$ depends on the confidence interval. The *margin of error (MoE)* quantifies estimation precision and helps to determine the potential amount of error that could occur when using a sample instead of the entire population:

$$MoE = z_{\alpha/2}\sqrt{\frac{\sigma^2}{n_s}}$$

The evaluation took 4 h, with two annotators reviewing different random samples. The samples were of type e.g. (Slide, contains, MC), and (LM, contains, MC). The first annotator evaluated 200 samples per model, while the second evaluated 183 Top-down and 180 Bottom-up samples. Evaluation stopped when all criteria were met. Results (Table 1) showed that the Bottom-up approach more accurately identified key concepts and their associations with the learning materials and the slides. However, a T-test found no statistically significant difference. Overall, across all evaluations, the Bottom-up pipeline emerged as the most effective and accurate method for EduKG construction in MOOCs.

6 EduKG Construction with Human-in-the-Loop

Our evaluation revealed that while the Bottom-up approach produced more accurate EduKGs, the overall accuracy was still relatively low. To address this, we integrate a Human-in-the-Loop approach in our pipeline, allowing course creators to review and refine the EduKG before publication. Once the main concepts in the learning material are extracted, instructors can preview them (Fig. 3, H1), edit or remove irrelevant concepts (Fig. 3, H2), and add missing concepts (Fig. 3, H3) and link them to the relevant slide(s) of the learning material (Fig. 3, H4). After finalizing the edits (Fig. 3, H5), the concept expansion step is applied and the verified EduKG is published and presented to learners. This process guarantees accurate EduKGs while striking a balance between automation and human expertise. Moreover, it ensures that learners receive an accurate and instructor-approved EduKG, minimizing the risk of disseminating incorrect or incomplete information.

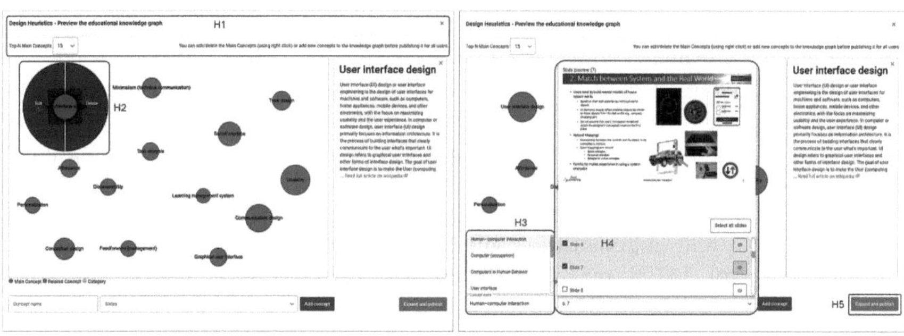

Fig. 3. UI of CourseMapper to Preview and Edit the EduKG.

7 Conclusion

In this paper, we explored Top-down vs. Bottom-up approaches for the automatic construction of Educational Knowledge Graphs (EduKGs) in the MOOC platform CourseMapper. We evaluated both approaches and found the Bottom-up approach to be more accurate and effective for EduKG construction at various levels. To further improve EduKG accuracy, we proposed a human-in-the-loop approach, allowing expert refinement while maintaining efficiency.

Disclosure of Interests. The authors have no competing interests to declare that are relevant to the content of this article.

References

1. Abu-Salih, B., Alotaibi, S.: A systematic literature review of knowledge graph construction and application in education. Heliyon (2024)
2. Ain, Q.U., Chatti, M.A., Bakar, K.G.C., Joarder, S., Alatrash, R.: Automatic construction of educational knowledge graphs: a word embedding-based approach. Information **14**(10) (2023)
3. Ain, Q.U., et al.: Learning channels to support interaction and collaboration in courseMapper. In: Proceedings of the 14th International Conference on Education Technology and Computers, pp. 252–260 (2022)
4. Ain, Q.U., Chatti, M.A., Meteng Kamdem, P.A., Alatrash, R., Joarder, S., Siepmann, C.: Learner modeling and recommendation of learning resources using personal knowledge graphs. In: Proceedings of the 14th Learning Analytics and Knowledge Conference, LAK 2024, pp. 273–283 (2024)
5. Alatrash, R., Chatti, M.A., Ain, Q.U., Fang, Y., Joarder, S., Siepmann, C.: ConceptGCN: knowledge concept recommendation in MOOCs based on knowledge graph convolutional networks and SBERT. Comput. Educ. Artif. Intell. **6**, 100193 (2024)
6. Dang, F., Tang, J., Li, S.: MOOC-KG: a MOOC knowledge graph for cross-platform online learning resources. In: IEEE 9th International Conference on Electronics Information and Emergency Communication (ICEIEC). IEEE (2019)
7. Gao, J., Li, X., Xu, Y.E., Sisman, B., Dong, X.L., Yang, J.: Efficient knowledge graph accuracy evaluation. arXiv preprint arXiv:1907.09657 (2019)
8. Grévisse, C., Manrique, R., Mariño, O., Rothkugel, S.: Knowledge graph-based teacher support for learning material authoring. In: Serrano C., J.E., Martínez-Santos, J.C. (eds.) CCC 2018. CCIS, vol. 885, pp. 177–191. Springer, Cham (2018). https://doi.org/10.1007/978-3-319-98998-3_14
9. Jhajj, G., Zhang, X., Gustafson, J.R., Lin, F., Lin, M.P.C.: Educational knowledge graph creation and augmentation via LLMs. In: Sifaleras, A., Lin, F. (eds.) ITS 2024. LNCS, vol. 14799, pp. 292–304. Springer, Cham (2024). https://doi.org/10.1007/978-3-031-63031-6_25
10. Jiang, L., et al.: Reinforced explainable knowledge concept recommendation in MOOCs. ACM Trans. Intell. Syst. Technol. **14**(3) (2023)
11. Joarder, S., Chatti, M.A., Sun, A.: A no-code environment for implementing human-centered learning analytics indicators. In: Companion Proceedings of the 14th International Learning Analytics and Knowledge Conference (2024)

12. Liu, T., Chen, Y., Chang, L., Zhu, C.: Knowledge graph-assisted collaborative filtering for course recommendation in MOOC. In: International Conference on Electronic Information Engineering and Data Processing (2023)
13. Manrique, R., Grévisse, C., Mariño, O., Rothkugel, S.: Knowledge graph-based core concept identification in learning resources. In: Ichise, R., Lecue, F., Kawamura, T., Zhao, D., Muggleton, S., Kozaki, K. (eds.) JIST 2018. LNCS, vol. 11341, pp. 36–51. Springer, Cham (2018). https://doi.org/10.1007/978-3-030-04284-4_3
14. Manrique, R., Herazo, O., Mariño, O.: Exploring the use of linked open data for user research interest modeling. In: Colombian Conference on Computing (2017)
15. Manrique, R., Marino, O.: Knowledge graph-based weighting strategies for a scholarly paper recommendation scenario. In: KaRS@ RecSys, pp. 5–8 (2018)
16. Mendes, P.N., Jakob, M., García-Silva, A., Bizer, C.: DBpedia spotlight: shedding light on the web of documents. In: Proceedings of the 7th International Conference on Semantic Systems, pp. 1–8 (2011)
17. Reimers, N., Gurevych, I.: Sentence-BERT: sentence embeddings using Siamese BERT-networks. arXiv preprint arXiv:1908.10084 (2019)
18. Shinyama, Y.: diner-python pdf parser. GitHub (2007). https://github.com/pdfminer/pdfminer.six
19. Xia, X., Qi, W.: Learning behaviour prediction and multi-task recommendation based on a knowledge graph in MOOCs. Technol. Pedagogy Educ. (2025)

MOOCS as a Tool for International Student Recruitment: A Cross-Country Analysis

Ekaterina A. Minaeva[1(✉)], Ulyana S. Zakharova[2], and Svetlana V. Zhuchkova[3]

[1] Boston College, 140 Commonwealth Avenue, Chestnut Hill, MA 02467, USA
minaeva@bc.edu
[2] Tomsk State University, Lenin Avenue, 36, Tomsk 634050, Russia
[3] HSE University, Potapovsky Lane, 16b10, Moscow 101000, Russia

Abstract. One of the promises of MOOC platforms that were widely discussed during the first two waves of MOOC popularity in 2010–2016 was its marketing potential for international student recruitment. However, the research on the effects of MOOC on international enrolment is currently scarce. Based on the data from Coursera and edX platforms for MOOC supply information, and Times Higher Education World University Rankings (THE Ranking) for national and international students' statistics, this research aims to explore whether the MOOC supply is positively associated with international students enrolment. Results of regression modelling reveal that, considering the whole sample and all other factors being equal, there is no significant association between the number of MOOCs university supplies and the percentage of international students at this university. However, the second model, which includes interaction term, and thus divides the overall effect of MOOCs by different countries, demonstrates that for some countries such an association does appear. These countries are the UK, the Netherlands, Germany, and Russia. For all four countries the detected effect is positive. Finally, the study presents MOOC description page content analysis to define the elements that might promote the university enrolment and push the MOOC learners through the Marketing Funnel from Awareness and Interest to Desire and Action. This paper might be of interest for the university international affairs and student recruitment deputies, to benefit from MOOC supply the university has, or vice versa for the online learning department managers to contribute to the university key performance indicators improvement designing and redesigning online courses for the international audience.

Keywords: MOOC · international student recruitment · Marketing Funnel theory · AIDA model

1 Introduction

Political turbulence and increased competition for talent push universities to elaborate on new tools, mostly online ones, which would allow them to preserve and increase their enrolment numbers. Massive open online courses (hereafter MOOCs) remain one of the crucial elements of the global education ecosystem, and the research shows that US and

E. Hamonic and R. Sharrock (Eds.): EMOOCS 2025, LNCS 15733, pp. 130–143, 2026.
https://doi.org/10.1007/978-3-032-00056-9_12

the EU university managers associate them mostly with driving student recruitment [1, 2]. Yet, surprisingly, not much empirical research is conducted to examine the use of MOOC as a marketing tool and its impact on student enrolment [3, 4]. The professional community today attempts to reflect on 15 years MOOC history, assess MOOC initiatives and shed light on good practice and challenges. The role and achievements of MOOCs in university internationalisation strategies deserve being on agenda, as well.

The increased competition for talent, financial considerations and other numerous benefits of education export made international education marketing one of the central aspects of international student mobility [5]. Over the past decades, driven by the increased number of actors, international education marketing has adapted many instruments and business models for student recruitment. As the market grows, attracting new students becomes more challenging, which calls for more developed and personalised communication channels between institutions and prospective students.

Reputation of universities plays a significant role in students' decisions regarding their study destination. Global university rankings, while not being equal to university reputation, remain one of the ways for institutions to be visible in the global market. However, one of the critiques of the hierarchical structure of global higher education rankings is that only few institutions are visible in the rankings and those are predominantly Western universities. In these conditions, well-designed MOOCs can be a good instrument for different types of universities to show their expertise and quality of teaching for an international audience.

One of the recent trends in MOOC is the emergence of the national MOOC platforms. For example, Japan has launched its own virtual campus which provides courses in English and Japanese, as well as information about studying in Japan and learning Japanese. In 2020, China created a similar platform in cooperation with Tsinghua University, providing courses from Chinese universities in English. The Russian platform Open Education is another example of the national education platform. A recent large-scale study showed that regional MOOC providers attract larger local populations, with more inclusive demographic profiles, and might be better positioned to fulfil learners' needs [6]. These platforms aim, among other objectives, at increasing the reputation of national education systems and enhancing interest in particular study destinations among international students. However, the international MOOC platforms such as Coursera and EdX remain the largest in terms of student numbers and courses supply. Therefore they are able to reach a wider audience of potential international students.

Furthermore, the evolution of the MOOC phenomenon is under the close attention of not only educators and researchers, but also representatives of mass media, including recognised newspapers and social network sites. In that regard, MOOCs platforms can serve as channels for promotion of educational programmes and as an instrument for student outreach and recruitment. Lastly, utilising MOOCs for the mentioned above purposes goes along with the strategic university plans for increasing international visibility. Though information on MOOCs impact on university visibility is rare, some leading universities publish the survey results showing that almost half of their MOOC learners have heard about their institution for the first time [7]. Still, having people as MOOC learners does not guarantee that they will enter the university.

Past research claims that adequate and complete information provided to students prior to enrolment is an important factor in students' decision-making regarding their study destination [8]. We argue that MOOCs can be a helpful instrument for guiding students through the stages of the decision-making, providing them with a first-hand online learning experience and familiarising with the structure, the content and quality of the selected educational programme.

To sum up, MOOCs could be a promising tool for international student recruitment. However, the evidence for that is scarce. A 2% increase has been revealed by J. Jacqmin for 72 French universities that offer MOOCs. She suggests two factors for that, which are a) institution visibility due to media buzz and Google searches around a MOOC (marginally significant but positive coefficient), and 2) direct information of MOOCs that bridge the gap between a university and potential students [9].

2 Theoretical Background

The choice of study destination is a complex process. There are many social, economic, cultural, political and educational factors that affect student decisions. As there are different groups of students with different motivations to pursue study abroad, the significance of factors among different groups varies. For example, for some students the ranking of the university is the most important motivation while for others it is the tuition fees and possible career prospects. There are specific decision-making factors that depend on a university's internationalization strategy and its openness to international students. Such factors include availability of information on study options in the host institutions [10], quality of education in the institution [11], students' familiarity with the format of studies in a foreign country [12], etc. By highlighting the advantages of the university and providing helpful information on the troubling issues for prospective international students, institutions can increase their attractiveness and engage with prospective applicants in a more efficient way.

In this regard, MOOCs can be a helpful recruitment tool in multiple ways. First, it can highlight the unique courses taught at the university and the high quality of its faculty and curricula. Second, it can provide additional information on the workload and complexity of studies, and give a student an understanding of how well he/she can cope with the studies. Finally, it can give a sense of belonging and familiarity with the faculty and university community. MOOC-learners can be encouraged to enter a university campus program by special offers, such as extra-scores for a successful MOOC completion at the entrance exams or a full substitution of the entrance exams with a MOOC. It is crucial that in order for these opportunities to work, a strategic approach to using MOOC as a marketing channel is needed.

One of the fundamental theories which describes the algorithm of customer engagement (in case of this research it is seen as engagement of potential students) and provides a detailed explanation of the stages of students' decision making process is the Marketing Funnel theory [13]. The theory is based on the 4-stage model of purchase. It states that in order to make a decision for purchase, the customer goes through Awareness, Interest, Desire and Action (AIDA model) [14], where Action is the purchase of a product. Getting to know the university via MOOCs, according to the Marketing Funnel framework, is the Awareness stage; choosing this as a MOOC provider is Interest, then considering this university as a probable place for further study is Desire, and finally applying to the university is Action. While we cannot trace the last step, which is Action, we can identify call-to-action messages in the MOOCs that aim to bring students to the last stage of decision-making.

There are several factors that come into play for the AIDA model for MOOCs to work. The first factor is the level of higher education at which MOOC learners are likely to apply. MOOC learners are hardly school leavers as online learning requires highly developed self-regulated skills that high school graduates have not acquired yet [15]. In this respect, recruiting MOOC learners for Master or PhD programs seems to be a good strategic choice. In addition, the human capital index could benefit from using MOOCs for recruiting professionals for vocational education and training programs [17], especially in those countries with an underdeveloped lifelong learning system.

The second factor is the readiness of institutions to provide English-taught programs. Reports from developed and developing countries show that international learners constitute a large share of MOOC students [7, 17]. While MOOC platforms try to diversify the languages of online courses, the largest number of MOOCs and the most popular MOOCs are offered in English [18, 19]. It indicates that prospective international students are proficient in English and not necessarily in the domestic languages of the universities' home countries [20]. In addition, students' decisions (particularly, when it comes to non-Anglophone students) are affected by concerns related to their success in a new study environment, workload and complexity of the international curriculum, as well as their ability to study in English, so in order for MOOC platforms to be a successful marketing instrument, universities should ensure that their web-sites and their education environment altogether signals the readiness to engage with the international audience.

The third factor is ensuring that MOOCs reflect the best teaching practices of the university. Howarth, D'Alessandro, and Johnson show that learners who have reached their course objectives for MOOCs but have broader educational goals and are satisfied with the pedagogical and delivery approach, would sooner consider the university-MOOC provider for study, then others [3]. Meanwhile, instructional quality of MOOCs is widely criticized, and research based on expert evaluations proves that is weak indeed [21]. In this respect MOOCs might provide a wrong impression of the level of instruction in the university and lead to the opposite result. Thus, it is essential that MOOCs reflect the high quality of education at the institution.

These considerations can help universities to tailor a competitive strategy for using MOOCs as an appropriate marketing instrument for attracting international students. However, available research does not allow answering the question whether MOOCs indeed are used by institutions for this purpose and whether availability of MOOCs from a specific university affects the number of international students at all.

Further research with profound analysis should shed light on whether there is such an impact, which countries and universities succeeded in unleashing MOOC potential in student recruitment, and what they do to bring people from MOOC learners into campus students. Current research is aimed at assessing MOOCs as a tool for international student recruitment for Times Higher Education Ranking universities having MOOCs on the most popular platforms (Coursera and EdX). It addresses the following research questions:

RQ 1: Is MOOC supply on an international platform associated with international students' enrolment for campus programs offered by the same university?
RQ 2: Is MOOC supply positively associated with international students' enrolment in countries with strong internationalisation strategies?
RQ3: What information about the course and university provided at the MOOC platforms can contribute to the marketing funnel for international student recruitment?

3 Methodology

3.1 Data Collection

To answer the research questions, we used data from three sources: Coursera, edX, and Times Higher Education World University Rankings (THE Ranking). The data was collected by the authors via a web scraping procedure (i.e., an automatic generation and retrieval of the student/enrolment data) during the period between September and October 2021.

The first two sources, Coursera and edX, were used to retrieve data about universities' MOOCs supply. These two platforms were chosen as they are international platforms with the highest number of users and courses in the world. Thus, Coursera has 97 million learners and 6000 courses while edX has 42 million learners and more than 3500 courses.

The latter data source, the THE Ranking, contains information about a key variable for our research – the percentage of international students at university – as well as a number of indicators measuring academic and scientific performance, which were used as control variables indicating universities' reputation. We chose this ranking among others since it provides non-processed data on the percentage of international students, and this data covers a period for several years making it possible to conduct panel data analysis. In this regard, we chose the period of 2016–2021, which is the period when no significant changes in the ranking methodology have been introduced. In order to have a strongly balanced panel sample, we kept in the analysis only those universities that appear in the ranking each year throughout the mentioned period. Overall, the final sample consisted of 896 universities from 77 countries, which resulted in 4676 observations for the subsequent analysis considering the longitudinal nature of the data.

3.2 Data Analysis

To answer the research questions, we employed linear regression analysis (regression modelling). The percentage of international students was considered a dependent variable; the number of MOOCs was used as an independent variable of interest. A set of control variables included different components of the THE ranking (more information on this is presented below), a year, and a country. The xt Stata package, devoted to longitudinal and panel data analysis, was applied to build the models.

Results of the preliminary test showed appropriateness of random and fixed-effects regression models over a pooled OLS regression model (statistics). Comparing random and fixed-effects models, we selected the random-effects model as a final one as this type of model allows us to include categorical variables into analysis (country in our case). The final models are presented in two specifications corresponding to two research questions: a main effects model for RQ1 and a model with interaction effect of number of MOOCs and country for RQ2. Both models were built with cluster-robust standard errors with university as a clustering variable.

In the THE Ranking, final universities' ranks are produced on the basis of five initial factors presented as standardized scores: Teaching, Research, Citations, International outlook, and Industry income. In regard to these factors, there are two details of data pre-processing conducted in our research that should be mentioned. First, these five factors are strongly correlated to each other with some correlation coefficients reaching 0.8 (Research and Teaching) and therefore cannot not be directly included into regression models. For that reason, these factors were transformed into three components that account for 91.5% of the initial variance using principal component analysis (PCA). Using varimax rotation, these components were extracted as uncorrelated ones in order to avoid strong multicollinearity in regression models. Based on the factor loadings, the extracted components could be referred to as academic reputation, international outlook, and industry income. Second, the initial five factors are based on more detailed indicators, and a share of international students is both a part of the international outlook factor (one of the independent variables) and a dependent variable at the same time. The described problem, known as endogeneity, was solved by using one-year lagged values of all the predictors in a regression model.

Since our sample consisted of 77 different countries, some of them were grouped before using in regression models. Thus, we selected several study destinations–the largest study destinations for international students: the USA, Australia, Canada, the UK, Germany, France, the Netherlands, Russia, and China while other countries were coded as 'Other'. The choice of countries was conditioned by their leading position in terms of international student enrolment and active engagement in international student recruitment and marketing (see Table 1). In addition, the selection aims to contain both Anglophone and non-Anglophone countries in order to provide possible insights on how MOOCs play out as an instrument for student recruitment.

Detailed description of the variables used in the analysis is given in Table 2.

Table 1. International student enrolment and active engagement in international student recruitment and marketing by country.

Country	Number of International Students	Share of International Students	National strategy for international student recruitment (as of 2017)
USA	1095299	6%	No
UK	601205	25%	Yes
Canada	256455	12%	Yes
Australia	429382	29%	Yes
Netherlands	94236	12%	Yes
Germany	319902	11%	Yes
France	370052	14%	No
China	492185	1,5%	No
Russia	295263	7%	Yes

To address RQ3 a content analysis has been performed. We derived a list of universities and their MOOCs for those countries which relieved a positive association at the previous stage. Webpages presenting information about these universities and each their course pages have been manually analyzed. The search was aimed at words representing the university as international and prestigious, and inviting the MOOC learners to continue their relations with the university, enrolling for other, on-campus programs.

Table 2. Description of variables used in the analysis.

Role	Variable	Description
Dependent variable	Percentage of international students	Discrete numeric variable. A percentage of international students at university, provided by the THE Ranking
Independent variable of interest	Number of MOOCs	Discrete numeric variable. Number of courses posted by university on Coursera and edX platforms. In cases where a course belongs to several universities such a course was assigned to each of these universities

(*continued*)

Table 2. (*continued*)

Role	Variable	Description
Independent (control) variables	Academic reputation	Continuous numeric variables. The components extracted by means of principal component analysis (PCA) on the basis of the initial raw scores included in the THE Ranking: Teaching, Research, Citations, International outlook, and Industry income. Using varimax rotation, these components were extracted as uncorrelated ones in order to avoid strong multicollinearity in regression models
	International outlook	
	Industry income	
	Year	Discrete numeric variable. The year for which all the previous statistics are considered. The variable is included in the models to take into account the common linear trend of change in percentage of international students
	Country	A set of dummy variables corresponding to the following countries: United States, United Kingdom, Canada, Australia, Netherlands, Germany, France, China, Russian Federation, and all other countries labelled as 'Others'. Explanation of choice of countries is provided in the text. The USA is presented as a reference category

4 Results

4.1 Results of the Regression Modelling

Results of regression modelling (Table 3) reveal that, considering the whole sample and all other factors being equal, there is no significant association between the number of MOOCs university supplies and the percentage of international students at this university. However, the second model, which includes interaction terms and thus divides the overall effect of MOOCs by different countries, demonstrates that for some countries such an association does appear. These countries are the UK, the Netherlands, Germany, and Russia. For all four countries the detected effect is positive: the more MOOCs universities of these countries offer, the higher the percentage of international students in these universities is.

Table 3. Results of regression modelling

Variables	Model 1	Model 2
Year	0,91***	0,90***
N of MOOCs (lagged)	0,00	0,00

(*continued*)

Table 3. (*continued*)

Variables	Model 1	Model 2
Academic reputation (lagged)	1,03***	1,03***
International attractiveness (lagged)	2,44***	2,41***
Reputation at the industry (lagged)	0,90***	0,87***
Country:		
The UK	13,95***	13,86***
Canada	3,87***	3,82***
Australia	10,64***	10,64***
The Netherlands	3,1	2,96
Germany	−1,69	−1,80*
France	3,13	3,16
China	−6,56***	−6,64***
Russia	2,79	1,63
Other	−3,55***	−3,60***
Country*Number of MOOCs		
The UK		**0,05****
Canada		0,01
Australia		0
The Netherlands		**0,02***
Germany		**0,20***
France		−0,16
China		0,02
Russia		**0,17*****
Other		−0,01
Constant	8,68***	8,81***
R2	0.5	0.49

4.2 Results of the Course Descriptions

Course-Level Analysis. At the course level the content analysis was aimed at spotting the course pages that contained an invitation to enrol only at this particular course (short-term strategy, one AIDA), invitation to additionally enrol to other courses offered by this university (to develop the consumer's loyalty, medium-term strategy, two or more AIDA processes, depending on the number of suggested MOOCs), and invitation to enter the on-campus programs (long-term marketing strategy, AIDA inside AIDA, enrolling a MOOC is connected to entering longer, more expensive and formal educational program).

The study showed that there are only 2,96% of course pages with an invitation for other long, on-campus programs of the university with the special offer, and all of them belong to one university, which is the Tomsk State University. The message is the following: "The certificate of completion provides extra-scores when enrolling Master programs provided by the National Research Tomsk State University. Get informed with these programs following the link <website>". 17,59% of pages included some invitation for other online courses of the same university, which is more peculiar to courses within specialisations, but sometimes to courses united by the field, as well. 3,95% course pages had some information about the expertise of the lecturers and reputation of the university but with no call to action, such as to get acquainted with the university or the department website.

As for the topic, we suggested that MOOCs about studying language or culture of the country that these universities represent should be considered as oriented mostly for the international students. There were only 1,58% of such courses.

As soon as only universities from countries with positive association of MOOC numbers and international students share have been analysed at this stage, we suppose that their marketing approaches to international student recruitment are the most active and effective among all the MOOC producers, though this should be checked in a comparative study.

University-Level Analysis. In addition to analysing the descriptions of the courses, we conducted an analysis of the university profile pages at Coursera and EdX for universities from the same four selected countries: Netherlands, Germany, UK and Russia.

The results for Netherlands, Germany and Russia show some consistency: in both countries the descriptions of universities include discourses that point at the international outlook of universities and their openness to international students. These discourses include highlighting the international reputation of universities, number of partially or fully English-taught programs, mentioning the number or share of international students at the university, highlighting different study options for international students (for example, Technical University of Munich features its international campus in Singapore). Some university descriptions also include a note that completing a course gives extra points during the admission to the Master and PhD level programs at the institution.

For the UK, however, the descriptions do not contain these narratives and most of them include only a high international reputation of a university.

4.3 MOOCs for International Students as the Main Audience

In order to have a better understanding of the marketing potential of MOOCs, we also conducted a targeted search of MOOCs that are fully or partially designed specifically for international audiences. Using the codes "International student", "Study abroad", "Language learning" and "Cultural adaptation", we found the following patterns. Only the US universities offer courses for current or prospective international students studying in the US, and there are only two courses offered by the University of Michigan (Preparing for Graduate Study in the U.S.: A course for international students) and University of Pennsylvania (Applying to the US Universities). The number of courses that provide foreign language training is significantly higher (36 courses), with English being the leading language provided mostly by the US institutions, followed by Chinese (provided by Chinese institutions) and Korean (provided by Korean universities). While the target audiences of language learning MOOCs go well beyond potential international students can be qualified as a fairly efficient marketing instrument for international student recruitment. However, the share of courses targeting international students as the main target audience remains highly insignificant and cannot be considered an established practice.

5 Discussion

The study investigated the association between a university MOOC supply and the international students' admission for campus programs offered by the same university, as well as MOOC elements that could contribute to student recruitment. The MOOC potential for internationalisation has been widely discussed [1, 2], though empirical research was scarce [3, 4]. Our research showed that though there is no association in the overall sample, positive results have been received in the subsample of leading internationally attractive universities, which are the Netherlands, the UK, Germany and Russia. These universities demonstrate some efforts to attract learners' attention to them as a good option for further, formal education, such as informing them about the university reputation and faculty expertise. Direct recruitment actions, as Jacqmin J. [9] suggested, such as providing extra-scores for the entrance exams for MOOC completers, are unique.

Coming back to the AIDA theoretical model in relation to international student recruitment, we outlined that getting to know the university via MOOCs, according to the Marketing Funnel framework, is the Awareness stage; choosing this as a MOOC provider is Interest, then considering this university as a probable place for further study is Desire, and applying to the institution is Action.

The summary of the results show that while universities aim to increase Awareness of their study programs, cause Interest among international students (enrol at the MOOC course), and, in some cases, feature information that can bring students to the Desire stage (for example, mentioning the international outlook of the institution, the number of English-taught programs or the preferential conditions of admission for MOOC learners). The latter two, which are the most important stages, are generally almost not tackled. For example, universities could add links to their admissions pages, interviews with international students who currently study in the university, provide helpful guidance on application process and inform about the scholarships, upcoming webinars for prospective students and other information that can lead a MOOC learner to Action, which is applying for the university on campus programs.

Given that addressing potential international students in these ways and bringing their attention to the university as a study destination is not cost-demanding, there is a missed opportunity of using MOOCs more efficiently for international student recruitment. Thus, the discussions on the marketing potential of MOOCs for international students that took place more than a decade ago during the first wave of popularity of online learning platforms are still not reflected and not included as an intended part of a marketing strategy for most universities providing MOOCs. As MOOCs market grows and online platform learning technologies advance, universities may use this gap as a potential advantage in order to advance their competitiveness and diversify their channels of engagement with prospective international students.

It is important to acknowledge that the second part of the research was performed with the first layer of the MOOC content only, which is the university presentation and course description ages. The MOOC course content analysis may be a promising avenue for future research. Elaborating the idea of a lagging effect of MOOC production for university internationalization, as well as the length of this lag should also be of interest for the researchers and supported with reliable methods and sufficient samples. As for methods, learner-level tracking could help to assess the conversion from MOOC participation to formal enrolment, but such a research requires consistent university databases and an access to them offered to the researchers.

The main research contribution of this paper is that our current results provide the first large-scale evidence of the association between MOOC supply and international students' admission. This finding implies several areas for university policy and strategy. First, the close collaboration of universities with MOOC platforms, particularly the joint collaboration between marketing, international and academic departments with MOOC platforms can help optimize the use of MOOCs for international student recruitment. By giving more attention on how the university appears at MOOCs platforms, universities can enhance their visibility with various strategies, such as mentioning the international outlook of the institution, the number of English-taught programs, or offering the preferential conditions of admission for MOOC learners, adding links to their admissions pages, interviews with international students who currently study in the university, provide helpful guidance on application process and inform about the scholarships, upcoming webinars for prospective students and other information that can lead a MOOC learner to Action, which is applying for the university on campus programs. Second, MOOCs can be used as a tool for international student integration and adaptation before their studies at the foreign university begins – such as the courses on academic writing and adaptation can be a good example of this strategy.

Overall, the study shows that while there is an association between MOOC supply and international students' admission, the potential of MOOCs for international student recruitment is still underexplored and can be used as a competitive advantage for universities communication and support strategies for international students.

Acknowledgements. The research has been supported by the Development Program of Tomsk State University (Priority 2030).

Disclosure of Interests. The authors have no competing interests to declare that are relevant to the content of this article.

References

1. Allen, E., Seaman, J.: Grade Change: Tracking Online Education in the United States. Babson Survey Research Group Report (2014). https://www.bayviewanalytics.com/reports/gradechange.pdf

2. Jansen, D., Konings, L.: MOOC strategies of European institutions Status report based on a mapping survey conducted in November 2016 – February 2017. Maastricht: European Association of Distance Teaching Universities (EADTU) (2017). https://eadtu.eu/documents/Publications/
3. Howarth, J., D'Alessandro, S., Johnson, L., White, L.: Massive open online courses and consumer goals. Int. J. Consum. Stud. **46**(3), 994–1015 (2022). https://doi.org/10.1111/ijcs.12742
4. Zakharova, U.S.: Online course production and university internationalization: correlation analysis. In: Calise, M., Delgado Kloos, C., Reich, J., Ruiperez-Valiente, J., Wirsing, M. (eds.) EMOOCs 2019. LNCS, vol. 11475, pp. 102–107. Springer, Cham (2019). https://doi.org/10.1007/978-3-030-19875-6_12
5. Minaeva, E., Wang, L., de Wit, H.: National agencies and private actors in international student recruitment. In: de Wit, H., Minaeva, E., Wang, L. (eds.) International Student Recruitment and Mobility in Non-Anglophone Countries: Theories, Themes, and Patterns. Routledge, New York (2022). https://doi.org/10.4324/9781003217923-2
6. Ruipérez-Valiente, J.A., Staubitz, T., Jenner, M., et al.: Large scale analytics of global and regional MOOC providers: differences in learners' demographics, preferences, and perceptions. Comput. Educ. **180**, 104426 (2022). https://doi.org/10.1016/j.compedu.2021.104426
7. Analytic Review on Electronic and Online Learning at Tomsk State University (2018). (in Russian). https://web.archive.org/web/20200923215357, https://ido.tsu.ru/science/projects/proj2018/report17-18.pdf
8. Rotar, O.: Online student support: a framework for embedding support interventions into the online learning cycle. Res. Practice Technol. Enhanced Learn. **17**(2) (2022). https://doi.org/10.1186/s41039-021-00178-4
9. Jacqmin, J.: Providing MOOCs: a FUN way to enrol students? Inf. Econ. Policy **48**, 32–39 (2019). https://doi.org/10.1016/j.infoecopol.2018.10.002
10. Mazzarol, T., Soutar, G.N.: Push-pull factors influencing international student destination choice. Int. J. Educ. Manag. **16**(2), 82–90 (2002). https://doi.org/10.1108/09513540210418403
11. Goel, L., de Jong, P.J., Schnusenberg, O.: Toward a comprehensive framework of study abroad intentions and behaviors. J. Teach. Int. Bus. **21**(4), 248–265 (2010). https://doi.org/10.1080/08975930.2010.526011
12. Brus, S., Scholz, C.: Promoting mobility: a study on the obstacles to student mobility. ESIB – The National Unions of Students in Europe (2007). https://ehea.info/media.ehea.info/file/ESU/85/9/ESIB_study_mobiity_582859.pdf
13. Strong, E.K.: The Psychology of Selling and Advertising. New York: McGraw-Hill book company, inc. (1925). https://hdl.handle.net/2027/uc1.$b38792
14. Townsend, W.W.: Bond Salesmanship. New York: H. Holt and company (1924). https://hdl.handle.net/2027/uc1.$b37470
15. Krause, S.D.: After the invasion: what's next for MOOCs? In: Invasion of the MOOCs: The Promise and Perils of Massive Open Online Courses, pp. 223–228 (2014)
16. Aboshady, O.A., Radwan, A.E., Eltaweel, A.R., Azzam, A., Aboelnaga, A.A., Hashem, H.A., et al.: Perception and use of massive open online courses among medical students in a developing country: multicenter cross-sectional study. BMJ Open **5**(1) (2015). https://doi.org/10.1136/bmjopen-2014-006804
17. Czerniewicz, L., Deacon, A., Small, J., Walji, S.: Developing world MOOCs: A curriculum view of the MOOC landscape. J. Glob. Literacies Technol. Emerg. Pedagogies **2**(3), 122–139 (2014)
18. Abeer, W., Miri, B.: Students' preferences and views about learning in a MOOC. Procedia Soc. Behav. Sci. **152**, 318–323 (2014). https://doi.org/10.1016/j.sbspro.2014.09.203

19. Boal, H.M.C., Stallivieri, L.: The influence of massive online open courses (MOOCs) on the internationalization process of higher education. In: Optimizing Higher Education for the Professional Student: A Balance of Flexibility, Quality and Cultural Sensitivity, pp. 21–38 (2005)
20. Minaeva, E.: Outbound student mobility in Russia: creating a path for brain circulation through higher education. Univ. Manag. Pract. Anal. **24**(2), 145–156 (2020). https://doi.org/10.15826/umpa.2020.02.020
21. Margaryan, A., Bianco, M., Littlejohn, A.: Instructional quality of massive open online courses (MOOCs). Comput. Educ. **80**, 77–83 (2015). https://doi.org/10.1016/j.compedu.2014.08.005

Experience Track

Eating Your Own Dogfood - A Project-Based Learning Experiment on an Open edX Platform

Thomas Staubitz[1(✉)], Stefania Trabucchi[2], and Eden Huthmacher[3]

[1] German University of Digital Science, 14482 Potsdam, Germany
thomas.staubitz@german-uds.de
[2] Abstract-Technology GmbH, 12101 Berlin, Germany
stefania.trabucchi@abstract-technology.de
[3] Axim Collaborative, Cambridge, MA 02142, USA
ehuthmacher@axim.org
https://german-uds.de , https://abstract-technology.de , https://axim.org

Abstract. The German University of Digital Science is a new online-only university catering to a world-wide audience. *Coding Camp 1: Python* was one of a first set of micro-degree programs offered in October 2024. It covered basic Python, Django, open-source development, version control, and agile project management. After introducing the basics, the program followed a project-based learning (PBL) approach. The learners had to choose between designing and developing an application of their own from scratch or contributing to the Open edX open-source project. Experts from two of Open edX' main stakeholders supported the learners to accommodate for the steeper learning curve. The paper at hand discusses the intentions, goals and views of the learners and the other involved stakeholders.

Keywords: Project-based Learning · Collaborative Learning · Online Learning

1 Introduction

The German University of Digital Science[1] is a new online-only university aiming to offer German university degrees to a world-wide audience. Students do not have to come to Germany to complete their study program, but can learn from wherever they are. This removes barriers to earning a European university degree-no visa, travel expenses, or high living costs. Graduates receive a state-approved German degree, enhancing their European job prospects. Before its official approval in Brandenburg[2] (March 2025), German UDS beta-tested

[1] https://german-uds.de.
[2] The German education system is a federal system. All universities are state-approved by the ministry of education of the federal state in which they are located.

E. Hamonic and R. Sharrock (Eds.): EMOOCS 2025, LNCS 15733, pp. 147–157, 2026.
https://doi.org/10.1007/978-3-032-00056-9_13

some of the study modules as micro-degree programs with real teachers and learners. With the start of the study programs in April 2025, life-long-learners in the micro-degree programs are learning alongside the regular students in the Masters and MBA programs.

The paper at hand examines a project-based learning approach in one of these micro-degree programs[3] offered in October 2024. This program's main focus was on Python/Django programming, but it also covered basics of related topics, such as agile project management, refactoring, clean code, version control, SQL, open-source development, and open-source licenses. The program's duration of 12 weeks, includes two preparation weeks, eight lecture weeks and two reflection weeks. The project work was conducted with two industry partners: Axim Collaborative, an NGO maintaining the Open edX project and Abstract-Technology, one of the main contributors to the project and the German UDS' development service partner, responsible for setup, customisation, and hosting of the system.

2 Related Work

Project-based learning has been widely used in various learning contexts for its educational advantages [8]. Back in the 1930's, Vygotsky delineated the *Zone of Proximal Development* [10]; a model claiming that students are capable of learning substantially better when they are not working isolated but can refer to some sort of guidance. This guidance can be provided either by the teachers themselves, by the learners' peers, or by a scaffold setup by the teachers. Later Mitra showed that the guidance provided by peers actually is very effective in his work on the SOLE project where a group of learners had to share one computer and was forced to learn collaboratively [6]. Condliffe, et al. [1], warn that the implementation of PBL can be challenging and requires a shift from a teacher- to a student-directed perspective and new forms of assessment. They encourage to add collaborative learning as one option to address the challenges [1]. Farrow, et al. [3], delineate *the project* as the vehicle to promote the student-centeredness altering the students' experience of learning [1]. The past two decades have witnessed a shift towards online learning. Examples are informal offers, such as the Khan Academy[4] or MOOCs; or the more formal offers that emerged from those MOOCs, such as Georgia Tech's online Computer Science Master[5], MIT's online Supply Chain Management Micro-masters[6], or the German UDS' fully online Masters' and MBA programs[7]. The Covid pandemic or the war in Ukraine, showed an increasing demand for this shift, although many teachers and organisations did not embrace this opportunity and switched back to their

[3] https://apps.lms.german-uds.academy/learning/course/course-v1:LMS+CODE_python-1+2024_OCT.
[4] https://www.khanacademy.org/.
[5] https://omscs.gatech.edu/.
[6] https://executive-ed.xpro.mit.edu/supply-chain-management.
[7] https://german-uds.de/study.

old ways as soon as possible. Archambault, et al. [4], point out that successful online education needs to focus on building relationships among the learners and incorporating active learning. Staubitz, et al. [9], have examined team-based collaborative learning and PBL in MOOCs and showed a significant improvement of the learning quality for the small subset of learners that embraces this form of learning, while the majority of learners, who enjoy MOOCs as a form of edutainment, are not willing or not able to put in this amount of extra effort. Chujfi, et al. [2], have successfully integrated the team processes into the assessment of team tasks and PBL. Building on these results and experiences, we have integrated a team-based PBL assignment in an online micro-degree program offered on the German UDS platform in October 2024.

3 Methodology

3.1 The Micro-degree Program

The micro-degree program consists of the phases listed in Table 1. Starting in Week4, the learners were guided through the process in weekly update meetings with the teacher—a one hour meeting per team and week. The program was offered in this constellation for the first time but the teacher of this course has a long history in offering MOOCs. Since 2013, he has created more than 30 courses with up to 20.000 participants. The numbers in this micro-degree program were much lower, 16 learners joined the course, 13 more or less actively followed the materials in Week1 to Week4. Seven learners actively participated in the project tasks, five of them successfully completed the course. The regular pricing of the micro-degree program is €900 but all of the enrolled learners

Table 1. Structure of the micro-degree program.

Phase	Description
Preparation	The learners were asked to participate in two of the Prep courses, which are offered on the German UDS open course platform free of charge for everybody. The two Prep courses were on the topics of Internet Basics[12] and Web Basics[13].
Week1	Python basics. Variables, control structures, functions, etc.
Week2	Object Oriented Programming in Python
Week3	Django as a Python web development framework, minimal HTML, SQL, Django template language.
Week4	Version control, intro to agile development frameworks, such as Kanban or Scrum, etc.
The weeks' contents consisted of lecture videos, multiple choice tests and exams, several hands-on coding exercises, and a short warm-up project.	
Week5–Week8	Project work in teams, office hours, presentations.
Reflection	At the end of the micro-degree program the learners had two more weeks to wrap things up and reflect on their learning.

joined the program for free, using an "earlybird" voucher that was offered to attract a larger number of learners and also to give ourselves more freedom to experiment. Due to the free nature of the course and the lack of other implications caused by a drop-out, the setting is, despite the numbers, more comparable to a MOOC than to a regular study program. A commonly used formula to calculate the completion rate for a MOOC [5,7] is

$$\text{completion rate} = \frac{\text{issued certificates}}{\text{enrolled participants - no-shows}}$$

Following this approach, and considering the "enrollees" who didn't start to be "no-shows", the completion rate of this program would be around 38%[14].

3.2 The Project Task

The guiding principles for the project tasks were:

1. it has to be a Python/Django project,
2. it should be meaningful to the learners or the learners environment,
3. and ideally a partner—industry partner or customer—is involved.
4. The contribution to an established open-source project was a plus.

Based on that, the micro-degree program offered two different tasks in the project phase as shown in Table 2.

Table 2. Offered project tasks and teams.

Team	Task
Team Green	Develop a Django application from scratch. The learners were asked to think about an application that would benefit their own life or the needs of an (ideally) real or imaginary customer. Create a project plan and implement an MVP. Features had to be prioritised, the team work had to be organised in an agile way and the code had to be under version control to allow collaboration and sharing.
Team Maintenance	Take over an open maintenance issue in the Open edX project. Open edX is an established open-source project, it serves as the basis for the German UDS' learning platform, it is Python/Django based, improving the platform has a direct impact on the learners' experience, and key players in the community—Axim Collaborative and Abstract-Technology—offered their support.

The focus of the rest of the paper at hand will be on the two learners who chose to work in Team Maintenance. At this point we will leave the three learners who chose to work in Team Green, even if their learning journey and approach really was impressive as well.

[14] For a MOOC this is a quite respectable number.

3.3 The Evaluation

Due to the small number of participants, we focused on a qualitative evaluation approach. The learners discussed their experience with the teacher and they were invited to discuss their experience in dedicated interviews with the industry partners. The survey results in the modules have no statistical significance but they support the more detailed qualitative data. The low sample size limits the generalisability of the results.

3.4 German UDS' perspective

The German UDS is offering practice-oriented study programs that include hands-on experience, ideally in direct cooperation with industry partners. Learners gain practical insights into real-world technologies and connect with potential employers for student jobs or early career opportunities. Involving organisations such as Axim Collaborative and Abstract-Technology in teaching fosters our community integration and strengthens relationships beyond business. We, therefore, consider the project a success from both organisational and instructional perspectives. While learners faced challenges, our grading approach ensured a safe environment without penalising failure-crucial in an unpredictable setting with many variables. To achieve this, the grading for this project consisted of three components:

1. Intermediate presentations during the weekly meetings between team and teacher (office hours). Informal progress updates to keep learners on track and prevent last-minute procrastination.
2. A final presentation allowed learners to share their journey. Each team member contributed, providing the teacher with evidence of their understanding.
3. A lab report documented both team and individual processes, providing a safe space for learners to fail without impacting their grades. The use of AI tools to polish their work was encouraged when documented. The report's format, incorporating personal experiences, resists simplistic AI-generated responses, while AI-assisted optimisation improved readability.

3.5 Learners' Perspective

The program's active learners came from diverse backgrounds (70% male, 30% female), with 50% having a migration background or studying abroad. Aged 30–70, most were employees of large companies, with one retiree. All held graduate degrees, with motivations split between learning Python and a general interest in teamwork[15]. Out of the 16 enrolled learners[16], 13 accessed at least one of the assignments in Week1 to Week4. Nine of them also submitted hands-on programming exercises, seven participated in the warm-up project, six in the

[15] The numbers were collected in the program surveys.

[16] This is the net number of enrolled learners and already excludes all testers, teachers, and other non-learning stakeholders.

final project that is the topic of the paper at hand. Of these six, two learners chose to work on the Open edX maintenance task. The other four, who chose to work on a self-designed application could be considered as a control group. However, the paper's focus, particularly considering the small sample size, is not differentiating between projects that involve industry partners and those who do not.

3.6 Industry Partners' Perspectives

The involved industry partners, Axim Collaborative and Abstract Technologies, have many common interests in joining this project, but there are also some subtle differences based on their respective roles in Open edX.

Axim Collaborative, as the NGO being responsible for the maintenance and sustainable development of the Open edX core platform, is always looking for ways to bring new contributors into the Open edX community and help them to succeed. One of the biggest challenges in open-source projects is attracting and retaining new contributors. Many developers hesitate to contribute due to the complexity of large-scale codebases, unclear entry points, or lack of guidance. Bringing students into the Open edX ecosystem benefits the entire community. More contributors mean more innovation, fresh perspectives, and ultimately a stronger, more sustainable platform. If even a small percentage of participants continue contributing beyond the course, that is a win for the Open edX project.

Abstract-Technology, as a company dedicated to delivering open-source Learning Management Systems (LMS) for educational institutions, carefully selects, designs, and customises innovative learning solutions for their clients. They proudly serve as a verified service partner of the Open edX LMS, which fits with their philosophy that is deeply rooted in the core principles of open-source: transparency, collaboration, and community. Abstract-Technology has actively supported initiatives that foster strong communities and the open exchange of knowledge in software development.

When the German UDS approached them with the idea of integrating real-world open-source contributions into their micro-degree program, it was an easy decision for both to support this initiative. For Axim Collaborative, the opportunity to introduce learners to Open edX's tech stack, while also fostering a deeper understanding of open-source collaboration, aligned perfectly with their goals as stewards of the project. By partnering with German UDS, they saw an opportunity to create a structured, guided introduction to Open edX development. This allowed them to engage with motivated learners, who might not have otherwise considered contributing to an open-source project. Abstract, as the technology provider for the German UDS, saw this initiative as a highly valuable opportunity that they could envision evolving into a long-term collaboration, benefiting the university as well as its students and last not least the company in their effort to hire new talent. The goals of the industry partners aligned well with the course goals and extended them with some aspects. We all hoped that the participants would, successfully onboard onto the Open edX tech stack using Axim's dedicated developer onboarding course on the Open edX training site[17], gain hands-on experience with open-source workflows, including version upgrades, repository tracking, technical feasibility testing, and other collaboration activities and become engaged members of the Open edX community. Both partners' engagement began with in-depths interviews conducted by the course instructor, which were delivered in Week4 of the micro-degree program. The interview with Abstract Technology provided a comprehensive overview of how a software development company operates. It explored methodologies, processes, tools, and the complexities of guiding open-source software along a commercial path. Additionally, it addressed key challenges such as why software projects can fail, offering a candid, insider perspective. The interview with Axim addressed similar topics but focused on the role of the gatekeeper and responsible maintainer of a large open source software project. Beyond knowledge-sharing, Abstract Technology's direct involvement extended to hands-on mentorship with the students facing challenges in setting up Open edX. Through a close, interactive approach, their developers worked side by side with the students, systematically analysing the setup process and troubleshooting technical roadblocks. This support took two distinct forms: first, a structured, step-by-step guidance model, where students were assisted in real-time whenever they encountered compilation errors or needed help interpreting tracking logs to debug and complete the installation. Second, a deeper analysis aimed at identifying not just individual mistakes but also broader open-source challenges that could impact future users. Axim provided the students with access to the Open edX project's communication channels and documentation.

4 Results

As mentioned in Sect. 3.1, the completion rate of the micro-degree program was around 38%. Looking at the participation patterns in graded assignments and exercises, the dropout reason can be clearly related to the project-based approach of the program and aligns with previous results [9]. This, however, also clearly indicates that completion rates cannot be the only metric of success. The two learners who initially participated in the projects and did not successfully complete the course, dropped out due to a lack of time caused by events unrelated to the course context. The learners who selected to work in Team Green, all listed a lack of experience and confidence in their skills as the main reason why they did not want to get involved into a large existing real world project. The learners in Team Maintenance struggled with project onboarding despite prior experience, facing steep entry barriers in setting up a local Open edX development environment. Only with late-stage support from one of Abstract's DevOps engineers were they unblocked, leaving insufficient time for the actual task. Since DevOps skills were not a core learning objective of the course, future iterations should include an early support session to prevent frustration. From this experience, Axim and Abstract identified a few key areas for improvement for their onboarding process:

[17] https://training.openedx.io/.

1. **Improved documentation:** The students' feedback identified gaps in documentation that require improvement. A key priority is the need for clearer, more structured, and version-specific documentation that ensures all installation steps are thoroughly explained. Task-specific guides should be developed to address common use cases, while separate documentation for Linux and macOS would help avoid confusion. Differing setup experiences based on operating systems were recognised. Open-source solutions often align more seamlessly with open-source OS than proprietary ones. Additionally, clearer statements on version requirements and compatibility would streamline the onboarding process for new users.
2. **Simplifying the installation process:** Particularly for Tutor on both macOS and Linux—remains an important goal. Regular maintenance reviews are essential to keep documentation up to date and to prevent outdated information from adding unnecessary complexity. Strengthening community support by offering expert-led sessions, improving response times to user queries, and developing a pre-configured environment for easier installation would further enhance accessibility. Moreover, introducing video tutorials or step-by-step screen recordings, despite the higher maintenance workload, could significantly improve the learning curve for newcomers.
3. **More structured onboarding support:** The setup process for the Open edX platform is complex, and we underestimated the level of assistance students would need. In future iterations, we would provide:
   - A dedicated onboarding session at the start of the project
   - Step-by-step setup guides[18] tailored to first-time contributors.
   - Guidance on how to locate reliable resources for troubleshooting, roadmap insights, bug resolutions, and expert support.
   - Identification of recurring technical issues that may not be isolated cases but rather systemic challenges that should be addressed at the project level for global improvements.
   - Office hours or a dedicated chat channel[19] (Slack or discourse) for troubleshooting
4. **Smaller, well-defined tasks:** Instead of assigning open maintenance issues, which can vary widely in complexity, we plan to curate a list of beginner-friendly tasks. These will focus on incremental improvements that learners can realistically complete within the course timeframe.
5. **Mentorship and peer support:** Encouraging learners to work in small teams and pairing them with experienced Open edX contributors could help ease the onboarding process. Having a mentor or peer to check in with regularly might prevent frustration from becoming a blocker.
6. **Encouraging long-term involvement:** While this was a short-term project, we would love to see some of these learners continue contributing to the Open edX Project. We will explore ways to keep them engaged, such as inviting them to Open edX community meetings, hackathons, or future contribution sprints.

[18] https://docs.openedx.org/en/latest/.
[19] https://openedx.org/community/connect/.

The results of the course end survey show that despite the obstacles, the learners in Team Maintenance were highly satisfied with the program. Both of them completed the survey. The answer options were on a 5-point Likert-scale. The course covered the expected topics (4.6), the materials were engaging (4.6), the content was up-to-date (5.0), I want to pursue further learning or projects in Python (5.0), the team-based project helped me to learn the dynamics of software development (4.5), I feel confident writing Python code(4.5), the course helped me understand the software development process (4.5), the technical aspects of the course worked smoothly (5.0), pace and duration of the contents were appropriate for my learning (4.0), I felt actively engaged and motivated throughout the course (5.0), The examples used in the course were relevant and helpful (5.0), the teacher explained the concepts clearly (5.0). In comparison, only one of four members of Team Green completed the survey with a similar at times a tad lower results. Again, due to the small number of responses, these results cannot be generalised in any way.

5 Conclusion and Future Work

This hands-on collaboration not only empowered the students but also provided invaluable feedback to the broader Open edX community, reinforcing the iterative and community-driven nature of open-source development. We saw strong engagement from those who persisted. The participants demonstrated enthusiasm and dedication, producing detailed lab reports that reflected a deep learning experience. All three partners are looking forward to continuing their partnership and repeating this offer for the learners in the future. The experiment has revealed where Open edX' onboarding material needs to be improved to flatten the steep learning curve. Despite the initial challenges, this collaboration was an invaluable experiment in integrating open-source contribution into formal education. In conclusion it was a win-win situation for all stakeholders: The students who completed the project walked away with real-world coding experience, Axim and the Open edX community gained fresh contributors and valuable feedback on improving its accessibility to newcomers, the German UDS was able to provide a useful task for the student project and the industry support strongly unburdened the workload from the teacher. Both Axim Collaborative and Abstract-Technology gained valuable insights how to improve processes and documentation. With some refinements to the onboarding process and project selection, we are confident that future iterations will be even more impactful. Projects connecting learners/students to real life problems, strongly contribute to a meaningful, competency-based education even if the main focus of the program's learning objectives are slightly missed. The experience they gained in setting up a development version of an open-source project, the insights into the workflows and decision processes of an open-source project, and the direct connection to their own learning environment, a system that they work with everyday for the time of their studies, outweighs the obstacles, pitfalls, and finally the lack of time to work on their actual task. As emphasised by the European EdTech

Alliance, a robust framework where academia, research institutions, and commercial providers collaborate is essential. By working together to test, evaluate, and refine software solutions beyond institutional barriers and competing interests, we can prioritise education as a universally accessible resource. Ultimately, the success of projects like Open edX depends on the shared commitment to making high-quality learning tools available to everyone, everywhere.

References

1. Project-based learning: A literature review. working paper (2017). https://eric.ed.gov/?id=ED578933. Accessed 08 Mar 2024
2. Chujfi, S., Traifeh, H., Staubitz, T., Refaie, R., Meinel, C.: Exploring collaboration and assessment of digital remote teams in online training environments. In: Babo, R., Dey, N., Ashour, A.S. (eds.) Workgroups eAssessment: Planning, Implementing and Analysing Frameworks. ISRL, vol. 199, pp. 27–53. Springer, Singapore (2021). https://doi.org/10.1007/978-981-15-9908-8_2
3. Farrow, J., Kavanagh, S.S., Samudra, P., Pupik Dean, C.: The promise of the project to student-centered learning: Connections between elements, curricular design, and practices of project based learning. Teach. Teach. Educ. **152**, 104776 (2024). https://doi.org/10.1016/j.tate.2024.104776. https://www.sciencedirect.com/science/article/pii/S0742051X24003093
4. Leanna Archambault, H.L., Rice, K.: Pillars of online pedagogy: a framework for teaching in online learning environments. Educ. Psychol. **57**(3), 178–191 (2022). https://doi.org/10.1080/00461520.2022.2051513
5. Meinel, C., Willems, C., Staubitz, T., Sauer, D., Hagedorn, C.: openHPI. No. 148 in 10 Years of MOOCs at the Hasso Plattner Institute (2022). https://doi.org/10.25932/publishup-56020
6. Mitra, S., Crawley, E.: Effectiveness of self-organised learning by children: Gateshead experiments. J. Educ. Hum. Dev. **3**(3), 79–88 (2014)
7. Nair, R.R., Staubitz, T., Meinel, C.: The influence of teacher interactions on sentiment development in MOOC discussion forums. In: 2023 IEEE Learning with MOOCS (LWMOOCS), pp. 1–6 (2023). https://doi.org/10.1109/LWMOOCS58322.2023.10306198
8. Saad, A., Zainudin, S.: A review of project-based learning (PBL) and computational thinking (CT) in teaching and learning. Learn. Motiv. **78**, 101802 (2022). https://doi.org/10.1016/j.lmot.2022.101802
9. Staubitz, T., Meinel, C.: Graded team assignments in MOOCs: effects of team composition and further factors on team dropout rates and performance. In: Proceedings of the Sixth (2019) ACM Conference on Learning @ Scale, L@S 2019, pp. 5:1–5:10. ACM, New York (2019). https://doi.org/10.1145/3330430.3333619. http://doi.acm.org/10.1145/3330430.3333619
10. Vygotsky, L.S.: Mind in Society: The Development of Higher Psychological Processes. Harvard University Press Cambridge (1978). (Original manuscripts [ca. 1930-1934])

Bridging Knowledge Gaps: The Potential of MOOCs for Political Science Education

Valentina Reda(✉) and Annalisa Squillante

University of Naples Federico II, Naples, Italy
{valentina.reda,annalisa.squillante}@unina.it

Abstract. The increasing demand for political knowledge and skills, driven by upskilling and reskilling, makes Massive Open Online Courses (MOOCs) a strategic tool for improving the global relevance of political science education. This paper analyzes the IPSAMOOC project, which offers an introductory cluster of seven political science courses, delivered on Coursera and edX. Using survey responses, the study aims at examining profiles of engaged learners, their experience with the courses, their motivation for participation, and their overall perception of the potential impact of political science education through MOOCs. The results confirm a growing international interest in the field and a high level of awareness among the involved learners. Indeed, MOOCs are identified as an effective tool to address widespread training demands, supporting academic and professional growth, and as a tool for expanding access to Political science education, especially in underserved regions such as the Global South, and supporting global SDGs. In this regard, MOOCs appear to be a valuable hub for political science university initiatives to achieve learning and civic goals and widen the disciplinary dissemination impact.

Keywords: MOOCs · Political science education · Professional & civic development · Global south

1 Scaling Political Science Education with MOOCs

In the fifteen years since the first MOOCs were offered, the landscape of digital learning has undergone profound changes from digitalization to AI [1], marked by the escalating processes of "datafication" and "marketisation" within higher education [2, 3], which posed major challenges to the university-led model of massiveness and openness of MOOCs. Nevertheless, the resilience of the format and the strategic vision of the institutions involved have ensured its continued relevance. Despite being declared too early obsolete [4, 5], MOOCs still occupy a central role in the multifaceted landscape of online education for at least two main reasons. Firstly, the "normalization" of their use. MOOCs, with their structured design, high-quality content, and usability, confirm their use as a versatile format for diverse training strategies [6]. Moreover, the pandemic accelerated their adoption, prompting institutions to implement fully remote or blended learning models, and "even those [institutions] who were reluctant to adapt have had

E. Hamonic and R. Sharrock (Eds.): EMOOCS 2025, LNCS 15733, pp. 158–167, 2026.
https://doi.org/10.1007/978-3-032-00056-9_14

to accept the use of distance-learning tools [...], and the result is a rather multifaceted world of teaching approaches" [7, 8]. Secondly, the key factors behind MOOCs' success have not lost their strength over time [9, 10]. These include the provision of affordable, high-quality content; the removal of geographical barriers; accessible learning opportunities that contribute to the empowerment of citizens; and the development of skills aligned with evolving labor market demands.

Building on these strengths, political science is uniquely positioned to capitalize on the potential of MOOCs, in the light of the discipline's global scope and interdisciplinary approach. As political knowledge becomes increasingly relevant in addressing contemporary challenges related to digitalization [11, 12] and consolidated local development issues [13], MOOCs offer an effective means of enhancing flexible and open access to learning content, and the professional applicability of political science education [14]. However, while research on MOOCs continues to attract the interest of scholars [15], the extant literature and experience still offers limited insights into their effectiveness and impact within this specific domain [16, 17]. Existing research on the teaching of political science has focused predominantly on the differences between online and in-person education, yielding conflicting results [18–22]. Instead, less attention has been paid to exploring the extent to which the massive and asynchronous nature of MOOCs may at least partially escape this dichotomy, as they are widely seen as effective tools for achieving both personal and collective goals. This may be particularly relevant for learners in the field. MOOCs have been recognized as 'the most appropriate element to fulfil the civic mission of disseminating, studying and deepening democratic values' [23], a concept which is particularly relevant to the Global South [24, 25]. Moreover, individual mechanisms and meanings behind learner behavior in MOOCs remain largely unexplored [26]. The IPSAMOOC project fits into this context. Based on a collaboration between the International Political Science Association (IPSA) and Federica WebLearning, the distance learning center of the University of Naples, the IPSAMOOC project promoted the publication of seven introductory courses covering key areas of political science, including comparative politics, international relations and political theory[1]. Strengthening IPSA's strategic goals[2], MOOCs are aligned within a global framework characterized by growing attention to the United Nations' Sustainable Development Goals (SDGs). To this end, the courses have been created with an attention to the accessibility of learning content and to the potential international need for lifelong learning and published on the main international platforms to take advantage of the growing recognition of their certifications. In fact, while MOOCs have been pioneering the process of "microcredentialisation" since their early stages, it is only recently that the interest of private technology firms seems to have led academic institutions to see nano and micro credentials as a way to attract career-focused learners and boost institutions' role in linking academia and industry globally[3].

[1] Courses: 1. Comparative Political Systems; 2. Comparative Research Designs and Methods; 3. Contemporary Issues in World Politics; 4. Democracy and Autocracy; 5. Global Politics; 6. Introducción a la teoría política; 7. Understanding Political Concepts.

[2] IPSA: Strategic plan 2023–2027, https://u.garr.it/a75tB, last accessed 2025/02/20.

[3] Coursera global skills report 2024, https://u.garr.it/ky6l8, last accessed 2025/02/20.

This study seeks to begin to analyze the extent to which political science MOOCs – within the traditional self-paced MOOC model, which remains the most scalable form of online education used by higher education institutions – can contribute to achieving these goals. To this end, in the following sections we will present the results of an exploratory survey, aimed at better understanding the profile and motivation, and gathering feedback from a group of engaged learners. The paragraphs will focus on four main aspects, corresponding to the sections into which the questionnaire was divided: their profile, to assess the characteristics of these learners; their experiences with the courses, to gather feedback on the perceived quality and effectiveness of the content and delivery format; the learners' motivations for participating in the courses and their takeaways; and their overall perceptions of the value of learning the discipline via MOOC.

2 Scaling Political Science Education with MOOCs

The global audience of IPSAMOOCs, from its launch in 2018 to December 2024, includes a widely distributed learner base, with an almost even split between those living in fully or flawed democracies (mostly from the most populous, i.e. the US and India) and non-democratic contexts (as classified by The Economist Intelligence Unit, 2024). Over 40% of the learners, are from the Global South, indicating a strong interest in political science education in this region and a critical need for specialized, high-quality education. Second, the educational background shows that the majority of IPSAMOOC learners have at least a bachelor's degree, even if a quarter have only a secondary education, suggesting that the project is reaching out beyond traditionally academically educated audiences. This heterogeneous learner population forms the sampling frame for the exploratory study on active learners, which was conducted through a survey administered between December 21, 2024 and January 10, 2025 and received 307 responses from engaged learners who voluntarily participated in the survey and explicitly expressed their interest in being part of a learning community for future interactions and participation in initiatives.

The profile of respondents matches the expectations of an active MOOC audience of lifelong learners: spread across demographic sections, with a good level of education, literacy and access to digital environments; familiar with online learning. All age groups are represented, albeit with a decreasing trend with increasing age, with one third of respondents falling in the 20–30 age group and around 20% in the 31–40 age group. Similarly, the gender distribution appears to be in line with the overall demographic composition of the wider MOOC audience, with a slight majority of men represented (at least 55% on average). In terms of previous education, a significant proportion of respondents on both platforms (over 80%) have at least one higher education qualification, with the majority split between those with a Bachelor's degree (36%) and those with a Master's degree (35%).

This is consistent with the demographics of a higher education level audience, but also with expectations of possible public interest in political science and with a rational use of online learning. The profile of lifelong learners is confirmed by their positioning on the student-worker continuum, since while the majority of respondents identify themselves mainly as workers or students (more than 65%, with a similar distribution), a proportion (almost 20%) identify themselves as neither students nor workers, thus suggesting their use of MOOCs as an orientation tool and transition support. The geographical distribution shows a diversified audience, with more than 60 different countries represented, and a broad regional distribution, underlining the capacity of political science courses to attract interest far beyond the Western world. The significant representation of participants from the Global South underlines their potential to function as a global and inclusive platform, promoting broader access to knowledge in the field across different regions and the related responsibility to deepen thematic and implementation needs.

Two elements of regional distribution seem interesting to complete the profile of these users. The first is the dual perception of access. While the vast majority of respondents report having good or excellent skills, extensive access to the internet and the ability to afford it, around 20% of them feel that internet access is still too expensive for everyone to have access. This suggests that factors that are often seen as barriers to MOOC participation – such as computer skills, internet access and affordability of connectivity – are relatively minor concerns for this sample, but are identified by respondents as contextual factors that exacerbate inequalities in access for the population as a whole. The second is the confirmation of a different habit in terms of access to online courses. The analysis of device usage highlights the general consistency with MOOC usage, with a strong preferences for portable (almost half of respondents) and desktop (around a third) computers in all regions, with significant minorities preferring access via mobile phones (18%) and tablets (5%). However, half of mobile phone users are concentrated in South Asia and Sub-Saharan Africa, where tablet use is also widespread.

Finally, their use of MOOCs confirms their engaged nature as learners with significant prior MOOC experience. Most respondents reported having taken several MOOCs, with two-thirds having completed at least two prior to the one for which they received the survey invitation; and the majority took more than one of the seven political science courses offered.

3 Learning Experience: Looking for Quality Contents, Community and AI Support

In terms of satisfaction and perceived usefulness, the courses met users' expectations. The responses show a consistently positive reception, with over 95% of learners rating the course as "excellent" or "good", indicating a general appreciation of the learning experience, both for the course as a whole – interest in the subject and quality of teaching – and for the composition of the materials available. Predictably, the most valued feature is video lectures, with more than 60% of respondents at both Coursera and edX finding them to be the most useful element of the learning experience. This is consistent with the nature of MOOCs, which prioritize accessible and engaging video content to facilitate self-paced learning. However, in descending order, readings were also highly valued, contrary to the main guidelines for MOOC development and the most visible trend on the major platforms. This is an important feature of the design of these courses, for which the presence of a significant set of texts and links to readings, selected from open access repositories and, to a minimal extent, from repositories accessible via most university circuits, was considered a distinctive feature, offering the possibility of more in-depth study and contact with other indispensable methods of access to study and in-depth analysis. Captions, quizzes and assignments were valued more as a complementary tool for learning than as a value in themselves. Finally, external resources were considered "very useful" by around 40% of respondents on both platforms. Despite the overall positive reception of these design elements, further insights were gained through open-ended responses about potential areas for improvement. Learner spontaneous feedback was divided between those advocating for additional video lectures and those favoring more reading materials. Notably, a few respondents from Sub-Saharan Africa and Latin America and the Caribbean emphasized the need for downloadable scripts and course resources for offline use and for translation of both video and text materials. Other important suggestions relate to the possibility of increasing student participation in "unexpected" ways, such as the inclusion of more complex evaluative or formative activities, such as written essays, and the establishment of a knowledge-sharing platform to promote intellectual exchange and community growth among IPSAMOOCs learners.

Calls for greater integration of AI-based student support tools were also noted, particularly from respondents in the MENA region and Latin America and the Caribbean. AI literacy emerges as a key factor in online learning, despite the fact that many AI tools are not yet integrated or have only recently been introduced in MOOC environments. The data shows that a significant portion of respondents relied on AI tools to enhance their learning experience. Given the different integration of AI in the two platforms, with a very focused structuring of Coursera's chatbot, the questions aimed to uncover the main functions for which users had used AI tools, either internal or external to the platform. The most frequently cited use was the generation of real-life examples related to course topics, highlighting the value of AI in making theoretical knowledge more practical and applicable. However, slightly less prominent but equally important functions were reported: Coursera respondents highlighted the use of AI tools to generate summaries, while edX learners reported a greater focus on creating practice questions, reflecting their emphasis on reinforcement and self-assessment. Interestingly, nearly 20% of respondents from Coursera courses had used the platform's recently released internal chatbot (in fact, a third of them were still unaware of it), finding it a useful tool for all available functions: to better understand complex course concepts or topics, get help with quizzes or assignments, find additional resources or references related to the course material, translate content or understand the course in a non-native language, contribute to discussion forums, or generate ideas for participation.

Overall, the feedback confirms the value of traditional course components and the need for further research to improve them and confirms AI as the main challenge for MOOC development. The findings highlight the flexibility of AI-enhanced functions to meet different learning needs and suggest that it is already widely used as a tool to deepen conceptual understanding and enrich guided and autonomous learning, which is likely to help improve retention and learning performance.

4 Learner Motivation: Political Science for Professional Development

Personal and professional development emerge as the main reasons for enrolling in a political science course. Around 20% of respondents indicated that they had enrolled on the course mainly to fulfil academic study objectives, while over 25% indicated professional development as their main objective; within this, around 50% of respondents indicated that the main impact of completing the course was to contribute to their continuing professional development (CPD) hours. In addition, about a quarter of respondents cited personal development as their main objective; with a higher percentage on edX, probably for reasons related to the platforms' access policies. In this case, the main perceived impact is directly related to the improved understanding of political science concepts. Elements such as the low cost of completion and the prestige of both the platform and the IPSA are considered secondary, but still relevant, with 7% and 5% of respondents respectively citing them as their primary motivation.

A significant level of motivation is confirmed by the choice of the enrollment option, where individual subscriptions predominate, indicating a high level of personal engagement. The individual subscription allows for the certificate, which about half of the learners have obtained, even if respondents report obtaining the certificate as a minority objective, suggesting that learners prioritize learning outcomes over credentials or external validation, in line with the profile of motivated, self-directed learners. The level of motivation is reinforced by the number of hours of study reported. Almost half of Coursera users spent 1–2 h per week, and almost a third spent 3–4 h per week, with the remaining 8% spending less than an hour. A similar trend is observed among edX learners, despite a greater share of audit-mode users.

The preference for individual enrollment is aligned with the mode of learning reported by respondents, which has been self-paced for around 90%. Furthermore, the fact – technical but not necessarily marginal – that the course was accessed mainly through the platform's internal search tool, i.e. by keyword or tag, confirms that this personal study program is part of habitual use of MOOCs for these learners.

Another useful pointer to understand learner motivation is the diverse topics of the MOOCs taken before the political science ones, and to the diverse backgrounds of the respondents – with less than half having a social science background, and the other half mostly split between humanities, economics and computer science. This data confirms the interdisciplinary interest in political science and suggests that these courses appeal to individuals who are not primarily trained in social sciences. More specifically, among the non-social sciences respondents, a substantial proportion of respondents come from the arts & humanities (33.7%), while a significant presence also emerges from the STEM area with physical science & engineering and computer science & data science backgrounds (21.7% combined). This heterogeneity suggests that political science knowledge is indeed seen as a convergence point for individuals with diverse interests, underscoring the discipline's ability to embrace interdisciplinarity and to provide analytical tools and useful knowledge relevant to critically address real-world challenges.

Therefore, the learner motivation for professional development underscores the potential of political science education to address diverse professional needs, particularly in non-Western countries, highlighting the discipline's crucial role in meeting this demand.

5 Perceptions of Political Science Education Through MOOCs

The perception of political science education through MOOCs was observed through the lens of the relationship that respondents identified between their course and IPSA's strategic goals and the UN's SDGs.

First, IPSA's strategic goals are directly related to the impact of political science on the development of scholars and citizens worldwide and on international academic cooperation. The first two areas in which respondents perceive that global distribution of online courses has the greatest impact is in "increasing outreach, visibility and reputability of political science research", with more than 20% of respondents identifying this as the primary contribution of the promotion of political science MOOCs, and "promoting the global standing of political science through enhanced outreach and knowledge dissemination", also identified by around 20% of respondents. This reflects the learners' recognition of the value of online learning and the educational initiative as a tool for the dissemination of the discipline, as also confirmed by the goal "foster scientific training and education in political science", which is third in the list of preference. This may also indicate that these objectives are perceived as closely related, if not overlapping. Additionally, the "promotion of academic freedom" is also acknowledged, with around 10% of learners identifying this as the main element of impact, indicating a shared perception of the IPSAMOOC as supporting the intellectual independence and integrity of political scientists. This perception appears particularly relevant for edX respondents from regions such as MENA and South Asia, where about 40% of respondents consider it a crucial strategic goal. The contribution to "equity, diversity, and inclusion" is also noteworthy, with more than 10% of respondents recognizing its role in fostering best practices within the discipline. This is particularly true for Global South learners, where our data reinforces the critical need for empowering underserved regions through human resource development, offering critical conceptual frameworks for political analysis, and cultivating the capacity to design effective policy responses to current and emergent challenges. Therefore, the perception of the IPSAMOOC project is that it not only fosters intellectual growth but also promotes civic engagement and empowers individuals – and practitioners – to participate in shaping their political realities.

Second, learners also identified a direct link to the SDGs. The largest proportion (29%) selected goals related to "peace, justice, and strong institutions", as well as "partnerships for the goals", reflecting a clear alignment with the course focus on political science and governance. Another notable share (26%) highlighted "quality education, decent work", and industry, innovation, and infrastructure, suggesting that participants also see the course as contributing to social and economic development objectives. In this sense, the IPSAMOOCs project serves as a testament to the transformative potential of online education in bridging knowledge gaps and empowering individuals to become active agents of change. In contrast, "no poverty, reduced inequalities, and gender equality" (12%), along with categories linked to environmental sustainability and health (ranging from 8% to 9%), garnered smaller, though still meaningful, recognition. Taken together, these results imply that while learners recognize the IPSAMOOCs broad applicability to multiple sustainable development aims, they perceive its strongest impact in areas most directly related to political science, institutional capacity, and educational advancement.

Expanding on the analysis with a regional perspective, the data show that learners from nearly all areas primarily associate the IPSAMOOC with "peace, justice, and strong institutions and partnerships for the goals". This is particularly evident in regions such as MENA, Sub-Saharan Africa, and Latin America & the Caribbean. A similar pattern emerges for "quality education, decent work, and Industry, innovation, and infrastructure". By contrast, SDGs concerning poverty, inequality, and gender (e.g., "no poverty, reduced inequalities, gender equality") see their highest mentions in MENA and Sub-Saharan Africa. Overall, these results confirm that while the IPSAMOOCs are broadly viewed as advancing multiple SDGs, learners especially recognize their contribution to the political, institutional, and educational dimensions of sustainable development.

6 Final Remarks

The growing multidisciplinarity of the training needs of lifelong learners for personal and professional growth offers an opportunity for subject areas that are under-represented in the MOOC universe. The great success of the introductory courses in political science included in the IPSAMOOC project demonstrates the interest in the subject from a vast international audience. This exploratory analysis confirms the main considerations that guided the design of the courses and the initiative. Firstly, there is widespread interest in developing knowledge and skills in the field of political science, as evidenced by the demand for more training in specific areas, not only to support a course of study, but also for personal growth and, above all, professional and career development. Secondly, MOOCs are recognized as an educational tool that can help learners achieve their learning objectives, due to the quality of the content and, above all, the flexibility of access and use. The limitations related to the lack of interaction are not seen as an obstacle, but as a critical issue to be worked on in order to find alternative solutions, which would for instance benefit from further AI integration, for engaging students through training activities of different formats and possible parallel community building initiatives. Thirdly, there is a general recognition of the value of teaching political science through MOOCs as a tool to achieve both personal and collective goals, with the strengthening of knowledge in the sector and research communities (SDGs and IPSA goals). Finally, the analysis confirms that engaged MOOC users tend to establish reinforcement and loyalty mechanisms on the international platforms. In this sense, the reflection suggests the need for a further commitment by organizations – universities and international academic associations – to increase the amount of content available and to define modes of action that allow a clearer identification of widespread needs and the definition of a response to the demand for interaction with the wider community. These preliminary conclusions are proposed as a starting point for further analysis aimed at defining an operational definition and planning new initiatives.

Acknowledgments. The authors thank IPSA and Federica WebLearning for their commitment to online learning in political science. Special thanks go to Federica Founder and President, Prof. Mauro Calise, and Director, Prof. Fortunato Musella, for their guidance of IPSAMOOC. This analysis was also carried out within the framework of the ALMA project (Advanced Learning Multimedia Alliance for Inclusive Academic Innovation), specifically as part of Work Package 2, Micro-credentials Observatory, which focuses on lifelong learning and innovative forms of certification.

Disclosure of Interests. The authors have affiliations with the organizations cited in the article, which did not interfere with the research methods, findings and presentation in any way.

References

1. Mairéad Pratschke, B.: Generative AI and Education. Digital Pedagogies, Teaching Innovation and Learning Design, 1st edn. Springer, Cham (2024). https://doi.org/10.1007/978-3-031-67991-9
2. Williamson, B., Hogan, A.: Pandemic Privatization in Higher Education: Edtech & University Reform. Education International, Brussels (2021)
3. Van Dijck, J., Poell, T., de Waal, M.: The Platform Society. Public Values in a Connective World. Oxford University Press, Oxford (2018)
4. Lohr, S.: Remember the MOOCs? After Near-Death, They're Booming, The New York Times (2020). https://u.garr.it/7FtUM
5. Warner, J.: MOOCs Are "Dead." What's Next? Uh-oh. One overhyped technology fades as another surges (2017). https://u.garr.it/gzHfJ
6. Brown, M., Costello, E., Donlon, E.: Digital education as social practice: major trends shaping online learning futures. Rivista di Digital Politics **1**(3), 455–484 (2021)
7. Capano, G., Verzichelli, L.: The Fate of Political Scientists in Europe: From Myth to Action. Springer, Berlin (2023). https://doi.org/10.1007/978-3-031-24643-2
8. Norris, T.: Educational futures after COVID-19: Big tech and pandemic profiteering versus education for democracy. Policy Futures Educ. **21**(1), 34–57 (2023)
9. Meinel, C., et al. (eds.): EMOOCs 2023: Post-Covid Prospects for Massive Open Online Courses-Boost or Backlash? Universitätsverlag Potsdam, Potsdam (2023)
10. Calise, M., Kloos, C.D., Reich, J., Ruipérez-Valiente, J.A., Wirsing, M. (eds.): Digital Education: At the MOOC Crossroads: EMOOCs 2019, Naples, Italy, May 20–22, 2019, Proceedings. vol. 11475. Springer, Berlin (2019). https://doi.org/10.1007/978-3-030-19875-6
11. Baldwin, R.: The Globotics Upheaval: Globalisation, Robotics and the Future of Work. Weidenfeld & Nicolson, London (2019)
12. Kneuer, M., Milner, H.V.: The digital revolution and its impact for political science. In: Kneuer, M., Milner, H.V. (eds.) Political Science and Digitalization. Global Perspectives, pp. 7–21. Barbara Budrich, Opladen (2019)
13. Asongu, S.A., Jacinta, N.: The role of lifelong learning in political stability and non-violence: evidence from Africa, AGDI Working Paper, No. WP/14/029, pp. 1–30. African Governance and Development Institute (AGDI), Yaoundé (2014)
14. Musella, F., Reda, V.: MOOCs as a Hub in political science. How online courses can reinforce strategies of academic associations. In: EMOOCs Ceur Proceedings, pp. 169–174 (2019)
15. Irwanto, I., Wahyudiati, D., Saputro, A.D., Rezkia Lukman, I.: Massive open online courses (MOOCs) in higher education: a bibliometric analysis (2012–2022). Int. J. Inf. Educ. Technol. **13**(2), 223–231 (2023)

16. Vieira Costa, A.L., Figueroa, A.M., Steuer, M.: Massive open online learning for democracy in political science: learners' reactions to connectivist elements. Soc. Sci. Humanit. Open **10** (2024). https://doi.org/10.1016/j.ssaho.2024.101113
17. Baudewyns, P., et al.: Teaching political science with a MOOC. Eur. Polit. Sci. **17**(2), 276–295 (2018)
18. Lantis, J.S. (eds.): Active Learning in Political Science for a Post-Pandemic World: From Triage to Transformation. Springer, Cham (2022). https://doi.org/10.1007/978-3-030-94713-2
19. Loepp, E.: Teaching Political Science Online. Guide. W. W. Norton & Company, New York, London (2022)
20. Hamann, K., Pollock, P.H., Smith, G.E., Wilson, B.M.: Distance education and the scholarship of teaching and learning in political science. Politics **37**(2), 229–238 (2017)
21. Bolsen, T., Evans, M., Fleming, A.M.: A comparison of online and face-to-face approaches to teaching introduction to American government. J. Polit. Sci. Educ. **12**(3), 302–317 (2016)
22. Daigle, D.T., Stuvland, A.: Teaching political science research methods across delivery modalities: comparing outcomes between face-to-face and distance-hybrid courses. J. Polit. Sci. Educ. **17**, 380–402 (2021)
23. Yeomans, M., Stewart, B.M., Mavon, K., Kindel, A., Tingley, D., Reich, J.: The civic mission of MOOCs: engagement across political differences in online forums. Int. J. Artif. Intell. Educ. **28**(4), 553–589 (2018)
24. Naidu, S.: The MOOC is dead - long live MOOC 2.0! Distance Educ. **41**(1), 1–5 (2020)
25. Zhang, K., Bonk, C., Reeves, T., Reynolds, T.: MOOCs and Open Education in the Global South: Challenges, Successes, and Opportunities, 1st edn. Routledge, London (2019)
26. Goglio, V.: The Diffusion and Social Implications of MOOCs: A Comparative Study of the USA and Europe. Routledge, London (2022)

Implementing Multilingual MOOCs in European University Alliances with the Help of AI Usage, LTI and Open Licenses: Technical and Organizational Challenges

Martin Ebner(✉), Sandra Schön, Katharina Gasplmayr, and Behnam Taraghi

Graz University of Technology, Münzgrabenstraße 36/I, 8010 Graz, Austria
martin.ebner@tugraz.at

Abstract. Producing and delivering MOOCs within European university alliances presents technical, organizational, and licensing challenges, particularly regarding multilingual accessibility, interoperability, and platform integration. This paper examines these challenges through a case study of the "Open Educational Resources in Higher Education" MOOC, developed with all partner institutions of the Unite! university alliance. The course was produced in all official alliance languages and used AI-driven tools (HeyGen) to generate multilingual instructor avatars for efficient localization. A key aspect of this MOOC was its open licensing approach. By adopting a Creative Commons (CC BY 4.0) license, the course materials were designed for reuse and dissemination across different educational contexts. To ensure broad accessibility, the MOOC was made available on the Austrian national MOOC platform iMooX.at and embedded within Unite! Metacampus, the alliance's federated LMS. For this, Learning Tools Interoperability (LTI) for cross-platform interactions was used. Through LTI, course activities and materials on iMooX.at were linked to Metacampus, allowing users to access materials, track progress, and interact within a unified learning environment. This strategy supported federated access and engagement across institutional systems. This paper outlines the technical and organizational strategies used in developing the MOOC, discussing key challenges and providing recommendations for openly licensed, AI-supported, and LTI-integrated MOOCs within European university alliances. The findings contribute to a deeper understanding of structuring cross-institutional MOOCs that are pedagogically, technologically, and organizationally sustainable while advancing open education principles in higher education.

Keywords: MOOCs · European University Alliances · Multilingual Education · Artificial Intelligence in Education · Learning Tools Interoperability (LTI) · Open Educational Resources (OER) · Open Licensing · Federated Learning Management Systems · Higher Education Digital Transformation · Cross-Institutional Online Learning

E. Hamonic and R. Sharrock (Eds.): EMOOCS 2025, LNCS 15733, pp. 168–178, 2026.
https://doi.org/10.1007/978-3-032-00056-9_15

1 Challenges of MOOCs in European University Alliances

Massive Open Online Courses (MOOCs) have become an essential component of digital education, offering scalable and flexible learning opportunities to a global audience. Within the context of higher education, MOOCs facilitate cross-institutional learning, enhance accessibility, and enable knowledge-sharing beyond traditional classroom settings. However, the implementation of MOOCs in European university alliances presents a distinct set of technical and organizational challenges, including interoperability across platforms, multilingual course delivery, copyright issues and institutional coordination (cf. [4–7, 14]). These challenges impact course development, delivery, and accessibility across multiple institutions. Institutional diversity complicates the coordination of MOOCs, as partner universities operate under different educational policies, infrastructures, and pedagogical approaches. This variation makes it difficult to establish standardized procedures for course design, assessment, and accreditation. Language barriers present another major challenge. A MOOC designed for a European university alliance must be accessible in multiple languages, requiring multilingual content adaptation. Differences in translation quality, terminology, and cultural relevance can affect the learning experience and engagement of participants. Easy access and technical integration are crucial but complex.

First, registration should be easy. Furthermore, universities use different Learning Management Systems (LMS) and digital tools, making it difficult to ensure interoperability between platforms. Without simple registration and seamless integration, students may experience inconsistent access to materials and course activities across institutions. Organizational complexity also plays a role. Coordinating multiple institutions, instructors, and administrative units can create logistical difficulties in course implementation. Differences in academic calendars, credit recognition, and institutional priorities can further complicate collaboration. Copyright and GDPR compliance introduce additional regulatory challenges. The use and redistribution of learning materials depend on national laws and institutional policies, making it unclear who is legally allowed to use and modify content. Additionally, GDPR regulations influence the choice of MOOC platforms, as institutions must ensure compliance with data protection laws. This can restrict the use of external providers and raise concerns about student data privacy and security. Certification and recognition are particularly complex when participants are not enrolled students at the issuing university or when a course is not part of a standard university curriculum. The awarding of ECTS credits requires formal agreements between institutions, which are often lacking in cross-institutional offerings. All these challenges highlight the complexity of developing and delivering MOOCs within European university alliances, requiring careful navigation of institutional, technical, and legal constraints.

European university alliances, such as Unite!, have recognized the potential of MOOCs to foster collaboration among partner institutions and strengthen the digital learning landscape. One notable initiative within this context is the development of the MOOC "Open Educational Resources in Higher Education", which was collaboratively produced by all partner institutions of the Unite! alliance. This course was designed to be fully multilingual, incorporating AI-generated instructor avatars through the tool HeyGen to enable efficient adaptation into all official alliance languages [7]. All course materials were developed under open licenses, "open educational resources" according the UNESCO OER recommendation [15]. Furthermore, the course was made available both publicly on iMooX.at and within the Unite! Metacampus, ensuring accessibility for external learners while also providing enhanced learning opportunities for Unite! members through federated LMS integration [12]. A key aspect of this implementation was the technical integration via Learning Tools Interoperability (LTI), allowing seamless cross-platform interaction and enabling users to track their progress across both platforms [11].

The aim of this paper is now to provide a comprehensive analysis of the technical, organizational, and legal challenges associated with implementing multilingual, openly licensed, AI-supported MOOCs within a federated university network. Specifically, we seek to answer the following research question: What are the key technical and organizational challenges in implementing multilingual MOOCs within a European university alliance, and how can AI and LTI support their successful deployment?

2 Our Case: An Alliance-Wide MOOC and Lecture About OER

The Unite! Seed Fund project "Unite! OER courses" aimed to spread knowledge about how and where to find and publish OER, as well as the principles of open licensing, including CC0, CC BY, and CC BY-SA. For this a massive open online course (MOOC) in all partner languages as well as a university lecture at Graz University of Technology were planned. The project and development of the MOOC started in October 2023 and the MOOC started in May 2024 on the Austrian national MOOC platform iMooX.at [3].

2.1 Providing the MOOC as Open Educational Resources

Since the course focused on Open Educational Resources (OER), publishing the materials under an open license was a given. The MOOC platform iMooX.at requires all hosted courses to have a Creative Commons (CC) license, further reinforcing this decision. Additionally, TU Graz, as the project lead, follows an OER policy that mandates open licensing for educational materials, ensuring that the MOOC seamlessly aligned with an open education framework.

Beyond institutional and platform-specific requirements, the CC BY 4.0 license (see Fig. 1) was essential for this collaborative, cross-university project. It ensures maximum reusability and adaptability, allowing institutions to freely modify and expand materials with proper attribution. Given the multilingual nature of the MOOC, the open license facilitated unrestricted translation and localization, supporting broader accessibility beyond the original consortium. Unlike normal copyright possibilities or more restrictive licenses (e.g., CC BY-NC-SA), CC BY 4.0 removed legal barriers for scalability across institutions, enabling seamless integration into different curricula. Additionally, open licensing fosters long-term collaboration, allowing other universities to contribute to and expand the course. Lastly, it aligns with Open Science and OER policies, such as UNESCO's OER Recommendation (2019), promoting equity and access in higher education. By adopting the CC BY 4.0 license, this MOOC serves as a model for collaborative, scalable, and multilingual OER development within European university alliances. It not only ensures broad accessibility and adaptability but also reinforces the principles of open education and knowledge sharing in higher education.

Fig. 1. The MOOC with the open license CC BY 4.0. Source: Screenshot of https://imoox.at/mooc/local/landingpage/course.php?shortname=OERinHE&lang=en (2025–02-18), CC BY 4.0 iMooX.at

2.2 Multilingual Offer with the Help of AI and Involvement of All Partners

To achieve multilingual videos the AI tool HeyGen was used to create videos of AI-generated instructor avatars. The original course was developed in German and then automatically translated into several official languages of the Unite! Alliance. While the avatars' speech was AI-generated, the other course components such as video illustrations, course texts, quizzes, and descriptions were created manually without significant AI involvement. This MOOC is likely one of the first worldwide to be produced simultaneously in multiple language versions, going beyond conventional subtitling approaches.

The process started with the development of the German-language version as the base course. The content was translated into multiple languages by humans, with partners adapting materials to national contexts. Video scripts were carefully drafted to minimize AI translation issues, AI examples were reviewed, and after positive approval the avatar parts were produced. Nevertheless, all visual design and video editing was handled by professionals, ensuring a high-quality learning experience. Finally, all materials were set up on the MOOC platform for launch (see Fig. 2).

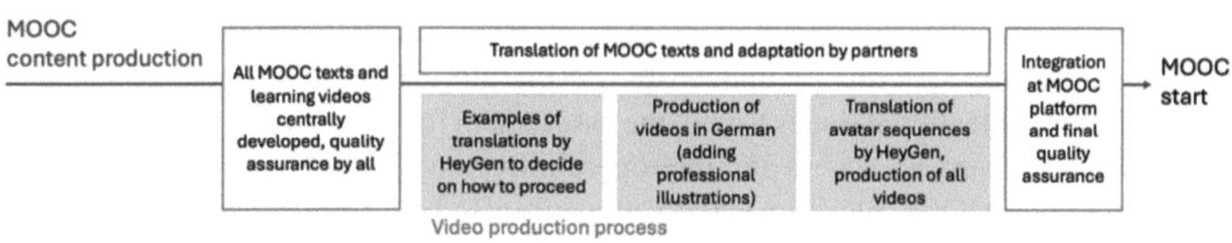

Fig. 2. Timeline of the production of the MOOC "OER in HE" and its videos using HeyGen. Source: Schön et al., 2025 [9]

The use of HeyGen's AI-driven translation helped streamline multilingual video production. However, certain challenges arose during translation, such as misinterpretations of technical terms (e.g., "repository" and "Open Science"), incorrect gender-based language translations, and issues with numbers and dates. To address these concerns, base texts were revised multiple times before final production of AI avatar videos. Due to the quality of the translation and pronunciation, as well as financial and partner preferences, the Finnish, Turkish and Catalan versions used English videos with subtitles; Polish included both English and AI translations (Fig. 3).

Fig. 3. Screenshots of videos in different languages produced for the MOOC "OER in HE"

The OER in HE MOOC was made available in several languages, corresponding to the languages of the Unite! partner institutions: German (TU Graz for Austria, TU Darmstadt for Germany), English (designed as an international version for the European higher education area), Finnish (Aalto University), French (Grenoble INP Graduate School of Engineering and Management, UGA Grenoble), Italian (Politecnico di Torino), Catalan (Universitat Politècnica de Catalunya/BarcelonaTech), Polish (Wroclaw University of Science and Technology), Portuguese (Universidade de Lisboa), and Swedish (KTH Royal Institute of Technology). In addition, the open licensing of the MOOC allowed further translations beyond the Unite! partnership, leading to three additional versions, namely Indonesian (Universitas Negeri Malang), Turkish (Atatürk Üniversitesi) and Arabic (University of Oran 2).

2.3 Integration into Higher Education and Learning Platforms

Alongside the MOOC, an additional official university course (lecture) on OER was developed at TU Graz and offered in English to all Unite! members. This course was made available via the Unite! federated LMS Metacampus, providing learners with additional materials, exercises, and the opportunity to earn the Austrian national OER certificate. The course expanded on the MOOC content by offering more detailed insights into finding, publishing, and applying open licenses. Furthermore, the Metacampus course also regulated all organizational issues to pass the assessment for the final grades successfully.

To facilitate seamless access and interoperability, the MOOC was published on the Austrian national MOOC platform iMooX.at, while also being embedded into the Unite! Metacampus using Learning Tools Interoperability (LTI). This dual-platform strategy allowed the course to be openly accessible while still offering exclusive features for Unite! members. Several LTI test pilots were already conducted within the Unite! framework before we attempted to implement it in a real productive environment and official university course (see [11]).

Learning Tools Interoperability (LTI) is a technical standard that enables seamless integration between different Learning Management Systems (LMS) and digital platforms, facilitating secure connections without extensive custom development. It has been used to link LMS with gaming platforms [16], online laboratories [8], or library systems [2]. However, its application for direct LMS-to-LMS integration within university alliances remains rare [11]. Two components are always involved in an LTI linkage: the LTI Tool Provider, which offers educational content or functionalities, and the LTI Tool Consumer, which integrates and enables access within its environment. Users initiate an LTI launch request from the Consumer LMS to access specific courses or modules in the Provider LMS. Administrators can configure synchronization of course participants and grade transfer, as well as three possible user-linking options: (1) linking an existing account in the Provider LMS, (2) automatically creating a new LTI account in the Provider LMS, or (3) allowing users to choose between these options. This flexible integration ensures seamless cross-platform access, enhancing interoperability between multiple LMS platforms in educational networks. The set-up used in our case is illustrated in Fig. 4.

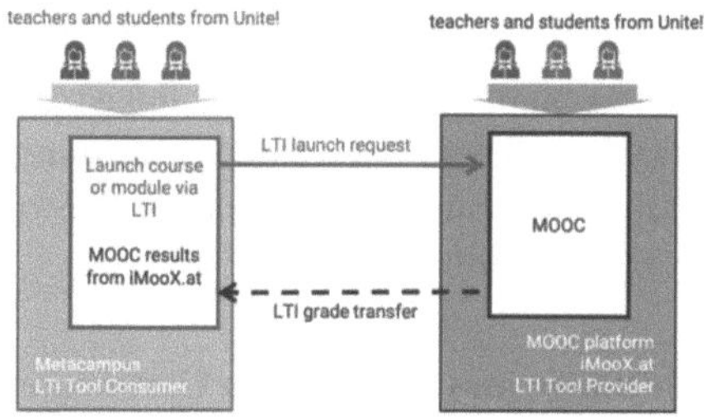

Fig. 4. LMS connection with LTI from users' perspective. Source: Schön et al., 2024 [11], part of Fig. 6 (right)

The Austrian MOOC platform iMooX.at was connected to a dedicated Metacampus course via LTI [11]. Participation in the MOOC "OER in Higher Education" was mandatory for the Metacampus course to ensure direct integration of content. To assess the feasibility of grade transfer between the systems—both for individual activities and the entire course—support staff conducted tests using real and test accounts on both platforms. To ensure low access hurdle, authentication on Metacampus was facilitated via eduGAIN for all Unite! members. Additionally, participants of the lecture were required to create accounts on iMooX.at, which were linked to their Metacampus accounts. Figure 5 illustrates how the MOOC from iMooX.at was integrated into Metacampus from the participants' perspective. While the term 'seamless interconnection' via LTI refers to the intended functional integration - which indeed worked smoothly once implemented by technicians and activated by the learners themselves - the description also reveals that the actual implementation process is (still) not truly seamless.

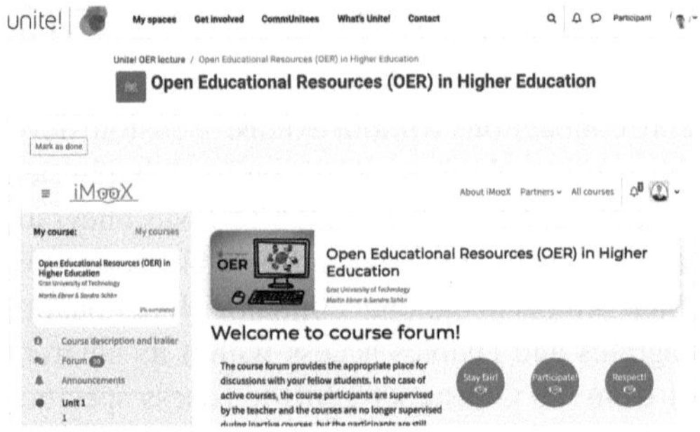

Fig. 5. The iMooX MOOC is integrated in the course in the federated LMS Metacampus (Screenshot). Source: Schön et al., 2024, [11], Fig. 7

The initial account linking between Metacampus and iMooX.at was only successful in Chrome and Edge, while later access also worked in Firefox; Safari was unsupported at the time (now resolved). Grade synchronization for both individual activities and full course grades was triggered automatically every 30 min. A user experience issue was identified, as the LTI tool provider displayed a full-screen content page without navigation, consistent with LTI's intended design. Further testing in real courses revealed a support challenge: Staff could not track linked student accounts, making troubleshooting difficult. Despite these issues, exam grade transfers from iMooX.at into Metacampus were successfully executed, confirming the feasibility of LTI-based grade synchronization for the 85 participants.

2.4 Certification: Open Badge and an Austrian Certificate

Certification in European university alliances is complex due to the absence of mutual recognition agreements. Typically, ECTS certificates can only be awarded to students enrolled at the issuing university, and partner institutions are not obliged to recognize external certifications. Since no formal agreements were established for this course, a multi-tiered certification approach was implemented: (a) all MOOC participants received an Open Badge and a certificate of participation from iMooX.at; (b) students enrolled in the university course were additionally awarded the Open Badge from Metacampus, acknowledging their achievement within the Unite! learning ecosystem; (c) those who successfully completed the university course received a Unite! course certificate; and (d) as a unique feature, participants could obtain the national Austrian OER certificate, since TU Graz is an accredited provider of continuing education programs, offering a formally recognized credential beyond the usual institutional and alliance-based certifications [10]. Finally, (e) students at Graz University of Technology additionally received their ECTS certificate for this course.

2.5 Results in Numbers and Note on Impact

The MOOC exceeded its enrolment target, with over 800 participants from Unite! institutions, highlighting the demand for multilingual OER in European higher education. By February 2025, more than 1,200 participants are registered, excluding those who left the course. The university course on OER on Metacampus had 85 registered participants, of whom 13 completed the course (10 from TU Graz, 3 from partner universities). The project's impact, including a staff training, is documented in separate contributions [13]. Notably, KTH integrated all course materials into a 2024 Open Science course, demonstrating their long-term sustainability in higher education.

3 Lessons Learned

To further emphasize the lessons learned, we highlight key takeaways that can support university alliances in developing and implementing multilingual, scalable, and interoperable MOOCs: (a) A balanced AI implementation is crucial for multilingual course offerings. While AI-driven translations and avatar-based content delivery offer significant advantages in scalability and efficiency, human oversight remains essential to ensure linguistic and contextual accuracy. A structured review process with native speakers should be integrated into production workflows to refine translations and maintain quality [1]. Experts responsible for careful preparation of the scripts, visualization and editing were therefore crucial for the professional results. (b) From a technical perspective, the integration of Learning Tools Interoperability (LTI) can provide seamless cross-platform access when using a federated LMS within university alliances. However, thorough testing and pilot implementations are necessary to address potential interoperability issues and ensure smooth user experiences. (c) A key factor in the scalability of MOOCs across institutions is the use of open licensing. The adoption of CC BY 4.0 licensing was instrumental in enabling the reuse, adaptation, and localization of course materials beyond the original partner network. This approach ensures that educational resources remain accessible, adaptable, and sustainable for a broader academic audience. (d) Additionally, hybrid certification models can enhance the recognition and value of MOOC participation. A combination of Open Badges, institutional certificates, and national certifications provides a flexible framework that accommodates diverse institutional policies. Future projects should explore how micro-credentials can be integrated into existing higher education systems to further increase recognition and acceptance.

The following table shows the challenges and mitigation strategies encountered during the implementation of a MOOC within a European university alliance, as demonstrated in our case study (see Table 1) from a technical, organizational and legal perspective.

Table 1. Challenges and mitigation issues when implementing a MOOC for a European alliance in relation to the case study

Category	Challenge	Mitigation Strategy (if)
Technical	Ensuring seamless integration of the MOOC across different LMS platforms via LTI	Extensive LTI testing and phased pilot implementations to ensure compatibility
	Browser compatibility issues affecting user experience and account synchronization	Identified and documented browser-specific problems, recommending Chrome/Edge

(continued)

Table 1. (*continued*)

Category	Challenge	Mitigation Strategy (if)
	AI-generated translations and avatars lacking accuracy and consistency	Manual review by native speakers and iterative quality assurance processes
	Synchronization of course grades between federated LMS systems	Automated grade transfer setup with synchronization intervals and manual checks
Organizational	Coordination among multiple universities with different policies and infrastructures	Flexible collaboration model with a shared core curriculum and local adaptations
	Managing multilingual course content across diverse institutional contexts	Use of AI-assisted translation with human oversight to maintain quality
	Adapting video scripts to avoid any problems with automatic translations	Test and develop strategies and adapt texts to avoid potential mistakes
	Videos need to be professionally edited in all languages by experts	No
	Lack of formal agreements for certification and mutual recognition of credits	Implementation of Open Badges, institutional certificates, and national certifications
Legal	Compliance with GDPR when using external MOOC platforms	Careful selection of platforms ensuring compliance
	Copyright and licensing complexities for shared educational materials	Use of CC BY 4.0 licensing to facilitate reuse, modification, and broad dissemination

4 Outlook

MOOCs and joint courses in European university alliances could benefit from key strategic developments. Establishing a microcredential framework at the alliance level would enhance recognition by aligning learning outcomes and facilitating mutual acceptance. Expanding the use of eduGAIN for authentication would simplify access across platforms, reducing participation barriers. Further testing and refinement of LTI could improve LMS integration, ensuring seamless access to learning resources, progress tracking, and certification issuance. OER remain fundamental for scalability, enabling cross-institutional course implementation and content reuse. These findings highlight the potential of AI-supported, openly licensed, and LTI-integrated MOOCs in fostering collaboration across European alliances. However, further advancements in microcredentialing, authentication infrastructures, and federated learning models are needed for MOOCs to become fully scalable and formally recognized. All proposed solutions are based on open standards and open licenses, supporting flexible and scalable digital education while strengthening digital sovereignty within European university networks. The use of OER further amplifies benefits, improving accessibility, open teaching, knowledge sharing, and sustainability (Jacob et al., in print). Prioritizing openness in both infrastructure and content ensure long-term impact while reinforcing principles of open science and education [13]. As MOOCs - as well as other joint courses - continue to be integrated into European university alliances, several strategic developments could enhance their effectiveness and recognition.

Acknowledgments. The presented work and development were done within the framework of the Unite! seed fund project "Unite! OER courses" within the Erasmus+ funding for the Unite alliance (2022–2026).

Disclosure of Interests. The authors have no competing interests.

References

1. Brünner, B., Ebner, M.: Rapid multilingual video production utilizing artificial intelligence. In: ED-MEDIA 2025 Conference (2025, in print)
2. Clossen, A.: Integrating the library in the learning management system. Libr. Technol. Rep. **54**(5) (2018)
3. Ebner, M.: iMooX - a MOOC platform for all (universities). In: 2021 7th International Conference on Electrical, Electronics and Information Engineering (ICEEIE), pp. 1–5 (2021). https://doi.org/10.1109/ICEEIE52663.2021.9616685
4. Ebner, M., Gasplmayr, K., Kreuzer, E., Leitner, P., Schön, S., Taraghi, B.: Implementation of MOOCs for microcredentials and European university alliances. In: Goundar, S. (ed.) Massive Open Online Courses – Current Practice and Future Trends. IntechOpen (2023). https://doi.org/10.5772/intechopen.1001466
5. Ebner, M., et al.: Aligning IT infrastructures for digital learning amongst the European university alliance Unite! - The Unite! digital campus framework and requirements (1.0). Unite! Community 2 Digital Campus, Graz University of Technology (2024). https://doi.org/10.3217/36yen-0wy21
6. Ebner, M., et al.: Examining IT infrastructures for learning and teaching in the European University Alliance Unite! In: Vogl, R., et al. (eds.) Proceedings of EUNIS 2024 Annual Congress in Athens, vol. 105, pp. 276–283 (2024). https://doi.org/10.29007/6n28
7. Ebner, M., Schön, S.: Der erste multilinguale MOOC zum Thema der Open Educational Resources: Rolle, Möglichkeiten und Herausforderungen des Einsatzes von KI bei der Erstellung von Videos mit Avataren der Lehrenden [The first multilingual MOOC on Open Educational Resources: Role, opportunities, and challenges of using AI for creating videos with teacher avatars]. Presentation at OEAD-Tagung, 14 November 2024, St. Pölten. Graz University of Technology (2024). https://doi.org/10.3217/jx9w7-qw453
8. Ruano, I., Estevez, E., Gamez, J., Gomez, J.: Standards for the integration of online laboratories with learning management systems. IEEE Access (2023)
9. Schön, S., Brünner, B., Ebner, M., Edelsbrunner, S., Hohla-Sejkora, K., Uhl, B.: Early findings from pilots in AI-driven education: effects of AI-generated courses and videos on learning and teaching. In: Auer, M.E., May, D. (eds.) 2024 Yearbook Emerging Technologies in Learning. LAIS, vol. 44, pp. 23–44. Springer, Cham (2025). https://doi.org/10.1007/978-3-031-80388-8_2

10. Schön, S., et al.: Development of an Austrian OER certification for higher education institutions and their employees. In: Otto, D., Scharnberg, G., Kerres, M., Zawacki-Richter, O. (eds.) Distributed Learning Ecosystems, pp. 161–182. Springer, Wiesbaden (2023). https://doi.org/10.1007/978-3-658-38703-7_9
11. Schön, S., et al.: Federated virtual learning management in a European university alliance: general challenges and first experiences using LTI to connect LMS in Unite! In: Bastiaens, T. (ed.) Proceedings of EdMedia + Innovate Learning, pp. 132–145. Association for the Advancement of Computing in Education (AACE) (2024). https://www.learntechlib.org/primary/p/224514/
12. Schön, S., Ebner, M., Gasplmayr, K.: Connecting platforms via LTI: the university course "OER in HE" and the connection of Metacampus with iMooX.at. In: Ebner, M., Gasplmayr, K., Schön, S. (eds.) Unite! Digital Teaching and Learning - Success Story Report, vol. 1, no. 2 (2024). https://doi.org/10.3217/v8nta-ayw79
13. Schön, S., et al.: A multilingual OER MOOC: a case study onproduction and usage in a university cooperation. J. Open Distance Digital Educ. **2**(1), 1–16 (2025). https://doi.org/10.25619/y956n017
14. Schön, S., et al.: The development of "teaching management patterns" from the perspective of IT infrastructure as a tool for consulting and further development in a European university alliance. In: Bastiaens, T. (ed.) Proceedings of EdMedia + Innovate Learning, pp. 146–155. Association for the Advancement of Computing in Education (AACE) (2024). https://www.learntechlib.org/primary/p/224515/
15. UNESCO: Recommendation on Open Educational Resources (OER). United Nations Educational, Scientific and Cultural Organization (2019). https://unesdoc.unesco.org/ark:/48223/pf0000370936
16. Winterhagen, M., et al.: LTI-connections between learning management systems and gaming platforms: integrating a serious-game prototype into moodle courses. J. Inf. Technol. Res. (JITR) **13**(4), 47–62 (2020)

Raising Awareness on Sustainability Through Digital Learning: An Institutional SPOC for All Newly Admitted Students, Moving Towards a MOOC Perspective

Frédéric de Lemos Esteves[1(✉)], Estelle Maes[1], Benoît Mayeur[1], Florianne Fassotte[2], Perrine Neuprez[2], Sybille Mertens[2], Bjorn Olav Dozo[1], and Valérie Defaweux[1]

[1] CARE Numérique, Université de Liège, 4000 Liège, Belgique
fdelemosesteves@uliege.be
[2] École de Gestion de l'Université de Liège, Université de Liège, 4000 Liège, Belgique

Abstract. The University of Liège (ULiège) has developed a Small Private Online Course (SPOC) on sustainability and transition, designed for new students. This initiative aims to raise awareness of environmental and societal challenges while offering students learning flexibility through an online format. The study reveals a high engagement rate (84%) and a strong success rate (86% to 94%), although involvement varies depending on student profiles: some prefer written materials or a selective approach to content.

Overall, students perceive the course as beneficial: 80% believe they have acquired new knowledge, and 83.2% find the online format suitable. However, tests are sometimes seen as a formality rather than a true learning tool. The study suggests enhancing the interactivity of assessments, adapting video formats, and promoting supplementary resources to enrich the learning experience.

ULiège is considering expanding the program's impact by transforming it into a Massive Open Online Course (MOOC), making it accessible to a broader audience, particularly within continuing education. This development aligns with a broader strategy to integrate Education for Sustainable Development (ESD) into higher education. The SPOC analysis highlights both opportunities and challenges associated with digital learning, emphasizing the importance of an interdisciplinary approach and continuous adaptation to students' needs to maximize the program's educational impact.

Keywords: Sustainability Education · Digital Learning Innovation · Higher Education Transition

1 Introduction

In response to major environmental and societal challenges, the University of Liège (ULiège) has placed sustainability and transition at the core of its strategic plan, aiming to prepare new generations for a more resilient and responsible world. This commitment underscores the growing need for enhanced education in sustainability. Studying the effectiveness of such education is therefore increasingly important [1].

E. Hamonic and R. Sharrock (Eds.): EMOOCS 2025, LNCS 15733, pp. 179–189, 2026.
https://doi.org/10.1007/978-3-032-00056-9_16

Academics must continuously explore how sustainability can be integrated into higher education institutions (HEIs) [2–4], as sustainable development is now recognized as HEI's fourth mission [5, 6]. This calls for the integration of sustainability at all levels and the adoption of inter- and transdisciplinary approaches [7, 8].

ULiège has developed a Small Private Online Course (SPOC) on sustainability and transition for all new students, with the goal of progressively evolving it into a MOOC accessible to a wider audience.

Based on Hueske *et al.* [9], this study examines the impact of the "Sustainability and Transition" SPOC through the concepts of *formalis* and *materialis*, while also exploring perception and participation. *Formalis* refers to organization and teaching methodology; *materialis* highlights the importance of concrete content. Perception concerns students' felt impact, and participation emphasizes the role of active engagement in learning.

1.1 Formalis (Mode of Delivery)

In this context, ULiège is transforming its educational practices by integrating Education for Sustainable Development (ESD) transversally into the curriculum for new students, through a structured 2-credit (ECTS) system. This approach aims to operationalize ESD principles by combining interdisciplinary training with disciplinary anchoring, in line with international recommendations on sustainability integration in higher education [10, 11].

This commitment is reflected on one hand in a mandatory interfaculty SPOC awarding the first ECTS, and on the other hand, in a second ECTS organized within each faculty, enabling disciplinary contextualization of sustainability issues. This dual approach combines global awareness of major environmental and societal challenges [12] with contextualized application in specific areas of expertise [13].

As an asynchronous digital training program, the "Sustainability and Transition" SPOC supports an innovative pedagogical model ensuring flexibility and accessibility, in line with Open and Distance Learning (ODL) principles applied to ESD [14]. Its instructional design follows a structured pathway, alternating educational video capsules and formative multiple-choice assessments, to enhance cognitive engagement and knowledge retention [15].

By involving experts from ULiège and civil society, this initiative adopts an interdisciplinary approach essential for a systemic understanding of sustainability challenges [16]. All content is structured into 54 video capsules on the institutional eCampus platform, ensuring effective knowledge transfer and compliance e-learning quality standards in higher education [17].

While literature highlights the potential of e-learning for sustainability education - especially in lifelong learning and adult education [14] - research on the integration of digital tools for ESD in higher education remains limited [18]. This gap underscores the need to explore how digital environments can foster student awareness and ownership of sustainability challenges [10].

The SPOC project offers a chance to empirically evaluate digital learning's impact on sustainability competencies. It is part of constructivist and socio-cognitive approach [19]. Its asynchronous, multimodal structure connects theoretical knowledge with interdisciplinary applications, supporting students' systemic understanding of socio-environmental challenges [11].

1.2 Materialis (Content)

The online course "Sustainability and Transition" is a mandatory course accessible to new students via the institutional eCampus platform. The structured, progressive, and conditional learning path allows students to progess step by step, completing assessments in a set sequence. The estimated workload is 12 h, comprising 54 expert-led video lectures from a multidisciplinary perspective. These lectures, spanning economics, law, philosophy, architecture, medicine, science, and sociology, total about 10 h, supplemented by 2 h of automatically graded assessments.

The course includes 29 assessments, each with three multiple-choice or multiple-response questions, auto-corrected. These are randomly drawn from expert-provided question banks (5 to 10 items per expert). To pass (60%), students have unlimited attempts.

The course is structured into four sequential modules aligned with multiple Sustainable Development Goals (SDGs), ensuring a holistic and accessible approach across disciplines.

Introductory Module: Eco-Anxiety. This module explores the psychological effects of environmental and societal crises, emphasizing resilience and proactive engagement. It supports SDG 3, "Good Health and Well-being," by addressing mental health and promoting strategies for individual and collective resilience.

Module 1: Environmental and Social Challenges. This module provides foundational knowledge of planetary boundaries and societal needs, highlighting contemporary challenges through a cross-cutting lens tied to SDGs 3-10 and 13-16 (Table 1).

Module 2: Systemic Analysis of Root Causes. Fostering holistic thinking, this module examines links between environmental and social crises. A systemic analysis of food systems illustrates impacts on ecosystems, food security, and consumption, aligning with SDGs 2, 9, 11, 12, 15, and 16.

Module 3: Responses and Action Levers. Adopting a forward-looking perspective, this module introduces sustainability and transition strategies. It presents actionable solutions at individual, collective, and institutional levels, emphasizing innovation, policy, and collaboration. It aligns with SDGs 8, 9, 11, 16, and 17 (Table 1).

1.3 Participation and Performance (Engagement and Involvement)

The first session of the course ran from September 16 to December 17, 2024. Participation and performance data were extracted from the institution's official learning management system, Blackboard Learn. For each course, the platform records the total time spent by each student, as displayed in the "Course Activity" section under the "Analytics" tab. However, this metric tends to be overestimated, as time continues to accumulate even when a student opens the course but remains inactive or leaves it running in the

Table 1. SDG Alignment by Learning Module

SGD\Modules	Introductory module	Module 1	Module 2	Module 3
SGD 2 - Zero Hunger			V	
SDG 3 - Good Health and Well-being	V	V		
SDG 5 - Gender Equality		V		
SDG 6 - Clean Water and Sanitation		V		
SDG 7 - Affordable and Clean Energy		V		
SDG 8 - Decent Work and Economic Growth		V		V
SDG 9 - Industry, Innovation, and Infrastructure		V	V	V
SDG 10 - Reduced Inequalities		V		
SDG 11 - Sustainable Cities and Communities			V	V
SDG 12 - Responsible Consumption and Production			V	
SDG 13 - Climate Action		V		
SDG 14 - Life Below Water		V		
SDG 15 - Life on Land		V	V	
SDG 16 - Peace, Justice, and Strong Institutions		V	V	V
SDG 17 - Partnerships for the Goals				V

background. The analyzed cohort includes 2,551 newly enrolled students from six faculties at ULiège: Science (4.3%), Medicine (30%), HEC (34%), Philosophy and Letters (1%), Law (30%), and Applied Sciences (0.3%). Thus, not all faculties or programs were represented in the study.

The course completion rate was 84%, with 2,139 students completing the entire learning path and passing all assessments with at least 60%.

In every faculty, average scores exceeded 60%, with success rates of 93.44% (Applied Sciences), 91% (Law), 92% (Medicine), 86% (HEC), and 94% for both Science and Philosophy and Letters. These results are noteworthy, considering students attempted each test only twice on average.

Time spent on the course is shown below (Table 2).

Over 35% of students spent under six hours, while 40% invested more than ten.

This suggests that nearly 60% did not watch all videos yet still passed. Full viewing was not required; simply opening a module and watching a few seconds allowed

Table 2. Time spent on the course

Time Spent on the Course	Percentage of Students
Less than 4 h	21%
Between 4 and 6 h	14,63%
Between 6 and 8 h	13,04%
Between 8 and 10 h	10,47%
Between 10 and 12 h	9%
More than 12 h	31%

progression. Transcripts were also available in downloadable PDF format. Conversely, 40% spent enough time to likely view all videos in full.

These findings reflect strong participation and engagement. The positive outcome is further supported by student perception data, discussed in the next section.

1.4 Perception (Student Reactions)

To analyze student perceptions, we administered a 37-question survey at the end of the online course. It explored motivation, satisfaction, communication, and student's sense of competence and control. Our analysis focused mainly on perceptions of course format and content.

Engagement and Time Spent

The course's structured, progressive format was generally well received, with 60% stating it improved engagement.

Video content engagement was relatively high: 35.2% reported watching at least half of the modules, and 38.2% said they watched all (Fig. 1A). Comparing self-reported data with platform stats—and given that all videos total about 10 h—we can infer that the 32.5% of students who spent 6–12 h watched at least half, while the 31% who spent over 12 h likely viewed them all.

Meanwhile, 22.5% reported watching less than half, aligning with eCampus data showing 21% spent under four hours.

Exploration of extra resources was moderate: 62.2% consulted, less than half or none. This may reflect the fact that core content alone was sufficient to pass assessments, reducing the need for supplementary materials.

Perception of Progression and Assessments

The course's sequential structure appears to have shaped students' perception of difficulty. While assessments were central to the learning path, opinions were mixed: 41.5% rated them as moderately satisfactory, and 38% evaluated them positively (Fig. 1B).

Given the high success rates with minimal attempts (as noted earlier), this contrast may indicate that assessments were viewed more as a hurdle than as an engaging learning tool.

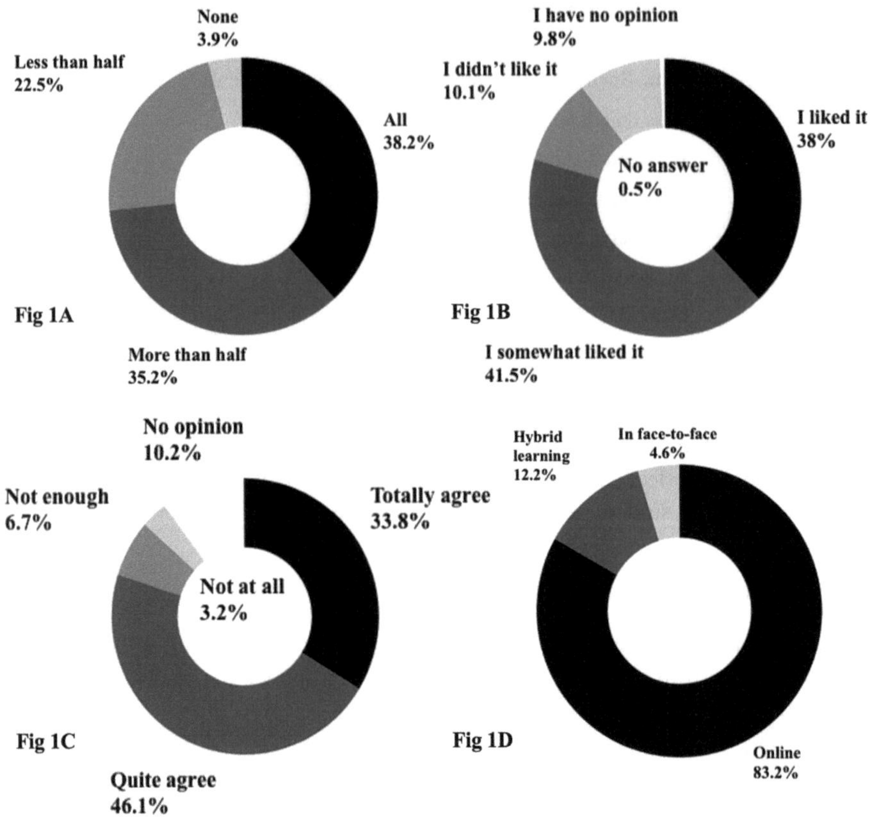

Fig. 1. Students' perception data. Figure 1A: engagement and time spent. Figure 1B: perception of progression and assessments. Figure 1C: impact on learning and satisfaction. Figure 1D: format and accessibility.

The effort required was generally seen as moderate to easy: on a scale from 1 (very difficult) to 5 (very easy), over 88% rated the course at least a 3, showing it was manageable. This perception aligns with the high 84% completion and success rate.

Survey responses also gave insight into how students viewed the course content: 86% found the materials (videos, transcripts, resources) appropriate and comprehensive, 12% were neutral, and just 2% expressed dissatisfaction.

Impact on Learning and Satisfaction

Despite being mandatory, students generally perceived the course's educational value positively: nearly 80% reported acquiring new knowledge (Fig. 1C). Over 72% felt that the assessment level matched the content, while just under 19% found it too easy. Combined with high success rates, these findings suggest the course met learning objectives with appropriate rigor, without hindering student success.

Satisfaction with the topics covered was also strong, with 75.2% expressing approval. Fewer than 10% wanted additional topics.

Format and Accessibility

From a technical standpoint, 72.9% of students were satisfied with the platform's usability and navigation. The alternation of video modules and assessments was perceived as an effective strategy.

The online format was particularly well received: 83.2% considered it the most suitable, compared to 12.2% who preferred a hybrid format and 4.6% who favored in-person instruction (Fig. 1D). This fully online approach proved motivating and satisfying for many students.

2 Discussion, Benefits, and Perspectives

2.1 Participation and Engagement

The analysis of participation data highlights a strong student engagement, with a completion rate of 84%. This is notable given the heterogeneity of student profiles across six faculties. However, the limited representation of some faculties (e.g., Applied Sciences at 0.3% and Philosophy and Letters at 1%) limits the generalizability of these results.

Time investment varied, reflecting diverse strategies. While 40% of students spent over 10 h on the course, more than 35% spent fewer than 6. This suggests that some adopted a selective approach, focusing on assessment-related content or using written materials (PDF scripts) instead of videos. The fully online format's flexibility enabled students to adapt their learning to individual needs and constraints.

2.2 Performance and Success

The consistently high success rate -averaging above 86% and peaking at 94% in Science and Philosophy and Letters- attests to the pathway effectiveness. The average of two attempts per test suggests that assessments were accessible and well-calibrated. However, this raises a key question: did they truly assess learning, or were they seen as a formality? The course's mandatory nature may have significantly influenced success, regardless of deep engagement.

Success likely stems from both institutional enforcement and thoughtful pedagogical design. The fully online format offered flexibility, while expert-led video modules added a professional and engaging dimension, enhancing student commitment.

2.3 Student Perception

Self-reported data confirm this positive perception: 80% of students felt they had acquired new knowledge, and 72.3% found the tests to be appropriately aligned with the course content. However, opinions on assessments were mixed: 41.5% rated them as "moderately appreciated." This may reflect a tension between their evaluative role and their pedagogical value—some students likely saw them more as constraints than learning tools.

Adherence to the online format was very high: 83.2% deemed it appropriate. The alternation between videos and assessments was well received, though video engagement varied. While 38.2% watched all videos, 22.5% viewed fewer than half, perhaps favoring transcripts or selecting content strategically based on assessment needs.

Use of supplementary resources remained low: 62.2% consulted fewer than half or none at all. This likely stems from the course design, where core content sufficed for success, reducing perceived need for extras.

2.4 Areas for Improvement and Future Perspectives

While results show strong engagement, they also reveal areas for improvement to enhance the learning experience. The satisfaction survey, though rich in insights, has not yet been systematically analyzed to inform the MOOC transition.

Three key areas for improvement emerge:

- **Optimization of assessments:** Transforming evaluations into genuine learning tools by incorporating more formative feedback and pedagogical explanations.
- **Better integration of video modules:** Given the partial engagement with video content, exploring shorter, interactive, or segmented formats could improve attention retention.
- **Enhancing the value of supplementary resources:** Increasing their appeal and accessibility to encourage deeper exploration of the provided content.

These adjustments will help optimize the learning model, using student feedback to strengthen the future MOOC's pedagogical impact.

3 Conclusions

This study makes a significant contribution to the literature on sustainability education by providing an in-depth analysis of the implementation of a mandatory SPOC and its potential transition to a MOOC format. While many sustainability MOOCs are designed for voluntary or specialized audiences, our SPOC stands out due to its mandatory nature within an academic curriculum, presenting a unique challenge in terms of pedagogical design. By comparing our SPOC with similar initiatives such as Stanford University's "Sustainability and Development" MOOC (2021) [22] and Harvard University's "Global Sustainability" MOOC (2022) [23], we have positioned our approach within an international context while highlighting the specific features of our program, especially its mandatory requirement, which will influence student engagement.

The results demonstrate that the SPOC model offers great potential for raising awareness about sustainability issues. However, to maximize this impact, it is crucial to facilitate its transition to a MOOC format that can address a wider audience. This evolution would better meet the needs of a heterogeneous audience, including students from other disciplines, professionals, and citizens wishing to self-learn. Adapting the program into a modular, remotely accessible MOOC with options for certification would offer greater flexibility and recognition of prior learning, in line with international recommendations on education for sustainable development (UNESCO, 2017; UNESCO, 2023) [24, 25].

This study also aligns with recent research by Ribeiro *et al.* (2022) [26] and Tisdell and Lee (2023) [27], who explored the impact of MOOCs on sustainability education in higher education. These studies highlighted challenges in adapting content to diverse audiences and managing student participation in digital environments. One of the major contributions of our study lies in how we integrated insights from these works to design a pedagogical structure that addresses diverse needs.

Additionally, our approach aligns with UNESCO's recommendations for sustainability education, emphasizing the need to make this education accessible to a global and diverse audience (UNESCO, 2017; UNESCO, 2023) [24, 25]. Furthermore, our study supports the arguments made by Cortese (2003) [12] and Lozano *et al.* (2013) [20], who advocate for the integration of sustainability into academic curricula to strengthen its legitimacy and impact.

The transition from SPOC to MOOC thus represents a strategic lever to broaden access to education on socio-ecological transition at a global scale. Drawing on recent research by Yuan and Powell (2013) [28], and global initiatives such as those at EDHEC, UCLouvain, and UNEP [10, 21], this transition will enhance the inclusivity of sustainability education programs and contribute to achieving the Sustainable Development Goals (SDGs) globally. We have demonstrated that the shift to a MOOC would bridge existing gaps in the educational offering on sustainability and increase the global impact of sustainability education.

In conclusion, this study demonstrates that the implementation of a mandatory SPOC on sustainability and its transition into a MOOC represents not only a significant advancement in sustainability education but also a pedagogical model adaptable to various institutional and professional contexts. This approach will reinforce the strategic and global impact of sustainability education, while addressing the contemporary challenges of socio-ecological transition and the emerging needs for training in this domain.

References

1. Markard, J., Raven, R., Truffer, B.: Sustainability transitions: an emerging field of research and its prospects. Res. Policy **41**(6), 955–976 (2012). https://doi.org/10.1016/j.respol.2012.02.013
2. Leal Filho, W., et al.: Sustainable development goals and sustainability teaching at universities: falling behind or getting ahead of the pack? J. Clean. Prod. **232**, 285–294 (2019). https://doi.org/10.1016/j.jclepro.2019.05.309
3. Niedlich, S., Bauer, M., Doneliene, M., Jaeger, L., Rieckmann, M., Bormann, I.: Assessment of sustainability governance in higher education institutions—a systemic tool using a governance equalizer. Sustainability **12**, 1816 (2020). https://doi.org/10.3390/su12051816
4. Starik, M., Kanashiro, P., Collins, E.: Sustainability management textbooks: potentially necessary, but probably not sufficient. Acad. Manag. Learn. Educ. **16**, 500–503 (2017). https://doi.org/10.5465/amle.2017.0188
5. Ozdemir, Y., Kaya, S.K., Turhan, E.: A scale to measure sustainable campus services in higher education: "sustainable service quality." J. Clean. Prod. **245**, 118839 (2020). https://doi.org/10.1016/j.jclepro.2019.118839
6. Trencher, G., Yarime, M., McCormick, K.B., Doll, C.N.H., Kraines, S.B.: Beyond the third mission: exploring the emerging university function of co-creation for sustainability. Sci. Public Policy **41**, 151–179 (2014). https://doi.org/10.1093/scipol/sct044
7. Lambrechts, W., Mulà, I., Ceulemans, K., Molderez, I., Gaeremynck, V.: The integration of competences for sustainable development in higher education: an analysis of bachelor

programs in management. J. Clean. Prod. **48**, 65–73 (2013). https://doi.org/10.1016/j.jclepro.2011.12.034
8. Leal Filho, W., Manolas, E., Pace, P.: The future we want: key issues on sustainable development in higher education after Rio and the UN decade of education for sustainable development. Int. J. Sustain. High. Educ. **16**, 112–129 (2015). https://doi.org/10.1108/IJSHE-03-2014-0036
9. Hueske, A.K., Aggestam Pontoppidan, C., Iosif-Lazar, L.C.: Sustainable development in higher education in Nordic countries: exploring e-learning mechanisms and SDG coverage in MOOCs. Int. J. Sustain. High. Educ. **23**(1), 196–211 (2022). https://doi.org/10.1108/IJSHE-07-2020-0276
10. Leal Filho, W., et al.: The role of planning in implementing sustainable development in a higher education context. J. Clean. Prod. **235**, 678–687 (2019). https://doi.org/10.1016/j.jclepro.2019.06.322
11. Sterling, S.: Living in the earth: towards an education for our time. J. Educ. Sustain. Dev. **4**(2), 213–218 (2010). https://doi.org/10.1177/097340821000400208
12. Cortese, A.D.: The critical role of higher education in creating a sustainable future. Plan. High. Educ. **31**(3), 15–22 (2003). https://scispace.com/papers/the-critical-role-of-higher-education-in-creating-a-50ij6e63tj
13. Brundiers, K., et al.: Key competencies in sustainability in higher education—toward an agreed-upon reference framework. Sustain. Sci. **16**, 13–29 (2021). https://doi.org/10.1007/s11625-020-00838-2
14. Azeiteiro, U.M., Bacelar-Nicolau, P., Caetano, F.J.P., Caeiro, S.: Education for sustainable development through e-learning in higher education: experiences from Portugal. J. Clean. Prod. **106**, 308–319 (2015). https://doi.org/10.1016/j.jclepro.2014.11.056
15. Mayer, R.E., Hegarty, M., Mayer, S., Campbell, J.: When static media promote active learning: annotated illustrations versus narrated animations in multimedia instruction. J. Exp. Psychol. Appl. **11**(4), 256 (2005). https://doi.org/10.1037/1076-898X.11.4.256
16. Watson, M.K., Lozano, R., Noyes, C., Rodgers, M.: Assessing curricula contribution to sustainability more holistically: experiences from the integration of curricula assessment and students' perceptions at the Georgia institute of technology. J. Clean. Prod. **61**, 106–116 (2013). https://doi.org/10.1016/j.jclepro.2013.09.010
17. Garrison, D.R., Kanuka, H.: Blended learning: uncovering its transformative potential in higher education. Internet High. Educ. **7**(2), 95–105 (2004). https://doi.org/10.1016/j.iheduc.2004.02.001
18. Lohrmann, C.: Online learning—do MOOCs contribute to the goals of agenda 21: "education for sustainable development"? In: Osburg, T., Lohrmann, C. (eds.) Sustainability in a Digital World. CSEG, pp. 211–224. Springer, Cham (2017). https://doi.org/10.1007/978-3-319-54603-2_18
19. Bandura, A.: Social Foundations of Thought and Action. Englewood Cliffs, NJ (1986). https://doi.org/10.4135/9781446221129.n6
20. Lozano, R., Lozano, F.J., Mulder, K., Huisingh, D., Waas, T.: Advancing higher education for sustainable development: international insights and critical reflections. J. Clean. Prod. **48**, 3–9 (2013). https://doi.org/10.1016/j.jclepro.2013.03.034
21. Otto, D., Becker, S.: E-learning and sustainable development. In: Encyclopedia of Sustainability in Higher Education, pp. 475–482 (2019). https://doi.org/10.1016/j.jclepro.2013.09.010
22. Stanford University: Sustainability and Development: A MOOC for Global Change (2021). www.stanford.edu
23. Harvard University: Global Sustainability: Understanding the Challenges (2022). www.harvard.edu

24. UNESCO: Education for Sustainable Development Goals: Learning Objectives. UNESCO Publishing, Paris (2017). https://doi.org/10.54675/CGBA9153
25. UNESCO: Education for Sustainable Development: A Transformative Approach to Global Learning. Report to the 78th United Nations General Assembly (2023). https://www.unesco.org/en/sustainable-development/education
26. Ribeiro, D., Silva, A., Marques, M.: Exploring the impact of MOOCs on sustainability education: a comparative study. Sustainability **14**(1), 23–45 (2022). https://doi.org/10.3390/su7032274
27. Tisdell, C.A., Lee, J.H.: Sustainability in higher education: MOOCs and the role of digital learning platforms. J. Educ. Technol. **31**(2), 65–78 (2023). https://doi.org/10.3390/su15129781
28. Yuan, L., Powell, S.J.: MOOCs and open education: implications for higher education (2013). https://doi.org/10.13140/2.1.5072.8320

Embedding and Evaluating a Pre-Covid-19 MOOC in an Interdisciplinary University Course More Than Five Years Later: E-Tutoring@UIBK and the MekoMOOC, A Case Study

Evelyn Feistmantl(✉)

University of Innsbruck, Innrain 52d, 6020 Innsbruck, Austria
evelyn.feistmantl@uibk.ac.at

Abstract. This paper aims to illustrate how the course concept for the E-Tutoring@UIBK lecture successfully utilizes the MekoMOOC, a Massive Open Online Course that has been available on the Austrian MOOC platform iMooX since October 1st 2019. More than five years later, the MekoMOOC serves as a vehicle for metacognitive analysis and critical reflection as well as a content pool to introduce students to a variety of media topics. E-Tutoring@UIBK was started with the objective of providing prospective teaching assistants and e-tutors with digital as well as didactic skills and competencies to effectively navigate the digital media landscape of the University of Innsbruck. For this purpose, the course integrates the timeless MOOC contents into its sessions at various points throughout the lecture. The students are tasked to reflect on the structure and didactic purpose of the MOOC's content structure and critically analyze its media composition in order to attain an improved understanding of how to design higher education courses themselves. Finally, the students are asked to produce a tutorial video on a subject matter of their choice. In doing so, students utilize skills and technical knowledge gained through the theoretical and practical aspects of the lecture as well as the MOOC.

Keywords: MOOC-Embedded Learning Design · Experiential MOOC Reuse · MOOC Longevity

1 Introduction and Methodology

This paper discusses the way that the Massive Open Online Course (MOOC) "#MekoMOOC20: Medienkompetenz in der Lehre" (MekoMOOC) has been integrated into the university lecture E-Tutoring@UIBK in order to showcase a long-term solution for sustainably (re)using MOOCs in teaching endeavors and, thus, guaranteeing their relevancy long-time. The author aims to address in what way E-Tutoring@UIBK is particularly suitable for such an implementation and how this integration may be replicable in other institutions. First, the online course and the lecture series are introduced. MOOC

E. Hamonic and R. Sharrock (Eds.): EMOOCS 2025, LNCS 15733, pp. 190–199, 2026.
https://doi.org/10.1007/978-3-032-00056-9_17

longevity challenges are addressed and the devised link between the MekoMOOC and E-Tutoring@UIBK analyzed in-depth in order to present a case for how an integration even of older MOOCs into in-person lectures may succeed. Furthermore, the relation between current Artificial Intelligence (AI) developments and MOOC production and trends are discussed. Lastly, the limitations of current AI and OER production endeavors are pointed out and a step-by-step guide for how to integrate a MOOC into a suitable university lecture is provided.

2 The MekoMOOC and E-Tutoring@UIBK

The MekoMOOC is the product of a collaboration between members of several Higher Education Institutions (HEI) and the University of Innsbruck. The first outputs of the project began as two early versions of the MekoMOOC: They started out as modular, supervised online courses (titled #MekoMOOC18 and #MekoMOOC19) that drew a wide audience of 1565 participants (Gröblinger et al. 2019), with 392 certificates issued during their runs. The final version of the MekoMOOC, titled "#MekoMOOC20: Medienkompetenz in der Lehre", was put online on the Austrian MOOC platform iMooX as a self-paced course on the 1st of October 2019. More than a thousand people have enrolled in it and 289 participants have been issued automated certificates, since (Gröblinger et al. 2019a). The lecture series E-Tutoring@UIBK (Information Technology Services/IT-Center – ZID 2025), on the other hand, is an in-person course consisting of sessions ranging from media didactics to hands-on trainings for using the technical systems offered at the University of Innsbruck. An elective course accreditable for Bachelor students, E-Tutoring@UIBK is open to students of all faculties.

Preservice teacher and e-tutor education thus far has relied commonly on integrating MOOCs with campus-based courses (Edumadze & Govender 2024; Sharma & Singhal 2020; Taguchi et al. 2019) in flipped classroom, blended learning or other hybrid learning formats. E-Tutoring@UIBK notably transforms the students' learning path by putting them in an instructional designer's role: The students are not simply passive learners but active e-tutors that are tasked to evaluate and analyze the MekoMOOC with a questionnaire before, during and after completing the course (cf. Kember & Leung 2005). Additionally, the MOOC is folded into E-Tutoring@UIBK at various points by way of the topic discussions. As a result, they are engaged in becoming e-tutors, namely teaching assistants with a background on e-learning matters. Their motivation for the completion of the MOOC relies on multiple factors: Their understanding of the reasoning behind going through the course in a pre-determined, question-guided manner and the project of designing and producing a video tutorial on the basis of, among other supplemented materials, the instructional videos in the MekoMOOC.

3 Challenges of MOOC Longevity

From the conception, coordination between the creators from different partner institutions to the creation and the maintenance of a MOOC, its timelessness needs to be factored into the equation (Bou-Vinals et al. 2019; Liu et al. 2019). Having been put online as a self-paced MOOC in 2019, after two runs with active supervision, the course creators needed to design it with continuously evergreen contents in mind: The topics give a generalized, comprehensive overview on media informatics, media didactics, media law, media usage and the impact of media.

With the fast-changing digital and online landscape in mind, there is a chance that contents may rapidly become outdated. Therefore, it is the responsibility of the institution operating the MOOC (Pomerantz 2018) to actively commit resources to maintaining it throughout its lifespan. Further academic institutional maintenance of MOOCs is essential because owners of MOOC platforms rarely take up responsibility for doing so. Events such as platform migrations may cause links to the course to break (MiriadaX 2025). The course may also be deleted if no owner actively downloads its contents or agrees to migrating it to a new system. MOOCs offer a static collection of modules and a set curriculum and learning path through the course. This, paired with the lack of personalization options when participants learn in a self-directed manner, may contribute to the high dropout rates: About 69% of MekoMOOC participants show up as "inactive" (Gröblinger 2019a). Yet, in connection with E-Tutoring@UIBK and the questionnaire, the MekoMOOC was one of the few course requirements that students did not mention as hindering their course success in their session reflections. In general, students self-reportedly underestimating the required total workload seemed to overall be the deciding factor for student dropout from the university course.

4 An Examination of the MekoMOOC and E-Tutoring@UIBK

The MekoMOOC consists of six lessons with an approximate workload of four hours each, with its contents ranging from an introduction about media law to an overview of media didactics. The modules about Open Educational Resources and knowledge management in particular seamlessly complement the contents of the lecture. E-Tutoring@UIBK is a university course being taught by a team of ten different lecturers (ZID 2025) on the digital tools in use at the University of Innsbruck, didactics and e-assessments at HEI. Generally applicable and quickly evolving subjects, like OER and AI, as well as transferable skills, such as instructions on how to learn to effectively use a learning management system (LMS), are the focus of the in-person sessions. The university course is open to all students at Bachelor level, thus guaranteeing a diverse, heterogenic student pool from different backgrounds and ongoing studies.

E-Tutoring@UIBK as a concept has been transformed multiple times throughout the years (cf. DMLT 2013; ZID 2025). By the time of the latest lecture runs, AI applications and use cases have developed exponentially. The MekoMOOC at first glance hosted outdated contents. However, an in-depth perusal of the MOOC proves informative: A comprehensive questionnaire based on existing evaluation frameworks to address the MOOC's instructional quality (Margaryan et al. 2014; Rice & Ortiz 2021, cf. Tan, K. H. et al. 2021) was compiled which guides the students through the MOOC in a reflective and purposeful way. Participants are asked to compare and contrast the contents of the MOOC to their knowledge about digital matters and evaluate the MOOC's instructional quality in detail (cf. Feistmantl & Pinzer-Bakay 2025).

4.1 The Systematic Deconstruction of the MekoMOOC

The question catalogue for the MekoMOOC is provided to them in the E-Tutoring@UIBK course on the university's LMS. Questions can be asked in a supervised forum of this simultaneously maintained online course. Unlike other tasks, the question catalogue so far has featured the least in students' frequently asked questions for this course, indicating the clarity and straightforwardness of the answers required within.

The questions needed to be answerable solely by going through the MekoMOOC in a structured manner. Question generation followed a systematic deconstruction process based on proven learning and knowledge acquisition theories and strategies, e.g., mind maps as perpetuated as learning vehicles by Tony Buzan (2005), spacing, interleaving, retrieval practice and elaboration (Madan 2023; Brown et al. 2014), and established question techniques (Krosnick 2018; Booth 2006).

First, students are asked questions on the MekoMOOC's structure, about their expectations and ideas for creating a MOOC, themselves. Considerations at the beginning of as well as the motivations for designing a MOOC are addressed (cf. Sanchez-Gordon & Luján-Mora 2017; Najafi et al. 2017; Najafi et al. 2015; Lopes et al. 2015). The students' critical thinking is facilitated further by way of asking them for suggestions for preventatively handling future (digital) challenges. They are encouraged to proactively seek to meet future expenditures while in the creation phase of a MOOC, a transferable experience they can then go on to use for prospective online teaching endeavors. A retrospective questionnaire allows students to analyze the project in its entirety: from the MOOC project's starting point to its usage to the participants profiting from the contents post-project (and post-funding) (cf. Rodriguez & Rodriguez Nieto 2019).

After these preliminary questions, the students are tasked to rate the structure of the lessons in the MekoMOOC along with more general questions about the lessons themselves: Each lesson is deconstrued, with students answering questions about the supplementary material and about the usefulness of the MekoMOOC's contents in the context of their diverse backgrounds and study areas, their personal experiences and (future) work aspirations. In addition to these, detailed questions about the videos steer the students' attention towards more practical, technical aspects that tie back to the lecture and are important for their own production of a video tutorial. As a result, they become active agents of their own learning (Little 2003).

Upon MOOC completion, the students are asked if they missed any information and what topics they would have liked to study more in-depth. For the latter they are given literature and course recommendations (cf. DMLT 2025; DMLT 2025a), which some have then gone on to work through independently. These questions take the students into the mindset of a teacher and prompt them to analyze their learning journey in depth.

The question catalogue is a powerful tool for furthering the students' understanding and their competence for analyzing an online course. This reflective activity (RA) (Araneta et al. 2024) combined with the university lecture allows them to obtain a comprehensive learning experience guiding them gradually into the role of an e-tutor or TA.

4.2 Linking the MOOC with the University Lecture

Teaching with the help of a MOOC in a higher education context is, to this day, a rare phenomenon (de Lima Guedes et al. 2022; Ferri, P. 2019; Jansen et al. 2015). The preparation of the MOOC, the implementation of the way that one would instruct and motivate the students to use it as well as what contents from the MOOC are included in the course material need to be selected carefully. The learning objectives as well as the course assessment have to be considered – a MOOC may supplement contents, however the main objective is to create a learning experience for the students that allows them to retain information as well as analyze and evaluate the teachings, themselves. As such, a MOOC may for example be added to a course's in-person sessions in a blended learning course format – the most common format for embedding a MOOC in a lecture series (Alario-Hoyos et al. 2023; de Lima Guedes et al. 2022; Israel, M.J. 2015). Nonetheless, E-Tutoring@UIBK selected to go a slightly different route: The MekoMOOC is used alongside the course, the only requisite for finishing it being a deadline for handing in the MOOC's completion certificate close to the last session of the lecture.

Within the first on-campus session, students are led through a tutorial on how to create the tutorial video that they have to complete in order to successfully finish the lecture: They are shown the studios that the University of Innsbruck offers them as well as various methods for creating a video. The students have to apply the same time management skills and discipline for successfully completing the MekoMOOC as they do for a mandatory video production self-learning course, reinforcing the need for effective self-management and self-motivation. On top of that, the videos of the MekoMOOC model to the students how to transfer knowledge effectively.

The interwovenness of the MOOC and lecture contents, especially in later sessions, guarantee an effective learning experience with structured interleaved learning periods, spaced retrieval practices and elaboration of obtained knowledge about theories and practical applications thereof (cf. Brown et al. 2014): The in-person session about OER, CC-licenses as well as accessibility for example complement the information covered in Lesson 4 and 6 of the MekoMOOC: Practical use cases for OER usage (Muuß-Merholz 2018) supplement the lecture, wherein student knowledge from the MekoMOOC is used for discussions about copyright restrictions, digital accessibility issues and OER. The students learn that the knowledge obtained from the MOOC can be applied and discussed in a reflective manner (Araneta et al. 2024), even if not all of them have finished the referenced modules. On the other hand, the lecture sessions on knowledge management and data protection remain largely independent from the MOOC, although the topics are touched upon in Lesson 6, too.

Meaningful learning can happen when students understand the usefulness and practical implementation of the material (Brown et al. 2014). Rote memorization is helpful in contexts that are situated at a lower level in Bloom's taxonomy, whereas the reflective understanding and application of knowledge is encouraged by the active examination of the MOOC. The questions train them to contest and reflect on how they are taught, how they retain information and how they might then go about teaching others about their expertise (Araneta et al. 2024). Autonomous learning, not to be misunderstood as self-instructed learning (Little 2000, 2007; Hamidullayeva & Fayziqulovna 2023), which has so far mainly been studied in language learning contexts, is proposed to play a crucial role in future academic course design.

The intention behind utilizing the MOOC to further students' learning is to help them improve their time management, discipline as well as accompany them on the first steps towards an autodidactic learning journey. Their self-efficacy in going through the MOOC ties into their ability to contribute to discussions in in-person sessions, which has proven to enhance learning success (Saliha, Samia 2024). The focus in this kind of interweaving of contents on participatory learning designs (Casanova et al. 2020) and a project-based learning approach gives students the necessary skills to obtain digital competencies and media literacy necessary for future work and study endeavors.

5 Discussion: (Re-)Using MOOCs in Times of AI

With the rise of AI and the ever-changing digital landscape, MOOCs form a background well of knowledge and information that one can draw from to support one's teaching. Concerns, such as the fair assessment of students' competencies, or their "AI-supported competency simulations" (Krommer 2025) largely fall to the wayside for an elective course that has the production of a tutorial video as one of the main assessment criteria and learning objectives. Generative AI and diffusion model development have come far, but the production of videos with AI may need many more improvements before it is at a level to reliably produce output comparable to that of a student's tutorial video. Students' knowledge about AI matters and their competency at using AI is another aspect that should neither be over- nor underestimated (cf. Tulis et al. 2024).

Due to the age of the MekoMOOC showing, this course could not simply be included in the E-Tutoring@UIBK lecture without preliminary considerations on the part of the course lecturers, in particular regarding possible AI implementations and the tasks required for the lecture. The question catalogue that accompanies the students on their learning journey through the MekoMOOC was devised with experiential reflections in mind. Successfully concluding the MOOC and handing in the answers to this question catalogue is one of the five main tasks students have to accomplish throughout the lecture: Regular reflections on the in-person sessions, their presence and active participation in class, the completion of a self-learning course on video production, a final presentation and the production of a tutorial video on a topic of their choice add up to a total of 5 ECTS that students stand to gain upon finishing the lecture. Few of these tasks lend themselves to a substitution through AI applications. Students are made aware of possible repercussions on their knowledge retention, performance in class and limitations of AI throughout the lecture. This preventative measure requires for course lecturers to be aware of the current developments of AI to the best of their abilities.

In times when MOOCs themselves can be created with the use of AI (e.g. Ebner & Schön 2024), the facilitation for students to use AI applications as tools rather than all-knowing entities must be improved upon. For this to work, the schooling of teaching personnel on the limitations and opportunities of AI is vital. On the other hand, the conception and production of OER might stand to gain much in the utilization of AI as a tool (e.g., as a sounding board for the creation of ideas). With DeepSeek as an Open-Source publication, the collaboration in the global community may soon bring forth new models with improved and more sustainable backgrounds than those that exist now (cf. Verma & Tan 2024). Future AI models might be able to integrate with LMS or they may provide a new way to aid the students in retaining knowledge: AI tutors already exist, however they offer limited functions as of yet.

6 Limitations

Keeping in mind the current limitations of AI and the project-based approach of the E-Tutoring lecture, the existing variety of applications for a MOOC in a lecture may prove insufficient for guiding the students towards their goal. New modes for using MOOCs in educational contexts are needed to integrate the online courses into innovative teaching contexts at HEIs. Additionally, the reuse of MOOCs from an instructor's perspective has thus far not been studied sufficiently in depth: Case studies and qualitative literary reviews promise a good starting point. Nonetheless, more quantitatively oriented research may prove informative for how many MOOCs have been used in what way at what level of education. A preliminary method for making the usage of MOOCs at HEIs more visible is by way of MOOC fellowships on iMooX (iMooX 2025).

Furthermore, MOOC dropout rates once a supervised course has transitioned into a self-paced format are empirically known to rise drastically; dropout rates of elective courses which utilize MOOCs have not yet been studied in-depth. For E-Tutoring@UIBK, dropout risks are largely mitigated by the fact that students take up an active role to identify themselves with (e-tutor) and the meaningful engagement with the material together with other students from an interdisciplinary background.

7 Conclusion

The unique point of departure for the conception of the E-Tutoring@UIBK university course as a formation for prospective e-tutors allows for a modified approach to the utilization of the MekoMOOC: Instead of "only" having the students complete the MOOC, they are to actively engage with the instruction practice by evaluating and assessing the MOOC's contents and instruction delivery, themselves. This reflective approach may not work in less project oriented educational contexts, however, it may be perfectly suited for teacher educational programs. In these settings, the MOOC integration can be replicated with the following steps:

1. A MOOC suitable for such an integration needs to be researched (an introductory MOOC to media competencies for teaching professionals is ideal),
2. A question catalogue regarding the MOOC has to be designed (the question catalogue as referenced in this paper has been published as an OER by Feistmantl & Pinzer-Bakay)
3. The questionnaire needs to be posed to the students
4. Several of the topics discussed in the MOOC need to be embedded in an accompanying lecture (through discussions of case studies and other methods)

The systematic deconstruction of the MekoMOOC is in ongoing development, with these questions forming a foundation for integrating it in future runs of the E-Tutoring@UIBK lecture. In 2010, MOOCs have been lauded as disruptive for the future of education at HEI (Haug et al. 2024). With a similar hype around AI applications nowadays, implications for MOOC creation and maintenance – in particular, MOOC ownership and OER licensing – cannot be specified as of yet.

Disclosure of Interests.. The author has no competing interests to declare.

References

Alario-Hoyos, C., Delgado Kloos, C., Kiendl, D., Terzieva, L.: Innovat MOOC: teacher training on educational innovation in higher education. Meinel. In: Schweiger, C., et al. (eds.) Post-Covid Prospects for Massive Open Online Courses: 8th European MOOCs Stakeholders Summit, EMOOCs 2023, (Potsdam, Germany, 14th-16th June 2023), pp. 229–237. Universitätsverlag Potsdam, Potsdam (2023)

Aldahdouh, A., Osório, A.: Planning to design MOOC? Think first! Online J. Distance Educ. e-Learn. **4**(2), 47–57 (2016). https://doi.org/10.5281/zenodo.48804

Araneta, M.G., Liotino, M., Olatunji, T.I., Fedeli, M.: Leveraging massive open online courses to foster reflective practice in blended university courses. Innov. Educ. Teach. Int., 1–13 (2024). https://doi.org/10.1080/14703297.2024.2320697

Booth, A.: Clear and present questions: formulating questions for evidence based practice. Libr. Hi Tech. **24**(3), 355–368 (2006). https://doi.org/10.1108/07378830610692127

Bou-Vinals, A.: #MekoMOOC18: Medienkompetenz in der Lehre. Lernziele. Universität Innsbruck (2018). https://www.uibk.ac.at/projects/mekomooc/lernziele_meko-mooc.html. Accessed 05 Mar 2025

Bou-Vinals, A., Brigo, A., Hoffmann, B.: Workshop: wie erstelle ich einen MOOC? 5. Österreichische Citizen Science Konferenz (Obergurgl, Austria, 26th–28th June 2019) (2019)

Brown, P.C., Roediger III, H.L., McDaniel, M.A.: Make it Stick: The Science of Successful Learning. Cambridge (USA), p. 207. The Belknap Press of Harvard University Press, London (2014)

Buzan, T.: The Ultimate Book of Mind Maps: Unlock Your Creativity, Boost Your Memory, Change Your Life. HarperCollinsPublishers Limited, London (2005)

Casanova, D., Huet, I., Garcia, F., Pessoa, T.: Role of technology in the design of learning environments. Learn. Environ. Res. **23**, 413–427 (2020). https://doi.org/10.1007/s10984-020-09314-1

de Lima Guedes, K.K., Davis, H.C., Schulz, J.: Integrating MOOCs into traditional higher education modules: a MOOC-based blend framework. Res. Learn. Technol. **30** (2022). https://doi.org/10.25304/rlt.v30.2702

Digital Media and Learning Technologies – DMLT: 179001 E-Learning Anwender Grundlagen und eTutorInnenausbildung. Universität Innsbruck (2013). https://lfuonline.uibk.ac.at/public/lfuonline_lv.details?sem_id_in=13W&lvnr_id_in=179001. Accessed 06 Mar 2025

DMLT: Crashkurs E-Didaktik. OpenCourses, Universität Innsbruck (2025). https://opencourses.uibk.ac.at/auth/RepositoryEntry/2981904/CourseNode/99925983867696. Accessed 30 Apr 2025

DMLT: OER-Zertifizierungskurs. OpenCourses, Universität Innsbruck (2025a). https://opencourses.uibk.ac.at/auth/RepositoryEntry/12058624/CourseNode/109846075778424. Accessed 30 Apr 2025

Ebner, M., Schön, S.: Open Educational Resources (OER) in Higher Education. iMooX (2024). https://imoox.at/course/OERinHE. Accessed 06 Mar 2025

Feistmantl, E., Pinzer-Bakay, F.: Reflexionsfragen zum MekoMOOC. Universität Innsbruck (2025). https://oer-repo.uibk.ac.at/edu-sharing/components/render/830d019d-dd86-44ee-8d01-9ddd8614ee43. Accessed 30 Mar 2025

Ferri, P.: MOOC, didattica universitaria digitale e Learning analytics. Opportunità e prospettive. Giornale Italiano Della Ricerca Educativa, Numero Speciale (Settembre 2019), 13–26 (2019)

Fowler, F.J.: Designing questions to be good measures. In: Designing Questions to Be Good Measures, 4th edn., pp. 86–113. SAGE Publications, Inc. (2009). https://doi.org/10.4135/9781452230184.n6

Fundación Telefónica: Miriada X.: https://www.miriadax.net – This website has not been reachable between 14.02.2025 and 17.04.2025 (2025)

Gordon, S., Luján, S.: Proceso de desarrollo y gestión de MOOC. Ciencia América **6**(2), 162–167 (2017)

Gráinne, C.: Designing effective MOOCs. Educ. Media Int. **52**(4), 239–252 (2015). https://doi.org/10.1080/09523987.2015.1125989

Gröblinger, O., Bou-Vinals, A., Hoffmann, B., Komar, J.L., Brigo, A.: MOOCs in citizen science. In: Proceedings of EMOOCs 2019: Work in Progress Papers of the Research, Experience and Business Tracks. EMOOCs 2019, Naples, Italy, 20–22 May 2019, p. 137 (2019)

Gröblinger, O., et al.: #MekoMOOC20: Medienkompetenz in der Lehre. iMooX (2019a). https://imoox.at/course/mekomooc2020Course statistics. Accessed 05 Mar 2025

Hamidullayeva, K.Z., Fayziqulovna, M.Z.: Project-based learning as an effective teaching approach to promote learner autonomy. Web Semant. Univ. J. Innov. Educ. **2**(3), 255–258 (2023)

Haug, N., Dan, S., Mergel, I.: Digitally-induced change in the public sector: a systematic review and research agenda. Public Manag. Rev. **26**(7), 1963–1987 (2024). https://doi.org/10.1080/14719037.2023.2234917

iMooX: MOOC Fellowships (2025). https://imoox.at/page/fellowship. Accessed 06 Mar 2025

Information Technology Services (IT-Center) – ZID: E-Tutoring@UIBK. Universität Innsbruck (2025). https://www.uibk.ac.at/zid/servicekatalog/servicebeschreibungen/e-tutoring-at-uibk.html. Accessed 05 Mar 2025

Israel, M.J.: Effectiveness of integrating MOOCs in traditional classrooms for undergraduate students. Int. Rev. Res. Open Distrib. Learn. **16**, 102–118 (2015). https://doi.org/10.19173/irrodl.v16i5.2222

Jansen, D., Schuwer, R., Teixeira, A., Aydin, C.: Comparing MOOC adoption strategies in Europe: results from the HOME project survey. Int. Rev. Res. Open Distrib. Learn. **16**(6), 116–136 (2015). https://doi.org/10.19173/irrodl.v16i6.2154

Kember, D., Leung, D.: The influence of active learning experiences on the development of graduate capabilities. Stud. High. Educ. **30**, 155–170 (2005). https://doi.org/10.1080/03075070500043127

Krommer, A.: KI-gestützte Kompetenz-Simulation (2025). https://www.linkedin.com/feed/update/urn:li:activity:7273459084895383552/. Accessed 07 Mar 2025

Krosnick, J.A.: Improving question design to maximize reliability and validity. In: Vannette, D., Krosnick, J. (eds.) The Palgrave Handbook of Survey Research, pp. 95–101. Palgrave Macmillan, Cham (2018). https://doi.org/10.1007/978-3-319-54395-6_13

Liu, M., Zha, S., He, W.: Digital transformation challenges: a case study regarding the MOOC development and operations at higher education institutions in China. TechTrends **63**, 621–630 (2019). https://doi.org/10.1007/s11528-019-00409-y

Little, D.: Learner autonomy and second/foreign language learning. In: The Guide to Good Practice for Learning and Teaching in Languages, Linguistics and Area Studies (2003). https://web-archive.southampton.ac.uk/www.llas.ac.uk/resources/gpg/1409.html. Accessed 06 Mar 2025

Lopes, A.P., Soares, F., Vieira, I.: How to feel "in love" with a math – a MOOC experience. In: Proceedings of INTED2015 Conference, Madrid, Spain, 2–4 March 2015, pp. 326–332 (2015)
Madan, C.: Using evidence-based learning strategies to improve medical education. Med. Sci. Educ. **33** (2023). https://doi.org/10.1007/s40670-023-01798-9
Muuß-Merholz, J.: Freie Unterrichtsmaterialien finden, rechtssicher einsetzen, selbst machen und teilen, 1st edn. Verlagsgruppe Beltz, Weinheim Basel, pp. 26 , 133 (2018)
Najafi, H., Rolheiser, C., Harrison, L., Håklev, S.: University of Toronto instructors' experiences with developing MOOCs. Int. Rev. Res. Open Distrib. Learn. **16**(3), 233–255 (2015). https://doi.org/10.19173/irrodl.v16i3.2073
Najafi, H., Rolheiser, C., Håklev, S., Harrison, L.: Variations in pedagogical design of massive open online courses (MOOCs) across disciplines. Teach. Learn. Inq. **5**(2) (2017). https://doi.org/10.20343/teachlearninqu.5.2.5
Padilla Rodriguez, B.C., Rodriguez Nieto, M.C.: How to run a massive open online course once the funding is over. In: Calise, M., Delgado Kloos, C., Reich, J., Ruiperez-Valiente, J., Wirsing, M. (eds.) EMOOCs 2019. LNCS, vol. 11475, pp. 156–161. Springer, Cham (2019). https://doi.org/10.1007/978-3-030-19875-6_18
Pritchett, N.: Effective question design. In: Brown, S., Bull, J., Race, P (eds.) Computer-Assisted Assessment in Higher Education. Kogan Page Ltd., London (1999)
Rice, M.F., Ortiz, K.R.: Evaluating digital instructional materials for K-12 online and blended learning. TechTrends Lead. Educ. Train. **65**(6), 977–992 (2021). https://doi.org/10.1007/s11528-021-00671-z
Tan, K.H., Chan, P.P., Mohd Said, N.-E.: Higher education students' online instruction perceptions: a quality virtual learning environment. Sustainability **13**(19), 10840 (2021). https://doi.org/10.3390/su131910840
Tulis, M., Kinskofer, F., Fischer, E.: Ergebnisse der quantitativen Erhebung zur Ki-Nutzung an Hochschulen. In: Brandhofer, G., Gröblinger, O., Jadin, T., Raunig, M., Schindler, J. (eds.) Von KI lernen, mit KI lehren: Die Zukunft der Hochschulbildung. Projektbericht, pp. 74–123 (2024)
Verma, P., Tan, S.: A bottle of water per email: the hidden environmental costs of using AI chatbots (2024). https://www.washingtonpost.com/technology/2024/09/18/energy-ai-use-electricity-water-data-centers/. Accessed 07 Mar 2025
Vizerektorat für Digitalisierung und Nachhaltigkeit: 110001 VU E-Tutoring@UIBK. Universität Innsbruck (2025). https://lfuonline.uibk.ac.at/public/lfuonline_lv.details?sem_id_in=24W&lvnr_id_in=110001. Accessed 05 Mar 2025

AI Chatbots for Educators: Transforming Online Learning in Higher Education

Irina Engeness[1](✉), Magnus Nohr[2], and Trine Fossland[3]

[1] Department of Languages, Literature and Culture, Faculty of Teacher Education and Languages, Østfold University College, Halden, Norway
irina.engeness@hiof.no

[2] Department of Education, ICT and Learning, Faculty of Teacher Education and Languages, Østfold University College, Halden, Norway

[3] Centre for Teaching, Learning and Technology, The Arctic University of Norway, Tromsø, Norway

Abstract. This study explores the experiences of pre- and in-service teachers using AI chatbots in Pedagogical Information and Communication Technology (ICTPED) Massive Open Online Course (MOOC), an online course designed to develop professional digital competence. Data was collected through an online questionnaire completed by 46 participants and follow-up interviews with eight students. The findings reveal that 52.2% of participants used chatbots to support their learning, while 47.8% did not. Participants primarily used chatbots to clarify course content, generate learning materials, and explore curriculum-related topics. Many students found chatbots to be valuable for developing conceptual understanding, providing instant feedback, and serving as brainstorming partners. Motivation for chatbot use included curiosity, ease of communication, and trust in the tool's feedback. Despite the reported benefits, some participants expressed concerns regarding the accuracy and reliability of chatbot-generated content. The study contributes to the growing body of research on AI in education by highlighting how chatbots can facilitate personalized learning experiences and self-regulated learning in online teacher education. Further research is needed to address challenges related to chatbot accuracy, over-reliance, and ethical considerations.

Keywords: AI Chatbots · Online Learning · Teacher Education

1 Introduction

The integration of chatbots in online education has emerged as a transformative approach, reshaping how learners and instructors interact with educational content [8, 10]. By leveraging artificial intelligence (AI) and natural language processing, chatbots provide instant support, personalized feedback, and interactive learning experiences. They address key challenges such as limited instructor availability and the demand for scalable educational solutions [11, 14]. As a result, AI chatbots have gained significant attention for their potential to enhance student engagement and self-directed learning in online courses.

E. Hamonic and R. Sharrock (Eds.): EMOOCS 2025, LNCS 15733, pp. 200–210, 2026.
https://doi.org/10.1007/978-3-032-00056-9_18

In massive open online courses (MOOCs), where large numbers of participants require scalable and flexible support, chatbots have proven to be particularly beneficial. They assist learners in navigating course content, answering frequently asked questions, and providing timely feedback, thereby enhancing engagement and motivation [8, 10]. Chatbots have been widely adopted in various educational contexts, from primary education to higher education and professional training. In STEM fields, chatbots offer step-by-step guidance and scaffolding tailored to students' performance levels, aiding in problem-solving and conceptual understanding [5, 6]. Similarly, in language learning, chatbots serve as conversational partners, promoting fluency, vocabulary acquisition, and self-directed learning [11, 14].

Despite their potential benefits, challenges remain in the effective use of chatbots in online education. Concerns about the accuracy and reliability of chatbot-generated content, over-reliance by students, and inclusivity issues, such as accessibility for diverse learners, have been highlighted in previous research [1, 13]. Additionally, ethical considerations related to data privacy and algorithmic biases require further exploration to ensure the responsible integration of chatbots in educational settings [1, 17].

The present study aims to explore the use of AI chatbots in the ICTPED MOOC, an online course designed to develop professional digital competence (PDC) among pre- and in-service teachers. As one of Norway's longest running and most popular MOOCs, the ICTPED course provides an ideal setting to investigate how educators engage with chatbots to support their learning. Specifically, the study examines how participants used the chatbots, their motivation for doing so, and the types of support the chatbots provided in achieving their learning goals.

By analyzing data collected from 46 participants through questionnaire and follow-up interviews with a subset of students, this study contributes to the growing body of knowledge on chatbot use in professional development settings by addressing the following research question: *How did the pre- and in-service teachers engage in learning with chatbots in the ICTPED MOOC?* The findings aim to inform future improvements in chatbot design and implementation in teacher education and professional development programs, addressing both the opportunities and challenges of AI-driven learning support.

2 Students' Use of Chatbots in Online Courses: What do We Know?

Chatbots have been widely adopted in diverse educational contexts, from primary education to higher education and professional training. In STEM fields, chatbots have been used to support problem-solving by providing step-by-step guidance and scaffolding strategies tailored to students' performance levels [5, 6]. These tools have also been employed in language learning, where they simulate conversational practice to enhance fluency and vocabulary acquisition, supporting self-directed learning in both classroom and extracurricular settings [11, 14].

The use of chatbots in online courses has shown significant benefits in fostering engagement and motivation. Studies demonstrate that immediate feedback provided by chatbots enhances learning outcomes especially in asynchronous learning environments where instructor interaction is limited [10, 12]. Massive open online courses (MOOCs), in particular, benefit from the scalability of chatbot technologies, which address learner queries and guide course navigation for thousands of participants simultaneously [8, 11, 18].

Chatbots have also been integrated into teacher education and professional development online courses. These courses, which often demand self-regulation and life-long learning skills, leverage chatbots to guide learners in setting goals, monitoring progress, and reflecting on their learning experiences [5, 9]. For instance, the "Learning Buddy" chatbot was designed to assist participants in professional development courses with setting SMART goals, fostering structured learning approaches [9]. In collaborative settings, chatbots have been shown to facilitate discussions and peer feedback, creating opportunities for professional growth among educators. In flipped learning environments, chatbots support active learning by personalizing feedback and enabling real-time interaction, which is particularly beneficial in professional development courses where participants may have diverse skill levels and goals [2, 9].

The benefits of chatbots in online courses are multifaceted. Chatbots enhance learning by providing instant, personalized feedback that reduces the need for instructor intervention [6, 10]. They also foster motivation and engagement through gamification and adaptive learning pathways, which align with learners' individual goals and preferences [5, 16]. Chatbots improve accessibility and scalability in online education, particularly in large-scale platforms like MOOCs. Their ability to function 24/7 ensures continuous support for learners, bridging gaps in instructor availability and accommodating diverse time zones [8, 11]. Furthermore, chatbots in professional development settings enable educators to engage in self-paced learning while balancing their professional responsibilities [2, 9].

Despite their potential, chatbots face several limitations that hinder their effectiveness. One key challenge is their limited contextual understanding, which can lead to inaccuracies or irrelevant responses, particularly in complex or domain-specific topics [1, 13]. This limitation is especially problematic in professional development courses, where participants expect advanced, reliable guidance which current chatbot technologies may struggle to deliver [1, 12]. Over-reliance on chatbots poses another concern, as it may reduce learners' critical thinking and problem-solving skills [5, 10]. Additionally, inclusivity issues, such as linguistic barriers and limited accessibility for participants with diverse needs, remain significant concerns [5, 11]. Ethical issues, such as data privacy and algorithmic biases, further complicate the integration of chatbots into educational systems [17]. Additionally, inclusivity challenges persist, particularly for non-native speakers and participants with diverse needs, highlighting the importance of culturally responsive and linguistically adaptive chatbot designs [11, 14].

In summary, the use of chatbots in online courses offers significant advantages, including personalized learning, enhanced engagement, and improved scalability. In teacher education and professional development, chatbots play a crucial role in fostering self-regulated learning, facilitating collaboration, and supporting lifelong learning goals. However, addressing challenges such as accuracy, over-reliance, inclusivity, and ethical concerns is essential for maximizing their potential. Therefore, more research is needed on how chatbots may assist online learning specifically in professional development courses, incorporating ethical safeguards, and exploring learning behaviors and outcomes.

3 Method

3.1 Participants and Setting

Data was collected through a questionnaire administered online to 228 pre- and in-service teachers enrolled in the ICTPED MOOC during spring semester 2024. In addition, we conducted interviews with 8 students who participated in the course.

The aim of the study was to explore the participants' learning experiences and students' use of subject-specific chatbots in the ICTPED MOOC. The questionnaire was designed to capture: (a) general information about the participants, (b) how they used the chatbots in the ICTPED MOOC and (c) how did students' interactions with chatbots contributed to achieving their learning outcomes.

The questionnaire consisted of 35 questions, employing a mix of formats, including a five-point Likert scale for quantitative measures and open-ended questions for qualitative insights. Table 1 shows the number of respondents to the questionnaire, their professional background and general evaluation of the ICTPED MOOC.

Table 1. The number of respondents to the questionnaire in 2023–24 and their general evaluation of the ICTPED MOOC

Years	Number of respondents	Male/female	Professional background	General evaluation of the ICTPED MOOC
2023–2024	46	Male = 15.7% Female = 84.3%	In-service teachers = 88% Pre-service teachers = 9% Other = 3%	Very little satisfied = 2.2% Little satisfied = 2.2% Somewhat satisfied = 6.5% Strongly satisfied = 65.2% Very strongly satisfied = 26.1%

3.2 ICTPED MOOC

The ICTPED MOOC, originally developed by researchers and development specialists at Østfold University College, was introduced in Norway in 2016. This MOOC is one of longest running and one of the most popular MOOCs in Norway. The course has an xMOOC structure, hosted on the Canvas platform, and aims to develop professional digital competence (PDC) among pre- and in-service teachers. Characterized by institutional focus, reliance on video resources, and automated assessments through quizzes, the ICTPED MOOC consists of eight modules completed over 20 weeks.

Each module begins with an introduction that includes Introduction video and textual information (accessible directly on the page) and embedded research articles, enhanced with relevant video content. Learners then engage in individual tasks and reflection questions, concluding each module with a multiple-choice quiz for summative assessment. Formative assessment is integrated in the modules in the form of small, strategically placed multiple-choice tests. Universal Design principles are embedded in the ICTPED MOOC, ensuring accessibility for all participants. Audio files are available on every webpage, and participants can also download each module in multiple formats, including audio files, podcasts, flat PDF files, or e-books. The complete list of modules in the ICTPED MOOC, along with the participants' progress plan, is provided in Table 2.

Table 2. Progress plan and the modules in the ICTPED MOOC.

Module number	Module name	Progress plan (week)
0	*Pre-course*	2
1	*ICT and learning*	3–4
2	*Digital studying techniques*	5–6
3	*Multimodal texts (examination module)*	7–9
4	*Cyber ethics*	10–11
5	*Classroom management in digital learning environments*	12–13
6	*Assessment for learning*	14–15
7	*AI in education*	16–17
8	*Flipped classroom (examination module)*	18–21

On successful completion of the ICTPEDMOOC, participants are awarded 15 European credit transfer and accumulation system (ECTS) credits.

In the final three modules, students were introduced to chatbots specifically trained on the curriculum for each module. These chatbots were created using OpenAI's technology for developing GPT models via the paid version of ChatGPT-4. To ensure accurate and subject-specific responses, the chatbots were trained using Retrieval-Augmented Generation (RAG) technology, based on the curriculum content of the respective modules. The chatbots were practically integrated into the course by being prominently displayed on the main page of each module. Students were informed about the availability and functionality of the chatbots through three instructional videos. To access the chatbots, students were required to have their own subscription to the paid version of ChatGPT.

3.3 Data and Analysis

To address the research questions in the study, the following questions were included in the questionnaire administered to the participants in the ICTPED MOOC (1) Have you used GPT/chatbots in modules 6, 7 and 8? (Participants were to provide yes/no answers) (2) How do you assess the use of the GPT/chatbots? (Applied on a five-point Likert scale.) and (3) How did you use GPT/chatbots in modules 6, 7 and 8? (Participants were to provide detailed descriptive answers.) The dataset consisted of responses from 46 participants to questions Q1, Q2 and Q3. All responses were collected anonymously and on a voluntary basis. A mixed-methods approach [7] was used to analyze the data, combining both quantitative and qualitative evidence to examine participants' engagement with the chatbots. To explore participants' learning experiences with chatbots, eight interviews were analyzed thematically [3, 4]. During the interviews the participants were asked the following questions: (4) How did you use the chatbots? (5) Why did you use the chatbots? (6) What support did the chatbots provide to you? The data were imported into NVivo 12 and coded using an inductive thematic analysis approach, meaning that no predefined categories were applied [15]. A thorough thematic analysis was conducted by the research team to identify key themes, with each sentence being carefully examined for its relevance to the subject under study.

4 Findings

4.1 Analysis of the Questionnaire

Participants' learning experiences with GPT/chatbots were analyzed by first reviewing their responses to Q1: *"Have you used GPT/chatbots in modules 6, 7, and 8?"* The results indicate that **52.2%** of participants reported using GPT/chatbots in their learning, while **47.8%** did not. In response to Q2, *"How do you assess the use of GPT/chatbots?"*, participants' feedback was distributed as follows: **0%** reported being *very little satisfied*, **0%** were *little satisfied*, **22.2%** were *somewhat satisfied*, **55.6%** were *strongly satisfied*, and **22.2%** were *very strongly satisfied*. The analysis of participants' responses to Q3, *"How did you use GPT/chatbots in modules 6, 7, and 8?"*, is presented in Table 3.

4.2 Analysis of the Interviews

In response to *Q4: How did you use the GPT/chatbots?* students reported using the chatbots to find relevant content in the curriculum, helping them navigate the material more effectively. Some students also used the chatbots to develop a deeper conceptual understanding, using the technology to clarify complex topics. In addition, several participants leveraged the chatbots to identify appropriate references from the curriculum, ensuring they were using the correct resources. The chatbots provided both brief and detailed answers, allowing students to choose the level of explanation they required. Finally, some students noted that tutorial videos generated by the chatbots were particularly helpful for enhancing their learning experience.

When asked *Q5: Why did you use the GPT/chatbots?* students provided a range of reasons reflecting their curiosity, positive experiences, and perceived benefits. Many

Table 3. Participants' Use of GPT/chatbots in ICTPED MOOC.

Theme	Explanation	Examples
Clarification and Understanding of Course Content	Many students used GPT/chatbots to verify their understanding of the material and clarify concepts they were uncertain about. This indicates that the tool served as a supplementary learning aid to reinforce comprehension	*"When I have been uncertain or needed someone to discuss my understanding with, I have asked the AI if I was thinking correctly. Of course, with a pinch of salt."*
Content Creation and Task Assistance	Several students reported using GPT/chatbots to generate content such as assignments, quizzes, and educational materials, highlighting its role in facilitating creative and instructional processes	*"It was interesting to use Chat GPT to write texts and become aware that the program is good at creating summaries, but that the information in the text can be very imprecise."*
Resource Gathering and Creating Summaries	Students utilized GPT/chatbots to gather and summarize academic resources, such as relevant literature, videos, and articles, especially when they had limited time	*"Find relevant literature for the reflection video in module 8."*
Exploration and Experimentation	Several students expressed curiosity about GPT/chatbots, exploring its capabilities as part of their learning process, especially since the topic is current and relevant	*"I have mostly used GPT related to tasks/work in module 7, but I think it has been useful to explore the possibilities since this is a current topic (and it can be a good tool when used correctly)."*

students expressed a desire to try a new tool and explore its potential in their learning process. Several participants highlighted their positive experiences with the chatbot, which motivated them to continue using it. The chatbot's ease of communication was also a significant factor, as students found it to be an accessible and convenient resource. Additionally, they recognized the chatbot as a useful tool in online courses, helping them engage with the content more effectively. Trust in the chatbot's feedback was another important reason, with students relying on it to provide relevant and reliable information. Some students even described their experience as "a new world for students," emphasizing the chatbot's transformative potential in their educational journey.

When asked *Q6: What support did the chatbots provide?* students highlighted their role as a valuable communication and brainstorming partner in the online learning environment. The chatbots offered an interactive platform where students could engage in discussions, clarify doubts, and explore ideas more effectively. By serving as a responsive and readily available resource, the chatbots helped students think through complex topics, refine their understanding, and generate new ideas. Their ability to provide instant feedback and suggestions made them a useful tool for brainstorming, allowing students to explore different perspectives and approaches within their coursework.

Overall, students found the chatbots to be a supportive companion in their learning process, enhancing their engagement and critical thinking in the online course.

5 Discussion

This study aimed to explore pre- and in-service teachers' learning experiences with AI chatbots in the ICTPED MOOC, focusing on their usage patterns, perceived benefits, and challenges. The findings align with previous research on the integration of chat-bots in online education, reinforcing their role in facilitating learning, enhancing engagement, and providing support across various educational contexts [5, 6, 11, 14].

Chatbots as Learning Facilitators: Consistent with prior studies that highlight chatbots' potential to support problem-solving and personalized learning in STEM and language education [5, 11]. Our findings demonstrate that participants used chat-bots primarily for clarification and understanding of course content. Many students reported leveraging the chatbots to verify their understanding, clarify complex concepts, and receive both brief and detailed explanations tailored to their needs. This reflects the adaptive and responsive nature of chatbots, similar to their use in STEM education, where they provide step-by-step guidance to enhance learning outcomes [6]. Additionally, chatbots were utilized as a tool for content creation and task assistance, with participants generating assignments, quizzes, and instructional materials. These findings echo research by [8], who emphasized the scalability of chatbots in MOOCs by assisting learners with course navigation and task completion. Participants also found chatbots beneficial for resource gathering and creating summaries, using them to locate relevant curriculum materials, academic references, and video content—an application that aligns with previous studies on chatbots' ability to facilitate self-directed learning [14].

Motivation and Engagement: The study findings highlight that participants were motivated to use chatbots for various reasons, including curiosity about the technology, positive past experiences, and the ease of communication offered by the tool. These findings resonate with research showing that chatbots enhance learner engagement by providing immediate feedback and promoting interactivity in online courses [10, 12]. In particular, several participants described their experience as opening "a new world for students," indicating a sense of empowerment and excitement, which aligns with previous studies emphasizing the motivational aspects of chatbots in online learning [9]. Moreover, the chatbot's perceived reliability and ac-accessibility contributed to students' trust in the tool as a valuable resource for online learning. Similar to findings by [11], who noted that chatbots improve accessibility in large-scale learning environments, participants in our study recognized the chatbots as a convenient and efficient means of obtaining support, particularly when instructor availability was limited.

Support for Self-regulated Learning: One of the key findings in this study is the chatbot's role as a communication and brainstorming partner. Participants found the chatbots to be valuable in exploring ideas, refining their understanding, and generating new insights. This aligns with previous research on chatbots' ability to foster self-regulated learning by guiding learners through goal setting, progress monitoring, and reflection [5, 9]. The ICTPED MOOC participants used chatbots to engage in reflective learning processes, confirming prior findings that these tools can act as intelligent learning companions that scaffold the learning process [2].

Challenges and Limitations: Despite the reported benefits, several challenges were identified in the participants' responses. Some students noted concerns regarding the accuracy of chatbot-generated content, aligning with existing literature that highlights chatbots' limitations in providing domain-specific, contextually accurate responses [1, 13]. This suggests the need for ongoing improvements in chatbot training to enhance content precision and minimize misleading or superficial explanations. Another key concern is the potential over-reliance on chatbots, which could impact students' critical thinking and problem-solving skills, as highlighted in previous studies [5, 10]. Some participants expressed hesitation about using chatbots extensively, indicating a preference for traditional learning methods or instructor-led guidance. These findings suggest the importance of integrating chatbots as a supplementary rather than a primary learning tool to balance independent learning with expert guidance.

6 Implications and Concluding Reflections

The results of this study suggest several practical implications for the implementation of AI chatbots in teacher education and professional development. *First,* chatbot design should prioritize subject-specific accuracy and contextual understanding to better support professional development courses, particularly in complex educational domains. *Second,* instructional strategies should emphasize the complementary role of chatbots, encouraging students to critically evaluate chatbot responses rather than passively accepting them. *Finally,* accessibility and inclusivity considerations should be integrated into chatbot design to accommodate diverse learner needs, as suggested by prior research [11, 14].

In summary, the findings of this study reinforce the potential of AI chatbots to enhance learning experiences in online teacher education and professional development programs. They provide valuable insights into how chatbots can support content under-standing, self-regulated learning, and motivation, while also highlighting areas for improvement such as accuracy, over-reliance, and inclusivity.

Future research should explore the long-term impact of chatbot use on teaching practices and investigate how different chatbot features can be optimized to meet the evolving needs of pre- and in-service teachers. Further studies should also focus on ethical considerations, including data privacy and bias, to ensure responsible AI integration in educational settings [1, 17].

Disclosure of Interests. The authors have no competing interests to declare that are relevant to the content of this article.

References

1. Aguilera-Hermida, A.P.: AI chatbots in education: the importance of accuracy. Int. Forum Teach. Stud. (2024)
2. Baskara, F.R.: Chatbots and flipped learning: enhancing student engagement and learning outcomes through personalised support and collaboration. IJORER Int. J. Recent Educ. Res. **4**(2), 223–238 (2023)
3. Braun, V., Clarke, V.: What can "thematic analysis" offer health and wellbeing researchers? Int. J. Qual. Stud. Health Well Being **9**, 26152 (2014)
4. Castleberry, A., Nolen, A.: Thematic analysis of qualitative research data: is it as easy as it sounds? Curr. Pharm. Teach. Learn. **10**(6), 807–815 (2018)
5. Chang, D.H., Lin, M.P.-C., Hajian, S., Wang, Q.Q.: Educational design principles of using AI chatbot that supports self-regulated learning in education: goal setting, feedback, and personalization. Sustainability **15**(17), 12921 (2023)
6. Cheng, L., Croteau, E., Baral, S., Heffernan, C., Heffernan, N.: Facilitating student learning with a chatbot in an online math learning platform. J. Educ. Comput. Res. **62**(4), 907–937 (2024)
7. Creswell, J.W.: Qualitative Inquiry and Research Design: Choosing Among Five Approaches. SAGE, Thousand Oaks (2012)
8. Deng, X., Yu, Z.: A meta-analysis and systematic review of the effect of chatbot technology use in sustainable education. Sustainability **15**(4), 2940 (2023)
9. Du, J., Huang, W., Hew, K.F.: Supporting students' goal-setting process using chatbot: implementation in a fully online course. In: IEEE International Conference on Engineering, Technology & Education (TALE), pp. 5–8 (2021)
10. Fidan, M., Gencel, N.: Supporting the instructional videos with chatbot and peer feedback mechanisms in online learning: the effects on learning performance and intrinsic motivation. J. Educ. Comput. Res. **60**(7), 1716–1741 (2022)
11. Han, S., Lee, M.K.: FAQ chatbot and inclusive learning in massive open online courses. Comput. Educ. **179**, 104395 (2022)
12. Hanshaw, G., Vance, J., Brewer, C.: Exploring the effectiveness of AI course assistants on the student learning experience. Open Praxis **16**(4) (2024)
13. Hellas, A., Leinonen, J., Leppänen, L.: Experiences from integrating large language model chatbots into the classroom. In: Proceedings of the 2024 ACM Virtual Global Computing Education Conference, vol. 1 (2024)
14. Jeon, J., Lee, S., Choe, H.: Beyond ChatGPT: a conceptual framework and systematic review of speech-recognition chatbots for language learning. Comput. Educ., 104898 (2023)
15. Patton, M.Q.: Qualitative Research and Methods: Integrating Theory and Practice. SAGE Publications, Thousand Oaks (2015)
16. Sáiz-Manzanares, M.C., Marticorena-Sánchez, R., Martín-Antón, L.J., Díez, I.G., Almeida, L.: Perceived satisfaction of university students with the use of chatbots as a tool for self-regulated learning. Heliyon **9**(1) (2023)
17. Song, X., et al.: Integrating AI in college education: positive yet mixed experiences with ChatGPT. Meta Radiol. **2**(4), 100113 (2024)
18. Wu, R., Yu, Z.: Do AI chatbots improve students' learning outcomes? Evidence from a meta-analysis. Br. J. Edu. Technol. **55**(1), 10–33 (2024)

Optimizing Embedding-Based Video Recommendation in Spanish Using LLMs for Automated Model and Parameter Selection

Ignacio Despujol Zabala(✉), Carlos Turró Ribalta, Jaime Busquets Mataix, and Sergio Puche García

Universitat Politècnica de València, Camino de Vera sn, 46021 Valencia, Spain
{ndespujol,busquets}@asic.upv.es, turro@cc.upv.es, spuche@upv.es

Abstract. This study investigates the automation of an embedding-based video recommendation system in Spanish through the application of Large Language Models (LLMs). The primary objective was to determine the optimal embedding model, search strategy, and chunking parameters for a system designed to deliver the top 5 most relevant videos in response to user queries. To achieve this, we developed an automated testing framework.

A dataset of 400 randomly selected videos from a pool of 50,000 was used. GPT-4 was employed to generate 10 questions per video, which were subsequently refined to remove irrelevant queries. These questions served as the basis for evaluating and comparing the performance of various models and configurations. The evaluation metric measured the percentage of instances in which the system accurately retrieved the source video within the top 1 and top 5 recommendations. This evaluation was conducted across different embedding models, search strategies, and chunking parameters.

Keywords: embeddings · recommendation system · LLM · AI model

1 Introduction

Video recommendation systems have become an integral part of modern digital platforms, enhancing user experience and driving engagement. Traditional recommendation systems often rely on collaborative filtering or content-based approaches, but these methods can be limited in their ability to capture the semantic and contextual nuances of video content, especially in question-based retrieval scenarios where users explicitly state their information needs.

1.1 Traditional Question-to-Video Recommendation Approaches

Early question-based video recommendation systems relied on simple keyword matching between user queries and video metadata. Collaborative filtering approaches, introduced by Goldberg et al. (1992), were adapted to this context by analyzing how similar users'

E. Hamonic and R. Sharrock (Eds.): EMOOCS 2025, LNCS 15733, pp. 211–221, 2026.
https://doi.org/10.1007/978-3-032-00056-9_19

queries led to similar video selections. Such systems recommended videos that were frequently watched by users who asked similar questions, regardless of the actual content's relevance to the query.

Content-based filtering, as detailed by Pazzani and Billsus (2007), found a natural application in query-based systems by matching question terms against video metadata like titles, descriptions, and tags. For instance, a query about "how to change a car tire" would trigger recommendations for videos containing these keywords in their metadata.

A fundamental approach underpinning many early question-to-video systems was the Bag-of-Words (BoW) model, described by Lewis (1998) as a simple yet effective text representation technique. In BoW, both user questions and video metadata were treated as unordered collections of words, disregarding grammar and word order. This representation allowed for straightforward similarity calculations based on term overlap. For example, a question like "How do I bake chocolate chip cookies?" would be transformed into a multiset of terms: {"how", "do", "i", "bake", "chocolate", "chip", "cookies"}, which could then be matched against similarly processed video descriptions. While computationally efficient, this approach suffered from an inability to capture word order relationships (failing to distinguish "how to train your dog" from "how your dog trains you") and semantic relationships between terms (not recognizing that "baking" and "cooking" are related concepts).

These early approaches faced significant challenges: poor handling of synonyms and paraphrases (users asking the same question in different ways), inability to understand the intent behind questions, and limited semantic matching between natural language queries and video content. Additionally, they struggled with the vocabulary mismatch problem identified by Furnas et al. (1987), when users and content creators used different terminology for the same concepts.

1.2 The Evolution Through Sparse Vector Representations

Information retrieval techniques became increasingly important as question-based video recommendation systems evolved. The Vector Space Model (Salton et al. 1975) represented both queries and video metadata as sparse vectors in a high-dimensional term space, enabling similarity calculations to rank videos by relevance to the query.

Term Frequency-Inverse Document Frequency (TF-IDF), introduced by Salton and McGill (1983), improved keyword matching by weighting terms based on their specificity. In question-based video retrieval, this meant that unique terms in a user's question (e.g., "carburetor" in an auto repair question) would carry more weight than common terms (e.g., "how" or "to").

Extending the basic Bag-of-Words approach, N-gram models (Cavnar & Trenkle 1994) incorporated some word order information by considering sequences of N adjacent words. This allowed systems to distinguish between phrases like "White House" (as a single concept) and the separate words "white" and "house". When applied to question-based video retrieval, N-gram models enabled more precise matching between query phrases and video content, particularly for questions containing distinct multi-word concepts or technical terminology. For example, a bi-gram representation of "how to make sourdough bread" would capture phrases like "sourdough bread" as distinct units, improving matches to relevant baking videos.

Latent Semantic Analysis (LSA/LSI) by Deerwester et al. (1990) helped address the synonymy problem by projecting queries and video descriptions into a lower-dimensional semantic space. This allowed systems to recognize that a question about "automobile maintenance" might match videos tagged with "car repair" even without exact keyword matches.

Query expansion techniques, surveyed by Carpineto and Romano (2012), were employed to augment user questions with related terms, addressing vocabulary mismatch issues. For instance, a query about "DSLR photography tips" might be expanded to include "camera," "lens," or "aperture" to better match relevant instructional videos.

While these sparse vector approaches improved question-to-video matching, they still struggled with understanding the semantic intent behind queries and the rich multimodal content of videos. Their inability to capture deeper question meaning and contextual nuances limited recommendation quality, especially for complex or ambiguous queries.

1.3 The Embedding Revolution in Question-Based Video Recommendation

The introduction of dense word embeddings revolutionized question-based video recommendation systems. Word2Vec, introduced by Mikolov et al. (2013a, 2013b), enabled systems to represent both user questions and video transcriptions in a continuous vector space that preserved semantic relationships in the vector values. This allowed for more nuanced matching between queries and videos, even with few exact keywords in common.

GloVe (Global Vectors), developed by Pennington et al. (2014), further improved semantic representations by analyzing global co-occurrence statistics. These embedding approaches enabled question-based systems to understand that a query about "beginner yoga poses" semantically relates to videos about "simple stretches for yoga newcomers" without relying on exact term matches.

The embedding revolution progressed further with sentence and document-level representations. Skip-Thought Vectors (Kiros et al. 2015) and later models like Universal Sentence Encoder (Cer et al. 2018) enabled encoding entire questions as dense vectors, capturing question meaning holistically rather than as a bag of words.

Transformative advancements came with the introduction of BERT (Bidirectional Encoder Representations from Transformers) by Devlin et al. (2019) and similar contextual embedding models. These approaches recognize that questions have context-dependent meanings and can capture nuances like:

Question Intent Classification: Distinguishing between informational questions ("How do solar panels work?"), instructional queries ("How to install solar panels"), and opinion-seeking questions ("Are solar panels worth the investment?").

Entity and Relationship Understanding: Recognizing entities in questions and their relationships, enabling better matching to relevant videos.

Context-Dependent Term Understanding: Capturing that "python" in a question about programming differs from "python" in a wildlife query.

Modern question-based video recommendation systems leverage these embedding technologies alongside specialized components:

Question understanding modules that parse user queries to extract intent, entities, and implicit information needs.
Cross-modal embeddings that represent both textual queries and video content (including visual features, audio, and transcripts) in a shared vector space, enabling direct relevance matching as described by Wang et al. (2018).
Transformer-based architectures like CLIP (Radford et al. 2021) that align natural language and visual content, allowing systems to match questions directly to visual concepts in videos.
Attention mechanisms that focus on the most relevant aspects of videos given a specific question, as demonstrated by Lei et al. (2020) in their moment-based retrieval system.

The most advanced question-based video recommendation systems now employ dense retrievers and re-rankers. First, efficient approximate nearest neighbor search finds candidate videos with embeddings similar to the question embedding. Then, more compute-intensive transformer models re-rank these candidates by deeply analyzing the relevance between the question and each video's content.

This evolution from simple keyword matching to sophisticated embedding-based semantic understanding has dramatically improved the ability of systems to recommend truly relevant videos in response to user questions. Modern systems can understand the intent behind questions, match them to appropriate content regardless of terminology differences, and even identify the most relevant moments within videos that address specific questions.

2 The Project

Our university has 53,000 public videos in its media system, a third of which are uploaded to its channel on YouTube. All these videos have automatically created video transcriptions (some of them with manual corrections) that can be transformed into embeddings and uploaded to a vector database.

We want to create a video recommendation service based on the user's questions that answers with links to the most related videos to a question based on the video transcriptions.

As we have seen, embedding-based approaches have emerged as a powerful alternative to capture the semantics of different texts and, by measuring the similarity between video transcription embeddings and user queries, deliver more accurate and relevant recommendations.

As video transcription texts can be very long, a technique called chunking is used. Chunking is a technique used to divide the transcriptions of videos into smaller segments, so the embeddings to be compared with the questions are shorter segments, enabling more fine-grained analysis and recommendation. Different chunking strategies, such as fixed-length chunking and sentence-based chunking, have been explored in the literature. Chunking is often enhanced by using chunk overlap, a technique that makes consecutive chunks have words in common, which increases the size of the vector database but captures better the content of related words.

The effectiveness of embedding-based systems relies on the choice of embedding model, search strategy, and chunking parameters. Furthermore, most of our video content is in Spanish and most of the questions will be in that language, and most embedding generation models available are tuned to work better in English.

So, selecting the best combination of searching strategy, embedding model and chunking parameters can make a big difference in the results obtained.

2.1 Using Large Language Models to Automate the Parameter Optimization

Large Language Models (LLMs) have demonstrated very good capabilities in natural language processing tasks, including text generation, translation, and question answering. Our theory is that, by leveraging LLMs, it is possible to automate the generation of diverse and relevant queries to compare different configuration parameters, thereby improving the quality of the video recommendation system.

3 Methodology

3.1 Research Questions

This study analyzes the feasibility of automating the evaluation of embedding-based video recommendation systems in Spanish by employing LLMs to generate a comprehensive set of queries and systematically testing different model configurations to identify the optimal parameters for delivering accurate video recommendations.

The research questions of this study are:

Q1: How much can the use of an automated system based in LLM generated questions improve the performance of a video recommendation system?
Q2: Which are the best configuration, model and parameters for a video recommendation system for educational videos in Spanish based in user's questions?
Q3: Can we achieve similar results using open source embedding models to the ones obtained with state-of-the-art paid models?

3.2 Procedure

370 videos from the collection were randomly selected, and their transcriptions were uploaded to a database.

These transcriptions were uploaded to ChatGPT-4 with the following prompt: "Generate 10 short-answer questions and their answers based on the text provided below. Return the result in CSV format, with the fields 'question', 'answer', 'video_code'. The questions must include all the necessary context to be understood without having access to the text. The text is:" and the transcription text.

The 3,700 generated questions were stored in the database to be used for the evaluation of different configurations of the retrieval system. The idea is to enter the questions in the retrieval system and see which videos are recommended, comparing the aggregated accuracy of the system in giving back the video from which the question was created.

For a specific configuration of the system and a parameter k (number of retrieved matching embeddings in order), the metrics calculated in the first version of the system were: embed generation time in seconds, retrieval time in seconds to process the 3,700 questions, percentage of cases in which the embedding appearing in the first position matched the correct video, percentage of cases in which the majority of the k embeddings corresponded to the correct video and percentage of cases in which any of the k embeddings corresponded to the correct video.

To have a figure for benchmarking the quality of the retrieval system with embeddings, a Python script was developed to do the same procedure using the BM25 algorithm. BM25 (Best Matching 25) is a ranking function widely used in information retrieval (IR) systems, such as search engines, to rank documents based on their relevance to a given query. It belongs to the family of probabilistic retrieval models and is based on the Bag of Words (BoW) representation. BM25 is an improvement over the older TF-IDF (Term Frequency-Inverse Document Frequency) model. This BM25 recommender gave only one answer that corresponded to the correct video for 67.38% of the question bank.

The next step was to select several embedding models to be evaluated. For this we used an open source embedding models leaderboard table available in the Hugging Face website (now available in https://huggingface.co/spaces/mteb/leaderboard_legacy). We selected the Retrieval category and selected several of the multilingual models that performed well with French and Polish languages.

Another Python script using LangChain library was created to calculate the different metrics with several embedding models, different chunking strategies, chunking sizes and overlaps and create with them a local vector database using FAISS. After creating the embeddings of the 3,700 questions and querying the vector database to see which videos were returned for a query, we compared the accuracy of the systems with the different metrics.

After a first evaluation round with fixed parameters (a chunk size of 1000, an overlap of 100 and recursive as the LangChain chunking strategy), we decided to evaluate BAAI/bge-m3 and intfloat/multilingual-e5 (small/base/large) (discarding Jina-embeddings and gte Qwen-2, that gave similar but slightly worse results) and hkunlp/instructor (base/large/xl) as open source models, and the best available embedding model available then from OpenAI, text-embedding-3-large.

Of the different chunking strategies that LangChain offers: fixed chunk size, semantic (in which the text is split at known sentence separating characters) and recursive (in which paragraphs and sentences are split recursively using separating characters -that can be chosen- until the chunk size is met), we decided to incorporate semantic chunking and two recursive strategies with splitting characters in different order.

In the next round we created a metric that added all the inverse distances of the embeddings corresponding to the same video with a weighting depending on their order in the k values, but the improvement in the accuracy was rendered insignificant by the use of rerankers in the next phase.

Later we incorporated a two-stage retrieval model using a reranker model. The system retrieves a higher number of embeddings in the first stage (higher k) and feeds the text associated with them to the reranker model in a second stage, that is slower but more accurate and gives a better result. The k value has to be chosen in a way that the retrieving time is within acceptable values. After trying several reranker models, we chose BAAI/reranker-v2-m3. This led to a significant improvement in the accuracy of the first result and let us add another improvement, mixing the results of the first stage with the results of a traditional BM25 ranker in a small proportion of 10% or less before feeding the documents to the reranker, so, if a question is more keyword based, the results improve.

In a later round we tried to improve the results by changing the library used for chunking to Llama2 and using its chunking strategies, "SimpleNodeParser", "TokenTextSplitter", "SemanticSplitterNodeParser" and "SentenceWindowNodeParser" but we got no improvement over the best results obtained with LangChain splitters. We also created a chunker with GPT-4 using the OpenAI API, but it was slower and didn't get better results than the best LangChain splitter either.

4 Results

4.1 Initial Phase

After selecting the embedding models and the ranges of the parameters to be tested (50, 100 to 800 with 100 spacing, 1000, 1600, 3000, 3200 and 5000), the overlap (0, 10, 20, 40, 50, 80, 90, 99, 100, 160, 180, 200, 250, 275, 300, 320, 350, 370, 375, 390, 450, 490, 500, 550, 590, 640, 650, 690, 700, 750, 790, 975, 1500), the k values (from 2 to 10, 15, 20, 30, 50) and 3 chunking strategies (semantic, recursive 1, recursive 2), we ran 2791 combinations and obtained the following results (Table 1).

Table 1. Initial accuracy by model.

Model	Accuracy of first result	Accuracy with "Most frequent in k" metric	Average retrieval time all questions
text-embedding-3-large (OpenAI paid)	77.94% (max) 74.24% (avg)	78.1% (max) 71.65% (avg)	2,042 sg
BAAI/bge-m3 (open source)	73.33% (max) 69.21% (avg)	73.7% (max) 64.78% (avg)	90 sg
intfloat/multilingual-e5-large (open source)	Similar to BAAI/bge-m3	Similar to BAAI/bge-m3	90 sg

The average retrieval time for all the questions with text-embedding-3-large is more than an order of magnitude over the time that the other models take (Table 2).

The other models get worse results, so they are discarded.

Table 2. Correct video among first k results

Model	k = 3	k = 5
text-embedding-3-large (OpenAI paid)	88.38%	92.6%
BAAI/bge-m3 (open source)	86.50%	91.30%
intfloat/multilingual-e5-large (open source)	86.50%	91.30%

The **optimal parameters for text-embedding-3-large are chunk_size = 600, overlap = 590, chunk strategy = recursive and the retrieval time = 2099** s. With these parameters the k = 3 percentage is 81.9%, not the best result for this metric.

The **optimal parameters for BAAI/bge-m3 are chunk_size = 400, overlap = 390, chunk strategy = recursive and the retrieval time = 73.33 s.** With these parameters the k = 3 percentage is 79.34%, not the best result for this metric.

The conclusions from this phase were that we were going to try to optimize the parameters for BAAI/bge-m3 to see if we could achieve or go over the performance of the OpenAI paid model. The improvements obtained by using the aggregated % metric instead of the first result are marginal, so this metric was discarded as the main metric to evaluate the system.

The time the OpenAI model takes is not practical for a production system, but, as the idea was to try to use the open-source models, no effort will be made to optimize it.

The overlap of the best solutions was very high, so the size of the embeddings database was incorporated to the metrics to control if it grew too much and to see if something could be done to make it smaller.

4.2 Reranker

The later trials, made to create a new metric that improved the results of the system by adding the different embedding corresponding to the same video, were discarded when the reranker approach was adopted, as it gave better results, so they are not commented.

A new parameter was introduced, the % of BM25 results fed to the reranker, and a new metric was created, the size of the embeddings database (as stated before).

132 different combinations were tried with the BAAI/bge-m3 model and the BAAI/bge-reranker-v2-m3, trying with k = 10, 20 and 50 and the best accuracy for the first result was up to 82.81% with 0% of BM25 results, chunk_size = 1300, overlap = 800, chunk strategy = recursive and k = 50 (with the reranker k becomes a parameter, as it increases the accuracy of the second stage and the retrieval time), but the retrieval time went up also to 882.44 s.

Selecting k = 10, 0% of BM25 results, chunk_size = 1300 and overlap = 800, the results are a little worse (81.9%), but the retrieval time goes down to 309.12 s and the embedding database size is 20.32 MB instead of 26.96 MB.

So, for the reranker a k value of 10 was selected as a compromise between accuracy and retrieval time.

The conclusion of this phase is that with a reranker the accuracy of the system improves significantly even with an open-source model and that retrieval times can be kept reasonable.

4.3 Optimizing Chunking Strategy

100 more trials were made trying to optimize the chunking strategy, testing the chunkers of the Llama 2 library and creating a chunker with GPT-4. None of them was better than the recursive or recursive2 strategies of LangChain.

A 5% of the results fed to the reranker came from BM25, as in keyword oriented queries it can improve very much the query result and the performance penalty in other situations is very low. The final results are listed below (Table 3).

Table 3. Final performance figures.

Accuracy (1st response)	82.23%
Accuracy (top 3 responses)	90.35%
Accuracy (top 5 responses)	93.32%
Retrieval time all questions	297.73 s
Database size (317 videos)	20.37 MB

Using SimpleNodeParser from Llama with chunk size = 1500, overlap = 800 and the same amount of BM25, is a little less accurate (81.84%), is a little bit slower (391.91 s) and creates a smaller video database of 15.85 MB.

5 Conclusions and Future Work

We have created a recommendation system using embeddings and improved its accuracy, from 77% with a paid embeddings model to 81% with a free one.

We have created a system that automates the tuning of the parameters of a system that can be used by any institution of online learning.

The best configuration for the BAAI/bge-m3 model is chunk_size = 1500, overlap = 800, chunk strategy = recursive, k = 10, BM25 = 5%.

For the future we have to extend the system to support 50,000 videos instead of 400, and several simultaneous users, so we have to move it to a system that can scale. Taking this into account, and after conducting research on what is available on the internet, we installed a Milvus server to store all the encodings.

The problem is that, for large amounts of embeddings, a simple index approach used is not fast enough, so we will have to choose from one of the index alternatives that Milvus provides, as search strategies play a crucial role in efficiently retrieving relevant videos from large-scale databases. Approximate Nearest Neighbor (ANN) search algorithms, such as HNSW and FAISS, are commonly used to accelerate the search process. However, the performance of these algorithms can be influenced by factors like index size, query volume, and desired accuracy.

References

Carpineto, C., Romano, G.: A survey of automatic query expansion in information retrieval. ACM Comput. Surv. **44**(1), 1–50 (2012)

Cavnar, W.B., Trenkle, J.M.: N-gram-based text categorization. In: Proceedings of SDAIR-94, 3rd Annual Symposium on Document Analysis and Information Retrieval (1994)

Cer, D., et al.: Universal sentence encoder. arXiv:1803.11175 (2018)

Devlin, J., Chang, M.W., Lee, K., Toutanova, K.: BERT: PRE-training of deep bidirectional transformers for language understanding. In: Proceedings of NAACL-HLT 2019 (2019)

Deerwester, S., Dumais, S.T., Furnas, G.W., Landauer, T.K., Harshman, R.: Indexing by latent semantic analysis. J. Am. Soc. Inf. Sci. **41**(6), 391–407 (1990)

Furnas, G.W., Landauer, T.K., Gomez, L.M., Dumais, S.T.: The vocabulary problem in human-system communication. Commun. ACM **30**(11), 964–971 (1987)

Goldberg, D., Nichols, D., Oki, B.M., Terry, D.: Using collaborative filtering to weave an information tapestry. Commun. ACM **35**(12), 61–70 (1992)

Kiros, R., et al.: Skip-thought vectors. In: Advances in Neural Information Processing Systems, 28 (2015)

Lei, J., Wang, L., Shen, Y., Yu, D., Berg, T.L., Bansal, M.: MART: memory-augmented recurrent transformer for coherent video paragraph captioning. In: Proceedings of ACL 2020 (2020)

Lewis, D.D.: Naive (Bayes) at forty: the independence assumption in information retrieval. In: Nédellec, C., Rouveirol, C. (eds.) ECML 1998. LNCS, vol. 1398, pp. 4–15. Springer, Heidelberg (1998). https://doi.org/10.1007/BFb0026666

Mikolov, T., Chen, K., Corrado, G., Dean, J.: Efficient estimation of word representations in vector space. arXiv preprint arXiv:1301.3781 (2013a)

Mikolov, T., Sutskever, I., Chen, K., Corrado, G., Dean, J.: Distributed representations of words and phrases and their compositionality. In: Advances in Neural Information Processing Systems, 26 (2013b)

Pazzani, M.J., Billsus, D.: Content-based recommendation systems. In: Brusilovsky, P., Kobsa, A., Nejdl, W. (eds.) The Adaptive Web. LNCS, vol. 4321, pp. 325–341. Springer, Heidelberg (2007). https://doi.org/10.1007/978-3-540-72079-9_10

Pennington, J., Socher, R., Manning, C.: GloVe: global vectors for word representation. In: Proceedings of EMNLP 2014 (2014)

Radford, A., et al.: Learning transferable visual models from natural language supervision. In: Proceedings of ICML 2021 (2021)

Salton, G., McGill, M.J.: Introduction to Modern Information Retrieval. McGraw-Hill (1983)

Salton, G., Wong, A., Yang, C.S.: A vector space model for automatic indexing. Commun. ACM **18**(11), 613–620 (1975)

Wang, X., Wu, J., Zhang, D., Su, Y., Wang, W.Y.: Learning to compose topic-aware mixture of experts for zero-shot video captioning. In: Proceedings of AAAI 2018 (2019)

The AIBook as a New Frontier in Conversational Learning Through a MOOC: A Case Study

Susanna Sancassani and Daniela Casiraghi(✉)

Politecnico di Milano, P.zza Leonardo da Vinci 32, 20133 Milano, Italy
{susanna.sancassani,daniela.casiraghi}@polimi.it

Abstract. In today's digital era, the development of an innovative AIbook - a digital, multimodal, and conversational text - redefines content delivery and learner engagement. Unlike traditional courses where videos and static texts are the main components, the AIbook serves as the privileged entry point to knowledge, supporting students as they perform exercises and navigate complex learning paths. More than a digital textbook, it constitutes a coherent and cohesive unit of communication that fosters continuous learning in an era when emerging technologies are reshaping educational paradigms. The MOOC "Imparare con l'IA" (Learning with AI), published in February 2025 on the *Edvance* platform as part of Italy's first digital education hub for higher education dedicated to advanced digital culture, exemplifies this transformation by centering its design on AI enrichment and fostering a dialogic relationship between the learner and the content.

Keywords: AIBook · Artificial Intelligence · New educational paradigms

1 Introduction

Generative artificial intelligence (GenAI) is profoundly reshaping our relationship with knowledge, revolutionizing traditional paradigms of information access, creation, and dissemination. This transformation is not only technological but also deeply epistemological, influencing how knowledge is organized, explored, and engaged with. Emerging formats such as "Perplexity Pages" provided by Perplexity AI [1], and the "Notebooks" provided by NotebookLM [2], exemplify this evolution, shifting from static, linear structures towards dynamic, conversational, and multimodal frameworks.

Together, these new tools and methodologies underscore a broader cultural and educational shift towards personalized, interactive, and multimodal learning experiences, significantly transforming the landscape of knowledge engagement and setting the stage for inclusive and democratized learning ecosystems.

Central among these innovative forms is the AIbook, which represents an advanced evolution from traditional books and e-books. Unlike conventional texts, an AIbook is not merely digital; it embodies a coherent and cohesive conversational logic, leveraging generative AI to dynamically interact with users through multimodal contents.

E. Hamonic and R. Sharrock (Eds.): EMOOCS 2025, LNCS 15733, pp. 222–231, 2026.
https://doi.org/10.1007/978-3-032-00056-9_20

2 From Book to eBook to AIBook: The Evolution of Knowledge Interaction

The transition from traditional printed books to digital formats such as eBooks and subsequently AIbooks represents not only a technological evolution but also a profound shift in cognitive patterns and knowledge interactions.

Historically, the printed book fundamentally altered human cognition, enabling the widespread dissemination of knowledge and fostering new forms of literacy. Marshall McLuhan, in his seminal work The Gutenberg Galaxy (1962) [3], argued that the advent of print technology significantly influenced human thinking, promoting linear, sequential, and analytical cognition. The structured format of printed texts facilitated deeper individual reflection, intensive reading, and the development of critical thinking skills, profoundly shaping modern intellectual traditions and societal structures.

With the emergence of eBooks, this paradigm of knowledge interaction underwent another significant transformation. Digital texts dramatically enhanced portability, allowing readers immediate access to vast libraries via electronic devices. Additionally, eBooks introduced dynamic capabilities such as hyperlinks, multimedia integration, and interactive elements, reshaping reading behaviors and promoting non-linear navigation through content. However, this transition has not been entirely seamless. Research indicates distinct cognitive implications for digital reading: while accessibility and flexibility have increased, studies by Mangen et al. (2013) [4], and Baron (2015) [5], have demonstrated that digital reading might affect deep comprehension, information retention, and sustained attention differently compared to print media. The hyperlinked, non-linear nature of digital texts can encourage scanning rather than intensive reading, potentially reducing the ability to deeply assimilate and critically reflect on content.

Today, generative AI technologies further evolve these paradigms through the concept of the AIbook. The AIbook surpasses the limitations inherent in both traditional books and eBooks, introducing dynamic, interactive, and conversational dimensions that leverage multimodal AI capabilities. An AIbook is an innovative medium leveraging artificial intelligence that redefines traditional concepts of textuality by introducing conversational, multimodal, and interactive dimensions. Unlike conventional books, an AIbook preserves coherence and internal consistency, maintaining the core qualities of a structured text, yet it transcends the limitations of linear and static information delivery. It dynamically interacts with readers through dialogues, responding adaptively to user inquiries, inputs, and learning behaviors. By integrating various media, such as text, audio, visual elements, and interactive content, the AIbook facilitates a richer, more immersive engagement with knowledge.

In this paradigm, coherence is achieved not simply through linguistic continuity, but through intelligent interactions that adapt to the user's learning path. This enables readers to explore content through conversational exchanges, where the AI actively supports knowledge construction and practical application of concepts. Thus, the evolution from books to eBooks, and now to AIbooks, signifies a deeper epistemological transformation, reshaping how knowledge is organized, navigated, and internalized. These changes underscore a broader historical trend towards personalization, interaction, and adaptability in learning environments, heralding a new paradigm for intellectual engagement in the digital age.

2.1 The "Author's Function" in the AIBook

Historically, the notion of the author has undergone profound transformations, shaped by cultural, philosophical, and technological shifts. In classical antiquity, authorship was closely associated with authority and rhetorical tradition, emphasizing the author's role as both creator and guarantor of textual meaning (Woodmansee, 1994) [6].

During the medieval period, anonymity was common, and texts frequently emerged as collective or collaborative creations, challenging the modern conception of individual authorship (Chartier, 1994) [7]. The Renaissance marked a pivotal transition towards individual recognition, paralleling the emergence of print culture and intellectual property rights, which gradually solidified the author's identity as an independent and authoritative figure responsible for textual authenticity (Eisenstein, 1979) [8]. Building upon these historical foundations, modern theories have critically reconsidered authorship. Michel Foucault (1969) [9] notably introduced the "author function" framing the author as a discursive construct contingent on socio-cultural and historical conditions, rather than a mere individual who creates a text. Similarly, Roland Barthes argued in his seminal essay "The Death of the Author" (1967) [10] for a paradigm shift away from the author as the definitive source of meaning toward the reader's active role in textual interpretation. This conceptual evolution profoundly influenced contemporary literary theory and pedagogy, positioning readers, and learners, as co-creators actively engaged in meaning-making processes.

Starting on these premises the AIbook fundamentally redefines the traditional notion of authorship by introducing the concept of a creator, whose role transcends conventional content production. Unlike an author, whose primary function historically involved generating and presenting fixed textual material, the creator of an AIbook designs both the content itself and the intricate system of rules and interactions that govern the AI at the core of the platform. This role requires the creator to strategically construct an adaptive learning ecosystem that continuously evolves based on user interactions. In this model, users shift from being passive consumers of predetermined knowledge to active participants, co-constructing their own personalized learning pathways through dynamic dialogue and engagement. The AI system, guided by the rules established by the creator, adapts in real-time, responding to user inputs, questions, and exploration patterns, thereby creating a highly individualized learning experience. This paradigm fundamentally redefines the traditional notion of textual authorship, emphasizing collaboration, personalization, and continuous interactivity, and reflects a broader transformation in educational practices toward more fluid, responsive, and participatory forms of knowledge engagement.

2.2 The Bibliography Function: Toward the Rigzomion

Extending the concept of the "author function" beyond its original literary boundaries, it becomes evident that other textual apparatuses, such as the index and the bibliography, also function as authoritative constructs guiding reader engagement and interpretation.

Just as the author's function organizes discourse and shapes textual meaning (Foucault, 1969), these auxiliary structures similarly dictate how knowledge within a book is navigated and legitimized. For instance, the traditional index, by imposing a predetermined framework, directs the reader's interaction, implicitly prioritizing specific concepts and connections (Genette, 1997) [11]. Likewise, the bibliography serves as a validation apparatus, reinforcing scholarly authority and delimiting interpretative pathways through explicit referencing practices (Bazerman, 1988) [12]. In contrast, contemporary digital innovations such as the AIbook challenge these traditional authorial apparatuses by introducing dynamically regenerating indices, such as the "Indaginarium," and rhizomatic bibliographic structures, exemplified by the "Rigzomion," which disrupt linear knowledge hierarchies and promote more personalized and exploratory forms of reader interaction (Deleuze & Guattari, 1987 [13]; Sancassani et al., 2023 [14]). Thus, transforming these textual components significantly alters the conventional authorial relationship, shifting the locus of authority toward reader-generated exploration and interpretation.

Gilles Deleuze and Félix Guattari's concept of rhizomatic knowledge, presented in their influential work A Thousand Plateaus (1987), offers a radical departure from traditional, hierarchical conceptions of knowledge. Using the botanical metaphor of the rhizome, a root system that expands horizontally without a central structure, they argue that knowledge does not develop in linear, structured patterns, like the branches of a tree, but rather emerges through an interconnected network of paths that expand endlessly in multiple directions.

Central to rhizomatic thinking are several key characteristics. First is connection and heterogeneity, the principle that any point within a rhizome can be connected to any other, irrespective of order or hierarchy. Second, multiplicity emphasizes that rhizomes are inherently complex, consisting of numerous, irreducible dimensions and meanings that resist simplistic reduction. Third, the concept of signifying rupture highlights the adaptability and resilience of rhizomatic structures, suggesting that even if one connection is disrupted, new ones immediately form elsewhere. Finally, Deleuze and Guattari introduce the notion of cartography and decalcomania, contrasting the openness of rhizomatic maps, which continually evolve, with static reproductions of established structures or "tracings."

Applied to educational contexts, rhizomatic knowledge proposes a learning environment in which knowledge creation is dynamic, learner-driven, and open-ended. Rather than following predetermined paths, learners are encouraged to explore, connect, and reconfigure knowledge in response to their interests and contexts. This pedagogical approach, termed rhizomatic learning, fosters creativity, autonomy, critical thinking, and adaptability, skills that are essential for navigating the complexities and interconnectedness of contemporary society.

The concept of the Rigzomion, a term derived from the fusion of "rigging" and "rhizome", represents an innovative evolution in how bibliographies function within AIbooks, transitioning from traditional linear listings to dynamic, interconnected frameworks. The term "rigging" refers metaphorically to the flexible, yet structured skeletal system used in 3D animation to give shape and control movement, while "rhizome," as conceptualized by Deleuze and Guattari (1987), describes knowledge as a non-linear, decentralized network of interconnected nodes. In conventional books, bibliographies serve as static compilations of sources selected by authors, guiding readers through fixed pathways of verification and further exploration. Conversely, within the AIbook environment, the Rigzomion functions as a rhizomatic apparatus integrating both content and operational rules, dynamically organizing knowledge through multiple, horizontal, and adaptive connections. This hybrid structure not only catalogs the diverse sources used for training the AIbook but also actively incorporates creator-defined flexible rules, continuously shaping user interactions and supporting personalized, exploratory, and self-directed learning experiences.

2.3 The "Index Function": The Indaginarium

The concept of the index has a long and intricate history, deeply intertwined with the evolution of books, reading practices, and knowledge management itself. Historically, indexes appeared as essential textual apparatuses designed to guide readers through complex or extensive materials, assisting them in locating specific information quickly and effectively. The earliest known indexes date back to classical antiquity: detailed indices were found accompanying scrolls and codices, particularly to support scholars in navigating extensive philosophical, legal, and religious works (Blair, 2010) [15]. However, these initial indexes were often rudimentary, consisting merely of ordered lists or outlines of topics rather than detailed alphabetical guides.

With the rise of manuscript culture in medieval Europe, indexing practices began to mature significantly. The expansion of universities and scholarly networks prompted a more structured approach to textual organization. Notably, medieval theologians and legal scholars developed sophisticated indexing methods, driven by the necessity to consult authoritative texts efficiently (Rouse & Rouse, 1979) [16]. These indices often employed thematic and hierarchical structures, reflecting a scholastic worldview that emphasized orderly categorization.

The invention of the printing press in the fifteenth century by Johannes Gutenberg amplified the complexity, accessibility, and importance of indexes. Printing technology made books more widespread, accessible, and numerous, and the index rapidly evolved from an optional scholarly convenience into an indispensable navigation tool (Eisenstein, 1979). Publishers recognized the practical and commercial advantages of thorough indexing, especially as printed volumes became more extensive and knowledge increasingly specialized.

During the Enlightenment and into the 19th century, the index solidified its role as a standardized and professionalized component of scholarly texts. Publishers employed specialized indexers who meticulously categorized content into precise alphabetical or thematic arrangements, reflecting a growing emphasis on clarity, accessibility, and efficiency. By the 20th century, indexing had become integral to virtually every genre of academic publication, reflecting not only the professionalization of knowledge management but also an increasingly pragmatic and user-centered approach to reading.

However, while traditional indexes provided substantial support in navigating fixed textual landscapes, they inherently embodied certain limitations: they reinforced linear reading patterns, imposed hierarchical structuring, and confined readers within predefined intellectual frameworks. In a sense, traditional indexing practices solidified the authority of the author, who dictated the primary pathways readers might follow to interpret the text.

Historically, the fundamental purpose of an index has been to facilitate the penetration of knowledge by enabling quick, efficient consultation of complex textual content. As an essential apparatus, the index serves readers by simplifying access, organizing vast information into clearly structured pathways, and making it manageable and navigable. By systematically categorizing and referencing key terms, concepts, and sections, traditional indexes enhance the usability of texts, empowering readers to locate specific information with precision and speed.

In recent times, digital technology and artificial intelligence have significantly disrupted this conventional practice, leading to innovative models of textual navigation and exploration.

In the AIBook the "index function "evolves in the Indaginarium. The term "Indaginarium" derives from the Latin "indagare," meaning "to explore" or "to inquire thoroughly." Unlike traditional static indexes, the Indaginarium functions dynamically, continuously regenerating and reorganizing itself in response to user interactions and evolving content.

Rooted conceptually in the rhizomatic philosophy of Deleuze and Guattari (1987), the Indaginarium replaces linearity and fixed categories with a fluid and adaptive model of knowledge exploration. Rather than presenting knowledge in hierarchical, author-centric categories, it employs fundamental, regenerating questions that serve as entry points into a complex, interconnected network of ideas. Each interaction between learner and text reshapes the scope and nature of subsequent inquiries, ensuring personalized and exploratory learning experiences.

The Indaginarium thus shifts the index's function from one of mere reference towards a conversational tool—one that interacts directly and iteratively with the reader. Knowledge no longer appears as static and authoritative; instead, it becomes responsive and negotiable. Learners, interacting dynamically with the AI-driven content, play an active role in constructing knowledge pathways, significantly diminishing traditional authorial control and fostering a learner-centered educational environment.

3 The AIbook "Learning with AI" as a Dynamic Learning Ecosystem: The Relationship Among Content, Smart Learning Design Methodology, and Conversational Strategies

The AIbook implemented in the Massive Open Online Course (MOOC) *"Learning with AI"* exemplifies a transformative approach to digital education, redefining interaction through a dynamic, conversational, and multimodal structure. Built upon the principles of Smart Learning Design (SLD) methodology (Sancassani et al., 2023), the AIbook moves beyond traditional static formats, guiding learners through progressive and non-linear learning events that leverage artificial intelligence.

Central to this innovative educational architecture is the Rigzomion created as a digital interactive space on Miro. This visual and hypertextual mapping connects various educational resources, support tools, and metacognitive strategies, linking them continuously to other digital materials. The Rigzomion expands dynamically, being regularly updated and enriched as new connections and insights emerge.

This structure aligns with the key learning events in the SLD model, which include:

- Exploration: Learners encounter new information, supported by AI in navigating reliable sources and clear conceptual structures.
- Elaboration: AI facilitates content synthesis and organization through mapping tools, glossaries, and conceptual comparison strategies.
- Application: The AIbook assists users in the practical application of knowledge, providing personalized support for exercises, simulations, and experiential activities.
- Discussion: AI-driven interaction fosters critical thinking, argument construction, and dialectical engagement with key concepts.
- Production: Active content generation is supported through iterative feedback and synthesis tools, enabling learners to refine their work.
- Consolidation and Metacognition: The AIbook promotes reflection on acquired skills through retrieval practice and continuous monitoring of the learning process.

Complementing the Rigzomion is the Indaginarium, an adaptive system of fundamental, dynamically regenerating questions related to the different learning events of the learning process, as described in the SLD methodology. It stimulates conversational learning interactions, continuously reshaping user pathways and fostering deeper engagement. By following the principles of Smart Learning Design and Biggs' Constructive Alignment (Biggs, 1996) [17], the AIbook ensures coherence between learning objectives, activities, and assessment, thus enhancing the practical transferability of knowledge.

The AIbook implemented in the MOOC *Learning with AI* exemplifies a transformative approach to digital education, redefining interaction through a dynamic, conversational, and multimodal structure. Built upon the principles of Smart Learning Design (SLD), the AIbook moves beyond traditional static formats, guiding learners through progressive and non-linear learning events that leverage artificial intelligence. Ultimately, this innovative medium positions learner as active participants who co-construct knowledge, driving learning beyond mere content consumption towards sustained and reflective engagement.

4 The Integration with the MOOC "Learning with AI"

The integration of the AIbook within the MOOC Imparare con l'IA creates a dynamic and interactive learning environment where students are actively engaged in applying their knowledge through "AItivities", structured exercises that leverage AI as a mentor rather than a mere tool. These activities guide learners in developing their ability to critically interact with AI systems, refining their skills in problem-solving, reflection, and knowledge application. Through the AIbook's conversational and multimodal support, students are encouraged to construct concept maps that visualize relationships between key concepts, create structured summaries that synthesize complex topics, and design personalized quizzes that reinforce retention and self-assessment. Furthermore, the AIbook facilitates the creation of iterative feedback loops, allowing learners to refine their understanding through AI-generated suggestions and guided revisions.

Beyond individual tasks, the AIbook also plays a key role in collaborative exercises, where students use AI-driven prompts to engage in structured discussions, develop case studies, and simulate real-world applications of AI-assisted learning. The Indaginarium within the AIbook encourages them to explore critical questions, formulating and refining queries that deepen their engagement with course materials. Similarly, the Rigzomion helps them navigate a flexible knowledge ecosystem where learning pathways are shaped by their inquiries.

By structuring these AItivities around active participation and reflection, the MOOC not only introduces AI as a learning assistant but fosters self-regulated learning, encouraging students to make deliberate decisions on how they interact with AI to enhance their personal and professional development. The AIbook thus transforms passive content consumption into an interactive, co-constructive learning experience, aligning with the SLD framework to cultivate adaptability, critical thinking, and lifelong learning skills.

5 Conclusions

The integration of an AIbook as the backbone of a MOOC introduces new possibilities for digital learning, fundamentally reshaping how learners interact with educational content. Unlike traditional MOOCs, which often rely on static instructional materials and asynchronous engagement, an AIbook fosters a dynamic, adaptive, and personalized learning experience. Through its conversational interface, multimodal resources, and structured learning pathways, such as the Indaginarium and Rigzomion, the AIbook enables continuous interaction between the learner and the content, shifting the educational model from passive consumption to active co-construction of knowledge.

By leveraging Smart Learning Design (SLD) principles and methodology, the AIbook enhances the flexibility and adaptability of MOOCs, allowing learners to navigate, apply, and critically engage with AI-supported content in a way that aligns with their unique learning needs. The ability to integrate AI-driven activities, such as concept mapping, reflective exercises, and iterative feedback mechanisms, ensures that MOOCs can evolve beyond traditional formats to become highly interactive ecosystems that foster metacognition and deep learning.

Moreover, the AIbook's potential to redefine authorship and knowledge organization by shifting the role of the instructor from a content provider to a creator of interactive learning environments, suggests a broader transformation in digital education. This shift necessitates further research into the cognitive and pedagogical implications of AI-driven learning models, particularly regarding learner autonomy, engagement, and knowledge retention.

Ultimately, the AIbook represents a significant advancement in AI-enhanced education, offering a scalable and innovative framework for MOOCs that aligns with the evolving demands of lifelong learning and digital literacy. As AI-driven learning continues to evolve, integrating AIbooks into MOOCs could set a new standard for accessible, flexible, and immersive online education, providing learners with adaptive, conversational, and contextually relevant learning experiences.

Data must be collected through surveys and interviews to assess the effectiveness of AIbooks in enhancing learner engagement, knowledge exploration, elaboration and consolidation, and personalized learning experiences, also supporting the "learning to learn" skills. The results will be used to refine the AIbook and, more broadly, to evaluate the effectiveness of this emerging format in relation to the specific educational contexts in which it is implemented."

Disclosure of Interests. The authors have no competing interests to declare that are relevant to the content of this article.

References

1. Perplexity AI. https://www.perplexity.ai/. Accessed 10 Mar 2025
2. NotebookLM. https://notebooklm.google/. Accessed 10 Mar 2025
3. McLuhan, M.: The Gutenberg Galaxy. University of Toronto Press, Canada (1962)
4. Mangen, A., Walgermo, B.R., Brønnick, K.: Reading linear texts on paper versus computer screen: effects on reading comprehension. Int. J. Educ. Res. **58**, 61–68 (2013)
5. Baron, N.S.: Words Onscreen: The Fate of Reading in a Digital World. Oxford University Press, Oxford (2015)
6. Woodmansee, M.: The author, art, and the market: rereading the history of aesthetics. Scriblerian Kit-Cats **27**(2), 218 (1995)
7. Chartier, R.: The Order of Books: Readers, Authors, and Libraries in Europe Between the 14th and 18th Centuries. Stanford University Press (1994)
8. Eisenstein, E.L.: The Printing Press as an Agent of Change, vol. 1. Cambridge University Press, Cambridge (1980)
9. Foucault, M.: Qu'est-ce qu'un auteur? Bulletin de la Société française de philosophie **63**(3), 73–104 (1969)
10. Barthes, R.: The death of the author. Aspen, 5–6 (1967)
11. Genette, G.: Paratexts: Thresholds of Interpretation, vol. 20. Cambridge University Press, Cambridge (1997)
12. Bazerman, C.: Shaping Written Knowledge: The Genre and Activity of the Experimental Article in Science, vol. 356. University of Wisconsin Press (1988)
13. Deleuze, G., Guattari, F.: A Thousand Plateaus: Capitalism and Schizophrenia. University of Minnesota Press (1987)
14. Sancassani, S., Baldoni, V., Brambilla, F., Casiraghi, D., Corti, P., Marenghi, P.: La ricerca del giusto mezzo: strategie di equilibrio tra aula e digitale. Pearson, Milano (2023)
15. Blair, A.M.: Too Much to Know: Managing Scholarly Information Before the Modern Age. Yale University Press (2010)
16. Rouse, R.H., Rouse, M.A.: Preachers, Florilegia and Sermons: Studies on the Manipulus Florum of Thomas of Ireland, vol. 47. Pontifical Institute of Mediaeval Studies, Toronto (1979)
17. Biggs, J.: Enhancing Teaching Through Constructive Alignment. High. Educ. **32**(3), 347–364 (1996)

Author Index

E. Hamonic and R. Sharrock (Eds.): EMOOCS 2025, LNCS 15733, pp. 233–234, 2026.
https://doi.org/10.1007/978-3-032-00056-9

MIX
Papier aus verantwortungsvollen Quellen
Paper from responsible sources
FSC® C105338

FSC
www.fsc.org

If you have any concerns about our products,
you can contact us on
ProductSafety@springernature.com

In case Publisher is established outside the EU,
the EU authorized representative is:
Springer Nature Customer Service Center GmbH
Europaplatz 3, 69115 Heidelberg, Germany

Printed by Libri Plureos GmbH
in Hamburg, Germany